Also by Mark A. Stelter

*The Gospel According to Christ: The Message
of Jesus and How We Missed It*

POST-CHRISTIAN NATION

The
Secular
Indoctrination
of America

Mark A. Stelter

WESTBOW
PRESS®
A DIVISION OF THOMAS NELSON
& ZONDERVAN

Copyright © 2024 Mark A. Stelter.

All rights reserved. No part of this book may be used or reproduced by any means, graphic, electronic, or mechanical, including photocopying, recording, taping or by any information storage retrieval system without the written permission of the author except in the case of brief quotations embodied in critical articles and reviews.

This book is a work of non-fiction. Unless otherwise noted, the author and the publisher make no explicit guarantees as to the accuracy of the information contained in this book and in some cases, names of people and places have been altered to protect their privacy.

WestBow Press books may be ordered through booksellers or by contacting:

WestBow Press
A Division of Thomas Nelson & Zondervan
1663 Liberty Drive
Bloomington, IN 47403
www.westbowpress.com
844-714-3454

Because of the dynamic nature of the Internet, any web addresses or links contained in this book may have changed since publication and may no longer be valid. The views expressed in this work are solely those of the author and do not necessarily reflect the views of the publisher, and the publisher hereby disclaims any responsibility for them.

Any people depicted in stock imagery provided by Getty Images are models, and such images are being used for illustrative purposes only. Certain stock imagery © Getty Images.

Unless otherwise noted, all Scripture quotations are taken from the Holman Christian Standard Bible, Copyright 1999, 2000, 2002, 2003, 2009 by Holman Bible Publishers. Used by permission. Holman Christian Standard Bible, Homan CSB, and HCSB are federally registered trademarks of Holman Bible Publishers.

ISBN: 979-8-3850-1050-9 (sc)
ISBN: 979-8-3850-1051-6 (hc)
ISBN: 979-8-3850-1052-3 (e)

Library of Congress Control Number: 2023920064

Print information available on the last page.

WestBow Press rev. date: 02/07/2024

To the men of Holy Smokes, who gather to share, laugh, and cry in friendship, fellowship, and fraternity. God Bless You All!

And to Men on Fire: a band of brothers dedicated to preparing and inspiring men for a life of service to Jesus Christ.

For the time will come when they will not tolerate sound doctrine, but according to their own desires, will accumulate teachers for themselves because they have an itch to hear something new. They will turn away from hearing the truth and will turn aside to myths. But as for you, keep a clear head about everything, endure hardship, do the work of an evangelist, fulfill your ministry.

—2 TIMOTHY 4:2-5

Contents

Forward xi
Acknowledgments xv
Introduction xvii

Chapter 1   Man as God: The Triumph of Secularism in
            American Culture 1
Chapter 2   Secular Totalitarianism: The Triumph of
            Secular Materialism 16
Chapter 3   A Shift in Worldviews 29
Chapter 4   Separation of Church and State 47
Chapter 5   The First Amendment: A Maligned Masterpiece 64
Chapter 6   The Academic Assault on Education: Removing
            God From The Classroom 81
Chapter 7   The Fall of Christian Thought 102
Chapter 8   The Academic Worldview: I Am An Atheist;
            Therefore, I Am An Intellectual 122
Chapter 9   A Scientific Assessment of Scientific Materialism 136
Chapter 10 A Rational Discussion of the Supernatural 153
Chapter 11 Has Science Proven The Existence of the
            Supernatural? 174
Chapter 12 Moral Relativism: A Brief Discussion of Secular
            and Christian Views 191
Chapter 13 Moral Truth v. Moral Relativism: Judging God
            and Finding Him Wanting 202
Chapter 14 The Truth About Truth 226
Chapter 15 The Intolerance of Tolerance 240

Chapter 16 Gorging on the Tree of the Knowledge of Good
            and Evil 256
Chapter 17 What Now Shall We Do? 265

Discussion Guide 287
Appendix 1: Suggested Books on Christian Apologetics 293
Appendix 2: Legal Resources for Christians 297
Bibliography 299
Index 305

Forward

Truth always prevails and darkness never overcomes the light. For followers of Jesus Christ, this statement is integral to the foundation on which we stand. We believe it, in part, because our personal faith journey is tested and buffeted with everything this world can throw at us. As we encounter difficult chapters in our life doubt is always conveniently available to become our "little friend." And there may be times we feel literally blinded by darkness. But as we persevere through our storms, doubt gives new birth to faith and what we hold true. And darkness always yields to the new light of dawn. For one who believes, faith builds faith.

As relevant our faith journey and life experience are to what we believe, nothing impacts the lens we view the world through more than Who we believe in. John Chapter 14, starting at Verse 5, records a conversation with Jesus and one of His disciples. It is fitting the Apostle who struggled with doubt asks Jesus, "Lord, we do not know where you are going, and how can we know the way?" Jesus responds, "I am the way, the truth and the life. No man comes to the Father except through Me." Oh, how we long to know where we are going and the way to get there! How desperate we are to have real truth and be able to hold onto it. For one who believes, Jesus IS the way, truth and life. And for the believer, where there is truth and life, light is always found.

The battle between good and evil, light and darkness, truth and lies, and life and death is nothing new. But the degree in which we acknowledge and actually find the willingness to fight this present battle is a deeply personal choice. As my friend and brother in Christ Mark Stelter writes, "There is a war waging for the very soul of America and most of us are not even aware of the battle. This is not a struggle over land or wealth, but a fight between worldviews. It is a war about the way Americans think and what they believe." It doesn't require genius to examine what much of this country—and the world—thinks and believes. If you look and listen it is abundantly crystal clear. Denial is not a river in Egypt. For one who believes, what we think ultimately manifests through how we live.

I'm grateful for the past many years of my life knowing Mark Stelter. I know what Mark believes and because of Who he believes in, how his personal relationship with Jesus impacts and influences his life as a writer and author, this book speaks for itself. More than just an outstanding wordsmith, Mark has the ability to peel the covers back on deep philosophical and spiritual issues presenting them in a way that affords easy reading. As you read, "Post Christian Nation: The Secular Indoctrination of America," you will find yourself drawn into a story part history, part current events, and most certainly insightful and diligently researched investigative writing. It is also happens to be a love story with a diabolical antagonist. If you're growing tired of incessant gas lighting and battling spiritual emasculation this book is a must read and a great antidote to both.

Many find it easy to identify and even eloquently articulate the problem. While Mark has done an outstanding job framing what we see happening to our Christian view, he offers practical steps toward doubling down and renewing and refreshing our faith. That is—for those who believe our faith is worth fighting for.

As much as it is an honor to know Mark as an accomplished author, I consider myself lucky to call Mark my friend. I know few men more genuinely honest, vulnerable-by-choice, and transparent than Mark Stelter. If you google, "Guy who loves Jesus but definitely doesn't have it all together," you'll find Mark's picture. One of the things I love most about him is his self-deprecating humility. That can be hard for a really smart guy and Mark is one of the smartest guys I know. But he's humble and broken enough to not have to pretend to be the smartest guy in the room. That requires being comfortable in one's own skin and I'm fortunate to be rubbing shoulders with a guy like Mark as we try to become more secure in who we are in Christ. For one who believes, one must never stop trying.

On a very personal note, I thank Mark for stacking hands with me and other men who meet weekly for "Men on Fire," a very diverse group of rag tag guys doing what we can to actively grow in our faith via a deeper personal relationship with Jesus. Mark has been with us since the beginning and his support, encouragement, and generosity have furthered the cause. The guys at "Men on Fire" don't meet for "Christian Cocooning." We meet to equip and prepare ourselves to courageously meet face-to-face exactly what Mark has written about.

For one who believes it is easy to see in what and Whom they believe. Thanks for believing, Mark!

Larry Strong
Lead Chaplain, Estes Park Police Department
Founder, Men on Fire

Acknowledgments

The great vice of acknowledging some is that I am bound to omit many deserving of acknowledgment. This is offset by the great virtue that at least a few of the many that I owe much to will receive appropriate recognition.

I begin by thanking Ryan Hayden, Kim Stelter, and Warren Wilkewitz, who thoughtfully and prayerfully read every word of my manuscript and made excellent comments and criticisms. Their devotion has made this a better book.

I also would like to thank Aaron Dorman, Jeff Hughes, Jesse Kirkpatrick, Kevin and Jan Morris, Caleb Ross, Justin Stelter, Scott Stelter, Angel Strong, Larry Strong, and Damian Valdez for their insightful comments, and even more importantly, for their incredible friendship.

Finally, I would like to acknowledge the conversations (seemingly endless, to them, I am sure!) I have had with my children—Stephanie, Michael, Nicole, and Jessica about Christianity, culture, and education. "I have no greater joy than this: to hear that my children are walking in the truth." —3 JOHN 1:4

Introduction

We live in an age where headlines and satire are indistinguishable. Issues never debated in the long course of human history are not only openly questioned, but those who hold to historical and self-evident truths are persecuted and even prosecuted.

Censorship is openly promoted to "protect free speech." Parents are routinely targeted for daring to speak about faith and social issues at school board meetings. Virtues such as chastity, prudence and equality have been swapped for formerly condemned vices such as pride and equity. Indeed, the grounding principles upon which Western Civilization has been built (and prospered for the past two-millennia) have been supplanted and summarily rejected and replaced. The world seems to have gone mad. Reason is out. Irrationally is in.

But no! You are not crazy. Author, lawyer, theologian, and former college professor Mark Stelter asks the first necessary question: "How did we get here?" Stelter shares his fascinating insights behind the moral and social entropy plaguing our culture and explains how a devious and scandalous plot to supplant our cultural soul has been playing out in the shadows. With his characteristic wit and sharp mind for reason, Stelter shines a spotlight on the persistent moral and theological erosion we are experiencing, as well as explaining the surprising forces behind it. Stelter does not present an unhinged conspiracy theory, but rather a thoughtful and well documented forensic investigation into the attempted murder of our culture by secularism.

Instead of bemoaning the dangers of godless thought, Stelter takes us on a journey of exploration into the dark bowels of the atheistic worldview as he expertly contests that dismal landscape with the inherent beauty of theism. In particular, he focuses on the enormous benefits and rational stability afforded to those who understand both personal and cultural Christianity.

By the end of this book, the reader is given so much more than compelling reasons to believe, but also a complex understanding of the powerful effect faith has in shaping both our lives and culture. Prepare to be challenged, informed, enraged, encouraged, and empowered as Stelter restores hope by applying the light of truth to what has been badly eroded by the darkness of ignorance.

Aaron Dorman
Lead Pastor, Christian Church of Estes Park

Chapter 1.

Man as God: The Triumph of Secularism in American Culture

Christianity is in crisis in America. The percentage of Americans who identify as Christian is declining and declining rapidly. In just the last decade, Christianity lost over 11,000,000 people—a 12% decline.[1] Of those raised in a Christian home, 23% have abandoned the faith.[2] At the current rate, by 2040 most Americans will no longer be Christians.[3]

This decline of Christianity is not because America is becoming a melting pot of different faiths. Christianity is not losing ground to other religions. In fact, people of other faiths—Jews, Muslims, Buddhists, and others *combined* make up only 7% of Americans, and their numbers have remained relatively stable. If Americans are not leaving Christianity for other religions, where are they going? The numbers tell the story:

In the 1950s, over 90% of Americans identified as Christian. As recently as 2009 more than 80% of Americans identified as Christian.

---

[1] "In U.S., Decline of Christianity Continues at Rapid Pace: An update on America's changing religious landscape," Pew Research Center: Religion & Public Life, October 17, 2019, https://www.pewforum.org/2019/10/17/in-u-s-decline-of-christianity-continues-at-rapid-pace/.

[2] Ibid.

[3] "Samuel Smith, "Religious 'nones' now as big as evangelicals in the US, new data shows," *The Christian Post*.https://www.christianpost.com/news/religious-nones-now-as-big-as-evangelicals-in-the-us-new-data-shows.

But by 2019, barely more than a decade later, that number had shrunk to 65%.[4] During that same period of time, those who identify as having no religious beliefs—a group pollsters refer to as "Nones"—has increased from 17% of the population to nearly 30% of the population.[5] This is an increase of over 30,000,000 people who say they have no religious affiliation whatsoever. There are now more Nones than there are Evangelicals in the United States—and Nones are growing much faster.[6] Even worse is the fact that the younger one is, the more likely they are to reject Christianity. Among Millennials (those born between 1981 and 1996), we have already reached a tipping point: about half of Millennials proclaim to be Christians and about half do not.[7]

What is perhaps most extraordinary is that this mass rejection of the Christian faith did not occur gradually over a long period of time. Rather, much of this abandonment of faith has taken place in the last 5 years and almost *all* of it has occurred within the last decade. The percentage of people in Generation Z (those born between 1999-2015) who claim to be atheist is *double* the percentage of Millennials who identify as atheist. This is a 100% increase in the number of atheists in the span of one generation.[8]

This indicates a recent cultural shift that has caused a dramatic change in the way Americans view Christianity—and God. While we will generally focus on Christianity in this book, the decline in Christianity almost mirrors a decline in the belief in God.

This profound change is evidenced not only in the rejection of Christianity by large numbers of people but also in the fact that many of those who remain Christian suffer a crisis of confidence in their faith. In truth, many Christians are more than a little embarrassed about being

---

[4] Frank Newport, "Percentage of Christians in U.S. Drifting Down, but Still High," Gallup, Inc., December 24, 2015, https://news.gallup.com/poll/187955/percentage-christians-drifting-down-high.aspx.
[5] "In U.S., Decline of Christianity Continues at Rapid Pace: An update on America's changing religious landscape."
[6] "Samuel Smith Religious 'nones' now as big as evangelicals in the US, new data shows," *The Christian* Post.
[7] "In U.S., Decline of Christianity Continues at Rapid Pace: An update on America's changing religious landscape."
[8] "Atheism Doubles Among Generation Z," *Barna Research,* January 24, 2018, https://www.barna.com/research/atheism-doubles-among-generation-z/.

Christians. They want to be true to the faith of our fathers, but think it ridiculous to believe in the supernatural. They want to believe that Jesus is the way to heaven, but think it intolerant to believe He is the only way. They like what Jesus said about loving our neighbor, but are uncomfortable with his comments on sin, judgment, and Satan. They resolve this conflict by revising their faith to conform to their secular beliefs. They are still believers, but they believe in a god that is subject to man's reason, man's science, and man's morality. If God does not conform to their understanding of reason, if His justice is not consistent with their sense of justice, if His will does not align with their will—then they ignore, reinterpret, or reject Him.

This dramatic shift is readily evident in our culture. We are "spiritual," rather than "Christian;" "seekers," rather than "believers;" and Jesus has been demoted from "Lord and Savior" to "wise philosopher and life counselor." Many churches have substituted the concepts of sin, redemption, and salvation with the more culturally acceptable concepts of equality, tolerance, and social progress. In short, Christianity is tolerated so long as it is indistinguishable from secular humanism. We imagine ourselves to be progressive Christians, or liberal Christians, or modern Christians—but the truth is that one who does not believe in the words of Jesus is no Christian at all. And so, we find ourselves in this middle ground—this no-man's land—where we believe in the "truths" of secularism, but we still cling loosely to our Christian faith in spite of the fact that is runs counter to everything we think we know. But with each passing day our Christian beliefs are pushed further and further to the periphery of our lives.

Why are so many people rejecting Christianity? Have there been amazing archeological findings that cast doubt on the Christian story? No, in fact the opposite is true.[9] Have there been new scientific discoveries that make the existence of God unlikely? Again, the opposite

---

[9] Archeology has provided strong evidence, especially in recent years, of the accuracy of the depictions of the towns, battles, and people mentioned in the Bible. See: H. Wayne House and J. Randall Price, *Zondervan Handbook of Biblical Archaeology: A Book by Book Guide to Archaeological Discoveries Related to the Bible* (Grand Rapids, MI: Zondervan, 2017) and Randall Price, *The Stones Cry Out: What Archeology Reveals About the Truth of the Bible*, (Eugene, OR: Harvest House, 1997).

has actually occurred.[10] Have philosophers shown that Christian orthodoxy is illogical, inconsistent, or in contradiction with itself? Not in the least. What then, has occurred that would explain the greatly increased skepticism about a faith that has withstood critical scrutiny for over 2,000 years?

The answer: *Americans have accepted a secular worldview that is entirely consistent with atheism and entirely inconsistent with Christianity.* These beliefs include religious irrelevancy, scientific materialism, and moral relativism. For ease of analysis, I call this set of beliefs *Secular Materialism* and describe them, broadly, as follows:

1. **Religious Irrelevance**
   Religious belief is based on faith, tradition, and ritual. Since the Enlightenment humankind has endeavored to throw off these chains and use the tools of reason, logic, and science rather than relying on the authority of the church. This is why the United States was founded as a secular nation with an impenetrable wall of separation between church and state. One's religious beliefs should have no influence on public policy and should, preferably, be banned from the public square and restricted to the confines of church, home, and individual conscience.

2. **Scientific Materialism**

---

[10] Modern science, far from being in conflict with the biblical worldview, has recently made startling discoveries that are consistent with biblical views. This has been especially evident in astrophysics and cosmology. See: Karl W. Giberson, *The Wonder of the Universe: Hints of God in Our Fine-Tuned World* (Downers Grove, IL: IVP Press, 2012); Hugh Ross, "Why I Believe in the Miracle of Divine Creation," in *Why I Am A Christian,* eds. Normal L. Geisler and Paul K. Hoffman, (Grand Rapids, MI, 2006), p. 135; and Paul Davies, *The Mind of God* (New York: Touchstone, 1992). Dr. Francis S. Collins, the Director of the National Institutes of Health and the head of the Human Genome Project has written a book arguing that biological evidence is consistent with the existence of God. See: Francis S. Collins, *The Language of God: A Scientist Presents Evidence for Belief* (New York: Simon & Schuster, 2006). Renowned philosopher Alvin Plantinga explains that there is no conflict between science and religion, there is a conflict between naturalism and science. See: Alvin Plantinga, *Where the Conflict Really Lies. Science, Religion, & Naturalism* (Oxford University Press, New York, 2011).

The material, natural world is all we can know and the scientific method is the only legitimate way of discerning facts about this world. Anything outside of the material world (the supernatural) is at best unknowable, and at worst, illusory.

3. **Moral Relativism**
Morality is a social construct, relative to time, place, and culture. One person's "truth" may not be another person's "truth." Because this is so, making universal truth claims is exclusionary and intolerant.

Secular Materialism, like any worldview, is complicated, complex, and includes many other subsets of beliefs that emanate from these as logical corollaries. The degree to which any individual subscribes to each subset of the Secular Materialist worldview will, naturally, vary with the individual. However, the maxims of Secular Materialism have become increasingly accepted as true among all Americans, and especially so among younger Americans with college degrees. This group is nearly synonymous with Nones who have abandoned the Christian faith. The degree to which Nones have been influenced by Secular Materialism is clear: 76% of Nones believe that religion is inconsistent with science,[11] 68% believe that morality is relative,[12] and 84% believe that man's highest goal in life is to "enjoy it as much as possible."[13] It is certainly more than a coincidence that those who have accepted the precepts of Secular Materialism have rejected Christianity. A comparison of the beliefs of Secular Materialism with the beliefs of Christianity reveals that Secular Materialism *directly contradicts* the Christian worldview:

1. **Religious Irrelevance v. Religious Reverence**

---

[11] "Religion and Science: Highly religious Americans are less likely to see conflict between faith and science," Pew Research Center, October 22, 2015, https://www.pewresearch.org/science/2015/10/22/science-and-religion/.

[12] "The End of Absolutes: America's New Moral Code." Barna Research, May 26, 2015, https://www.barna.com/research/the-end-of-absolutes-americas-new-moral-code/ and "A Generation in Transition: Religion, Values, and Politics among College-Age Millennials," Robert P. Jones, *Public Religion Research Institute*, April 19, 2012, https://www.prri.org/research/millennial-values-survey-2012/.

[13] Ibid.

Christian theology holds that not only is Christianity reasonable and logical but that reason and logic emanate from God. Christians point to the historical fact that the Constitution does not call for a separation of church and state but rather protects religious belief by prohibiting the establishment of any religion by the government while at the same time guaranteeing the free exercise of religion by all. Religion in America was, up until very recently, an almost omnipresent and ubiquitous part of our culture, present nearly everywhere and influencing practically every aspect of public life, from our schools to our courts. This is consistent with the Christian belief that God is omnipresent and not only created the world but sustains it. Secular Materialism's attempt to limit the influence of God is irrational, sinful, and impossible.

2. **Scientific Materialism v. The Transcendent and Supernatural**
The Christian view is that God is imminent and transcendent and reality consists of the material and spiritual, the natural and supernatural. God is here in this material world and God transcends the material world. God is supernatural and eternal and one can know God in many ways, including through the supernatural intervention of the Holy Spirit. Jesus believed this world was passing away and the faithful would live forever in the eternal, supernatural kingdom of God. Scientific materialism rejects any knowledge of the supernatural and thereby rejects any belief in miracles, angels, demons, heaven, hell, or God.

3. **Moral Relativism v. Absolute and Eternal Truth**
Christians not only believe in absolute, eternal, and unchanging truths, but that Jesus Himself *is the truth*. Christians believe God ordains morality and that God cannot act immorally. Whatever God does is moral because morality is part of His essence. Christians believe not only in absolute truth and God-created morality, but in sin, redemption, and salvation. Moral relativism holds that morality is relative and truth is subjective

to time, place, and culture. Man establishes what is right and wrong, true and false, good and evil—not God.

It is clear that the Secular Materialist view of the world and the Christian view of the world are not simply two worldviews, they are two *opposing* worldviews. One can either believe the truths proclaimed by Secular Materialism or the truths proclaimed by Christianity, but one cannot believe the truths of Secular Materialism and believe in Christianity. The acceptance of the worldview offered by Secular Materialism is, I believe, the major reason belief in Christianity is declining so rapidly in America. One simply cannot, logically, adhere to both Secular Materialism and Christianity simultaneously. This explains all 3 cultural phenomena we are currently facing: the rise in Nones, the rejection of Christianity, and the cognitive dissonance experienced by so many Christians who want to believe but think their faith is inconsistent with science and reason.

The doctrines propounded by Secular Materialism are a worldview, as subjective and filled with assumptions and presuppositions as any other worldview. They are not a set of scientific facts based on experiment, evidence, and logic, but simply a set of assertions about the way the world is. We will explore in great detail these assertions to reveal that not one of them has been proven by science and that they often are inconsistent with reason, logic, and experience. And yet the propositions of Secular Materialism are often taught, directly or indirectly, as if they were unbiased discoveries about the nature of our universe.

Secular Materialism, or some variation of it, constitutes a major part of the curriculum at most colleges and universities. Any college student who is paying attention knows that she is supposed to believe these things—or at a minimum give them very serious consideration. Having a visceral dislike for all religious truth claims, rejecting the supernatural, understanding that morality is relative, and venerating the individual and his self-actualization is nearly synonymous with having a liberal education in our current culture. Believing these things is what constitutes being enlightened, tolerant, and sophisticated. Unfortunately, these "truths" of Secular Materialism are, for all practical purposes, identical to the "truths" of atheism.

Students are not taught that God is irrelevant; they are taught that our religious beliefs are to be strictly separated from our public lives. Students are not taught that God does not exist; they are taught that the supernatural does not exist. Students are not taught that God is not the author of morality; they are taught that morality is a man-made construct relative to time and place. Students are not taught that Man is God; they are taught that the individual is the highest authority and his self-actualization is the purpose of life.

Christianity and its rich theology and philosophy is considered, like all other religious beliefs, to be unworthy of academic discussion for the simple reason that they are religious beliefs. This explains why such a dramatic number of students enter college as Christians and leave as Nones.

It is no wonder that millions of Americans—including millions of Christians—are struggling with their faith in God. They have not been told that God does not exist, but they have been indoctrinated with views that make belief in God *intellectually impossible.*

The acceptance of a secular worldview—combined with a bombardment of scorn, derision, and mockery for those who dare question it—has left millions of Christians feeling alienated and confused, like strangers in their own land. Christianity—as an influence on the public life of the nation—is being systematically removed from our culture at large and limited to the confines of our churches and homes. The mere mention of Christianity is considered boorish in social settings, a distraction in the business world, inappropriate in policy discussions, and outright illegal in the classroom. It is as if an agreement has been struck where belief in God is tolerated so long as this belief plays no significant role in our lives. We have, it seems, acquiesced to a radical separation of faith from *everything* else, such that the space left for Christianity is so minor that even most atheists would be comfortable with it. God has been given one hour of worship on Sunday morning, but He is strictly forbidden from showing up anywhere in our culture outside of the walls of the church. The tacit agreement is: sing praises to your God all you like on Sunday, but leave Him at the church when you return to the real world on Monday.

Deep in our inner being we know that something has gone horribly awry. We feel a sense of profound loss—a loss of vitality, of vibrancy, of significance. Like a person afflicted with Alzheimer's, we know Christianity has lost something, but we don't quite know what.

Tragically, the secularization of America has been so successful that we are only vaguely aware of *what* we have lost. There was never a moment when Christians went to battle with secularists for the life of our culture. Rather, Christians embraced Secular Materialism because we believed the lie that our faith life is separate from our intellectual life. We succumbed to the indoctrination we received in our secular schools that faith has its place, but that place is confined to the personal and the private. We bought the myth that this separation of faith from almost every aspect of our live is appropriate because faith is neither rational nor scientific and therefore should play no role in government or academics. But most importantly, we have been taught a set of beliefs that make Christianity intellectually impossible.

But it doesn't have to be this way. There is another path. This alternate resolution is to concede that our Christian beliefs and Secular Materialism are in conflict, but to conclude that it is *Secular Materialism* that is unreasonable, not our Christian beliefs. This is a difficult path. Not because the case for Christianity and against Secular Materialism is so difficult, but because even to consider that our secular beliefs may be misplaced requires that we question what we think we know. This takes a good deal of thought that is at once contemplative, critical, and creative. In other words, it requires that we engage in the rarest kind of thinking: that we question what we have been taught.

Because our culture has become so secularized, we mistakenly feel that our Christian faith is inconsistent with science and logic. The truth is one can believe in God and not give up an ounce of reason or logic. Secular Materialism is radical and new. It was *not* the view held by Socrates, Plato, Aristotle, Copernicus, Da Vinci, Michelangelo, Galileo, Descartes, Pascal, Locke, Newton, Beethoven, Hegel, Kant, Madison, Jefferson, Lincoln, or Kierkegaard—to name only a few! After all, most of the world's greatest philosophers, artists, writers, and scientists were Christians—not secularists. Their genius and their Christianity were not at odds with each other. The only reason we feel the tension between our knowledge and our Christianity today is because we have been taught a view of the world that is opposed to Christianity.

The great irony of our blind allegiance to Secular Materialism is that it fails to stand under close scrutiny. While it parades itself as the rational choice and sets itself up as the irrefutable champion in the battle between reason and Christianity, the fact is that much of Secular Materialism is intellectually bankrupt. The secular emperor has no clothes but no one dares question his intellectual nakedness.

I had the privilege of serving as a college professor for almost 20 years. My students inspired me to write this book. Even though I taught at colleges in the Bible Belt, a disturbing number of my students had blind faith in the "truths" of Secular Materialism. It was through listening to the worldviews of these students that I realized an entire generation of people had been indoctrinated with a philosophy that not only made Christianity untenable, but also could not itself survive critical analysis. When I asked them to defend their secular worldviews, most of them had no defense whatsoever. Instead, they looked at me as if I were insane. These were not views to be defended; they were absolute truths to be accepted without question. (I know, it is ironic that one of the secularist absolute truths is that there are no absolute truths.) When I asked an open and sincere question about these beliefs, this did not usually result in an intellectual discussion wherein postmodernism, secularism, and relativism were intelligently defended. Instead, the mere fact that I dared to question these truths invited personal attacks on my alleged lack of "tolerance." (I know, it is ironic that tolerance is one of the hallmarks of secularism—unless one questions the truths of secularism.) If I dared to mention the Bible in these discussions, I was immediately informed that using the Bible as a source was illegitimate. Never had my students suggested the same of the works of Freud, Marx, or Dawkins. Indeed, never had *any* other source been regarded as "illegitimate." Aside from the Bible, *all* thoughts from any and every source were considered not only legitimate, but equal. This was part of their indoctrination. If I mentioned Christianity I was informed—or often even *warned*—that any discussion of Christianity was violation of the "separation of church and state doctrine" and was illegal in the classroom.

Post-Christian Nation

What was particularly alarming about the standard response of students to any discussion of religion was that with few exceptions the responses were adamant and uniform. While I could barely get a hand to raise if I asked questions about the day's assigned reading, and while it was sometimes even difficult to have students share their own personal opinions on issues related to the course, they were as certain as they were bold about their opinion on matters relating to Christianity: Religion is based on faith, not reason; it is a personal matter, the claims of which are entirely subjective; it is unverifiable scientifically, and therefore of little use in intellectual discussion; and, its discussion in the classroom is prohibited by the separation doctrine of the United States Constitution. These sentiments (and sentiments is what they may most generously be described as because not one of them is a fact) were expressed with such glee that my students acted as if I should affix a gold star to their foreheads for providing the perfect answer.

My friends, this is not education—it is indoctrination. The fact was that while almost all of my students knew the secular answers very few of them could defend these answers. The secular mantra my students had on the tip of their tongues was, alas, not the result of protracted, arduous philosophical discussion during their high school years. No, far from it. My students came to me indoctrinated with a dogma that had been fed to them by the current authority in power. The final irony being that Secular Materialists (the current authority in power) have successfully dispatched the Church (the former authority in power) under the premise that people should make up their own minds and not be dictated to by the current authority in power! Of course, exchanging one authoritarian dogma for another is not much progress. The king is dead, long live the king. Or as Peter Townshend sings in, *We Won't Be Fooled Again*: "Meet the new boss; Same as the old boss."[14]

The truth is our children are being taught a worldview that is belief masquerading as fact, indoctrination masquerading as education, and subjective opinion masquerading as objective truth. Most parents, teachers, and students are not aware of it, but make no mistake: our schools are teaching atheism under another name. And the result is

---

[14] Peter Townshend, *The Who*, "We Won't Be Fooled Again," (1971).

that our children—even those who consider themselves Christians—are finding it very difficult to believe in a faith that runs counter to everything they think they know.

Having spent nearly 20 years of my life as a teacher and more than 20 years as a student, I am unaware of any topic, save religion, that is so discriminated against in our classrooms. I have engaged in (or sometimes merely endured) discussions on homosexuality, lesbianism, transgender issues, transvestite behavior, sadomasochism, masculinity, femininity, racism, sexism, xenophobia, nationalism, imperialism, capitalism, socialism, communism, Marxism, nihilism, liberalism, conservatism, libertarianism, fascism, genocide, anorexia, bulimia, suicide, abortion, euthanasia, global warming, sociopathy, psychopathy, criminal deviance, sexual deviance, totalitarianism, apartheid, ethnic cleansing, child labor, human trafficking, sexual harassment, and the patriarchy. Indeed, the above list of topics reads like a college course catalogue—and I have no problem whatsoever with the discussion of these topics. What I strongly object to is that faith, belief, religion, and God are not included in this rather inclusive list of important social topics. Particularly when it is indisputably true to say that nothing else comes even close to Christianity in the impact it has had—for better and for worse—on Western culture.

The purpose of this book is *not* to turn our schools into churches. It is not to teach that Christianity is the one true religion, the best religion, or even better than other religions—although I believe it is all of these. It is not to teach that the Christian worldview is "right" and secular worldviews are "wrong." It is certainly not to eliminate any subjects from being taught in our high schools, colleges, and universities. My purpose is just the opposite: to teach more, not less; to broaden, not narrow what our children are taught; and to seek more context, more depth, and more questioning; not merely indoctrinate our children with atheist dogma.

Our current educational system from high school through graduate school has all but eliminated any mention of the single most significant event of the Western world: Christianity. This is ludicrous. This not only weakens our understanding of Christianity, but it weakens our understanding of Secular Materialism, atheism, and every other worldview. Indeed, forbidding Christian thought from the classroom diminishes all of us—believers, doubters, and unbelievers alike. It is a preposterous position for any institution of learning. It is never wise to prohibit thoughts, viewpoints, and worldviews. To prohibit discussions about Christianity is nothing less than the censorship of what is objectively the single most important topic in the history of humankind. It is the moral equivalent of burning books. And it is time it stopped.

There is a war waging for the very soul of America and most of us are not even aware of the battle. This is not a struggle over land or wealth, but a fight between worldviews. It is a war about the way Americans *think* and what they *believe*. Secular Materialism replaces God with pseudo-science; truth with relativism; and salvation with self-actualization. It is atheism wrapped in scientific clothing and our children are being indoctrinated with this worldview—softly and indirectly in elementary school and stridently and directly by the time they reach graduate school. And this atheistic worldview teaches them that there is no God, there is no moral truth, and there is no purpose aside from grasping for some happiness in a very short life.

This war of worldviews battling for our hearts and souls is waged with words, but it will determine the fate of our nation as surely as if it were waged with bullets. The enemy is well-armed, well-trained, and well-organized. And they are winning. Adherence to an exclusive secular worldview is not only an enemy of Christianity, it is an enemy of education. Eliminating Christian thought from our schools is not only an assault on Christianity, it is an assault on truth. It requires the rewriting of history, the reinterpretation of literature, the prohibition of free speech, and the suppression of free thought.

What began decades ago in elite universities has now completely infiltrated our entire public education system. It is no longer just the radical atheist professor at Yale who espouses Secular Materialism, but the talk-show host, the stand-up comedian, and the barista at our local coffee shop. We have learned our lessons so well that schools no longer need teach an atheist worldview—it is firmly and deeply engrained into our culture. All "educated" people know that it is one thing to hold Jesus in respect as a man of great wisdom and kindness and that it is quite another to believe in such anachronistic and superstitious things as miracles, sin, redemption, and salvation. We "know" in every fiber of our sophisticated selves that such things are unreasonable, illogical, and unscientific. As such we can continue to believe in them as a matter of faith, but we can no longer consider them as actual possibilities in the real world.

And so, we trudge through our lives devoid of purpose or meaning and sophisticated enough to know it is naïve to believe there is any purpose or meaning. We read novels and watch television programs whose characters are equally filled with angst and anxiety and who seem to have no spiritual lives whatsoever. We have succeeded in completely removing our religious beliefs from every aspect of our lives, save church—and even there it is often hollow and ritualistic. We mistakenly blame this emptiness on our faith itself, thereby confirming our secular teaching, when in fact it is our secular teaching that has made our faith seem false.

One cannot long hold onto rituals that have no meaning; onto a belief we no longer believe. And how can one believe? We have been taught the truths of Secular Materialism and we have believed them. Ironically, these truths are not based on any scientific discoveries, rational conclusions, or logical inferences. They themselves are dogmatic beliefs, not proven, but merely accepted. Secular Materialism is our new national religion and to doubt its doctrines is heresy.

The hour is late. It is time we critically examine these culturally accepted truths. It is time we recognized that what we have been taught directly contradicts our Christian beliefs. It is time these "truths" were challenged—as all truth claims should be challenged. Only then will we discover whether Secular Materialism provides a more reasoned, more logical, more rational explanation of our world than does Christianity. Until we do this, Christians will continue to lose a battle we do not even realize is being waged.

While this book is specifically a call to action for Christians, the same fight against Secular Materialism should be joined by all believers of any faith. A study of the worldviews of Buddhists, Muslims, Hindus, Jews, and others, as well as Christians, would enlighten the minds of students and provide a contrast to the only philosophy currently permitted in our schools: Secular Materialism. The elimination of all "God-talk" from the classroom impoverishes the souls and minds of our children. It is a bias against even the possibility of the existence of God. As all totalitarian states know, the best way to eliminate a point of view is not to argue against it—it is to never mention it. And that is, whether intentionally or accidentally, what happened in our public schools. This, in turn, has resulted in our schools being soulless places where not only has the study of God been eliminated, but also the search for meaning and purpose, because one cannot discuss such topics in any serious fashion without at least considering the possibility of a Creator. Because the United States was (and still is) a predominantly Christian nation, the secular attack has been on Christianity. But the truth is the fight is between theism and atheism. The goal is not only the elimination of Christian thought from our culture, but the elimination of any theistic worldview.

While I welcome and encourage the discussion of *all faiths* in our public schools, as a Christian, I write this book for those Christians and those seekers who want to accept Christianity but think that their reason gets in the way of their faith. As we will discover, one can be a Christian and an intellectual at the same time. "Come, let us reason together, says the Lord."[15] Come indeed. Christianity does not fear critical inquiry. It does not prohibit questions. An authentic Christian journey is an exhilarating discovery of the truth that will enable us to once again share our faith with confidence so that we may proclaim the words of Jesus, "You will know the truth, and the truth will set you free!"[16]

---

[15] Isaiah 1:18, Barker, *Holy Bible, New International Version*, 1984.
[16] John 8:32.

CHAPTER 2

SECULAR TOTALITARIANISM: THE TRIUMPH OF SECULAR MATERIALISM

Christianity has fallen on hard times. There was a time when Christianity was the dominant worldview in our culture and its basic theological premises were commonly understood and accepted. It was considered not only a religion, but a body of deep intellectual thought and profound philosophical insight. After all, Christianity replaced the Greek and Roman views of the world not only as a religion, but as the favored philosophy of the world's intellectuals. A very incomplete list of brilliant Christians includes Origen, Anselm, Augustine, Aquinas, Erasmus, Galileo, Newton, Bacon, More, Montaigne, Descartes, Milton, da Vinci, Berkeley, Pascal, Locke, and Kierkegaard.

Today, critics of Christianity mount sieges of every imaginable variety from every conceivable source in every possible direction and the faithful seem either incapable or unwilling to defend their faith. Angry atheists write irrational rants against Christianity such as *The End of Faith*, *The God Delusion* and *God Is Not Great*—and they become bestsellers. Television documentaries breathtakingly claim to "reveal new evidence" found about Jesus that is almost always anti-Christian, not to mention historically inaccurate. Programs claiming that the bones of Jesus have been found, that "lost gospels" long suppressed by the church have been unearthed, or that Jesus was married to Mary

Magdalene all produce high ratings—and all are demonstrably false. Traditional signs and symbols of Christianity are removed from public view, ministers are imprisoned for holding Bible studies in their homes in violation of city zoning ordinances, school children are forbidden from singing Christmas songs and are expelled for having the audacity to wear a rosary or bring a Bible to class.[1]

Supreme Court decisions have all but banned even the mention of God in public primary and secondary schools. Christmas songs are forbidden,[2] Christmas break has become "Winter Break," Easter is "Spring Break,"[3] and leading the class in prayer is one of the few offenses that will actually get a teacher fired.[4] Courts have ruled it unconstitutional for a high school football team to pray that no one gets injured during a game;[5] that a teacher cannot silently read his own Bible to himself during a class break;[6] that Christian student groups may be banned;[7] and that a simple cross as a memorial to fallen soldiers cannot be placed in a public park.[8] Church postings on social media are removed for being "exclusionary," or engaging in "hate speech."[9]

---

[1] *Stratechuk v. Board of Education*, 577 F.Supp.2d 731 (2008, cert. denied); *Fetterolf v. Borough of Sewickley Heights* (2:18-cv-00939), July 20, 2018; and http://religion.blogs.cnn.com/2011/10/05/school-tells-girl-wearing-rosary-violates-dress-code/comment-page-15/; https://www.ocregister.com/2015/08/21/california-boy-banned-from-wearing-rosary-at-school/; and http://wdtprs.com/blog/2012/06/rosaries-forbidden-in-a-school-because-they-are-gang-signs/, respectively.

[2] *Stratechuk v. Board of Education*, 577 F.Supp.2d 731 (2008, cert. denied).

[3] See Ted Olson, "Taking Christ Out of Christmas' Leads to Lawsuit," Christianity Today Online, Dec. 2002.

[4] *School Dist. of Abington Township, Pa. v. Schempp*, 374 U.S. 203 (1963); *Engel v. Vitale*, 370 U.S. 421 (1962).

[5] *Santa Fe Independent School Dist. v. Doe*, 530 U.S. 290 (2000).

[6] *Roberts v. Madigan*, 921 F.2d 1047 (1990).

[7] *Christian Legal Society v. Martinez*, 561 U.S. 661 (2010).

[8] *American Humanist Association v. Maryland-National Capital Park and Planning Commission*, 588 U.S. ___(2019) The U.S. Supreme Court, in a split decision, reversed the holding of the 4th Circuit and determined the cross could stay. Sadly, the Court pretended that the cross was not a symbol of Christianity, at least not exclusively, using some rather tortured reasoning. For example, the Court wrote that the Swiss flag has a cross on it, but apparently the cross does not symbolize Christianity on the Swiss flag. Although I applaud their decision, I find their reasoning cowardly and disingenuous. The case may be found at No. 17-1717, 588 U.S. ___(2019).

[9] My own pastor's Facebook page was removed from circulation because he had the unmitigated audacity to proclaim Jesus as the exclusive way to salvation. Whether this

The list goes on and on.[10]

Robert Bork, a former Yale Law School professor and U.S. Supreme Court nominee writes on this current separation doctrine:

> That was not the historical meaning of the First Amendment. The first Congress, which proposed the First Amendment for ratification by the states, also appointed chaplains for the House, Senate, and armed forces. The early Congress regularly petitioned the president to issue Thanksgiving Day proclamations addressed to God. The framers and ratifiers could not conceivably have anticipated that the Supreme Court, sitting in a courtroom with a painting of Moses and the Ten Commandments, would hold it an unconstitutional establishment of religion for a high school to have a copy of the Ten Commandments on a wall.[11]

Social commentator Christopher Lasch, one of the more distinguished members of the academic elite himself, concluded that most of his colleagues' view religion with "indifference to active hostility."[12] Bork agrees: "The major obstacle to religious renewal is the intellectual classes, who are highly influential and tend to view religion as a primitive superstition."[13]

Fred Barnes, a distinguished but rare member of the national press writes:

---

proclamation is true or false, it is an essential teaching of most Christian churches, just as the teaching that "there is no god but Allah and Muhammed is His Messenger," is a central teaching of Islam. To remove such statements as "exclusionary" seems ludicrous.

[10] For some insight into the radicalism of some atheist organizations see the website for the Freedom From Religions Foundation. They proudly list the litigation they have engaged in, including such heroic actions as attempting to have the Star of David removed from a Holocaust Memorial for being "exclusionary."

[11] Robert H. Bork, *Slouching Towards Gomorrah*, (HarperCollins, New York: 1996), 289.

[12] Christopher Lasch, *The Revolt of the Elites and the Betrayal of Democracy*, (W.W. Norton, New York: 1995), 215.

[13] Bork, 294.

> [There is a] peculiar bias in mainstream American journalism against traditional religions. ...Whenever religion comes in contact with politics or public policy, as it increasingly does, the news media react in three distinct ways, all of them negative. Reporters treat religion as beneath mention, as personally distasteful, or as a clear and present threat to the American way of life.[14]

Researchers S. Robert Lichter and Stanley Rothman conducted interviews with 240 members of mainstream media establishments in the United States, including *The New York Times, The Washington Post, The Wall Street Journal, Time* and *Newsweek* Magazines, *U.S. News and World Report*, all of the news departments at CBS, NBC, ABC, PBS, and all of the major public broadcasting stations. During these interviews they found that only 8% of mainstream media journalists attend church or synagogue on a weekly basis and a full 85% *never* attend church or synagogue. Perhaps more incredibly, a full 50% are self-professed agnostics or atheists.[15]

Carl Cannon, Washington Editor of RealClearPolitics writes: "Although the number fluctuates, some 40 percent of the American people describe themselves as evangelical Christians. Yet, in traditional U.S. news organizations, such believers are a rarity. The news coverage tends to reflect this disconnect. Evangelicals are often dismissed, particularly in political reporting, as exotic; or, worse, as a menace to civil society."[16]

Comedians and popular television programs treat Christianity with a disrespect they would never show to Muslims, Buddhists, or even atheists. Christians are regularly portrayed as simple-minded nincompoops, conservative reactionaries, or intolerant bigots. But mostly Christianity is simply not mentioned at all. It is an odd truth

---

[14] Fred Barnes, "Faithful Bigots," Forbes Media Critic, vol. 1, no. 2, 1994, 10.
[15] S. Robert Lichter, Linda Lichter, and Stanley Rothman, *The Media Elite: America's New Power Brokers* (Hastings House, 1990), Figure 124-1.
[16] Matthew Brown, "Newsroom Religion: Is There a Dearth of Religious Journalists in the Nation's Newsrooms?" https://www.deseretnews.com/article/865578660/Newsroom-religion-Is-there-a-dearth-of-religious-journalists-in-the-nations-newsrooms.html.

that in a nation of over 150,000,000 Christians, faith is almost never mentioned in our literature, television programs, or movies. It is as if faith were non-existent, or at best, unimportant to people in our culture. Reflect, for a moment, the treatment Christianity is given by each of the following institutions:

- public primary and secondary schools
- colleges and universities
- governmental agencies and bureaucracies
- businesses
- radio programs
- documentary television programs
- newspapers and magazines
- local and national newscasts
- comedians and social commentators
- television dramas, situation comedies, and talk shows
- mainstream movies
- novels
- music

A thoughtful review reveals three striking facts: First, the institutions and media listed above are so comprehensive that they cover, in some fashion, almost every waking moment of our lives. Second, the above list includes every culture-making institution in the nation, save the church and the family. Third, in this extraordinarily broad list of activities, Christianity is most often entirely ignored, derisively ridiculed, or affirmatively attacked. Our current interpretation of the separation doctrine has tragically left our public schools, colleges, and universities indistinguishable from those in officially atheist nations: the mention of God is illegal. The same is true for every interaction with our government, from the post office to the courthouse. Business, while not prohibited from engaging in Christian activity, have largely decided it is best not to (recall the ridicule, protests, and attempted government discrimination when Chick-fil-A became embroiled in the homosexual marriage controversy) and most movies, television programs, and novels treat religion as if it was simply non-existent. Seldom do our fictional characters attend church, mosque, or synagogue and they move through their lives as if they never considered the possibility of God for a moment. Those films, songs, or novels that do address God are generally segregated as "Christian genre," further enforcing the idea that faith is somehow separate and distinct from our "normal" lives. Would it kill a mainstream radio station to play a Christian song occasionally? Would it destroy the book if the characters, when facing some existential crisis, considered the possibility of the existence of God? Would it destroy the enjoyment of a film if we saw one of the characters, for a brief second, coming out of church or saying a simple prayer at dinner?

If a visitor from outer space came to Earth and observed our television, film, music, and literature he would report back to his Leader that Earthlings seemed totally unaware of even the concept of God.

The result of this onslaught against Christianity and its almost complete removal from our culture was not, until recently, a wholesale abandonment of Christianity by Americans. That took some time. The Christian faith has been so strong in America for so long that it is no exaggeration to say that the United States was the world's citadel of Christianity. For 400 years this land has been a refuge for those seeking religious freedom and that freedom was enshrined by the Founding Fathers in the very first amendment to our nation's constitution. Our Christian roots run too deep to be easily discarded. But through decades of mistakes, misinterpretations, and malice, the foundational beliefs of the Christian faith have been severely weakened. We have sown the wind and we are now reaping the whirlwind. Not only have millions of people left the faith, but for many Christians their faith amounts primarily to tradition and ritual, having no real relevance to their lives.

David Wells, professor of Historical and Systematic Theology at Gordon-Conwell Theological Seminary writes:

> It is one of the defining marks of Our Time that God is now weightless. I do not mean by this that he is ethereal but rather that he has become unimportant. He rests upon the world so inconsequentially as to not be noticeable. He has lost his saliency for human life. ...It is a condition we have assigned him after having nudged him out to

the periphery of our secularized life. His truth is no longer welcome in our public discourse. The engine of modernity rumbles on, and he is but a speck in its path.[17]

It Was Not Always This Way

To appreciate how far we have fallen—and to realize the heights to which we could return—we need to know where we started. In spite of what is taught in many of our schools, the truth is that the United States, while never formally a Christian nation, was most assuredly a nation of Christians. George Washington admonished his countrymen, "It is the duty of all nations to acknowledge the providence of Almighty God, to obey His will, to be grateful for His benefits, and humbly to implore His protection and favor."[18] Our fifth president, John Quincy Adams, thought the birth of our nation was metaphysically connected with the birth of Christ. He wrote, "Is it not that in the chain of human events, the birthday of the nation is indissolubly linked with the birthday of the Savior?—that it forms a leading event in the progress of the Gospel dispensation? Is it not that the Declaration of Independence first organized the social compact on the foundation of the Redeemer's mission upon earth?—That it laid the cornerstone of human government upon the first precepts of Christianity?"[19] Thomas Jefferson, who wrote in the Declaration of Independence that we are "endowed by our Creator with certain unalienable Rights" reflected, "[C]an the liberties of a nation be thought secure when we have removed their only firm basis, a conviction in the minds of the people that these liberties are of the gift of God? That they are not to be violated but with

---

[17] David F. Wells, *God in the Wasteland: The Reality of Truth in a World of Fading Dreams*, (Eerdman's, Grand Rapids, MI: 1994), 88.

[18] George Washington Papers, Series 8, Miscellaneous Papers ca. 1775-99, Subseries 8A, Correspondence and Miscellaneous Notes: Correspondence and Miscellaneous Notes, 1773-1799, The Library of Congress.

[19] John Quincy Adams, "An Oration Delivered Before the Inhabitants of the Town of Newburyport, at Their Request, on the Sixty-First Anniversary of the Declaration of Independence, July 4th, 1837." Whether Adams rather exalted view of the United States is correct or not is not the point. The point is a time existed in our history where such statements could be made by without the slightest amount of controversy.

His wrath?"[20] Is it even imaginable that a presidential candidate would make such claims today—or that a public school teacher would even be able to reveal this part of our history to her students?

Not so long ago the Supreme Court, in holding that the Bible may be taught in public schools, wrote, "Why may not the Bible, and especially the New Testament, without note or comment, be read and taught as a divine revelation in [schools]—its general precepts expounded, its evidences explained and its glorious principles of morality inculcated?"[21] Such a comment today would subject one to jeers and ridicule. A proponent of reading the Bible in public schools would no doubt be castigated by the media as one who wishes to unpatriotically overthrow our proud secular history and cast us back into the Dark Ages of a theocratic state! Never mind that it was common practice for Bible studies and even prayers (God forbid!) to be recited in public schools until the 1970's—and there is no evidence that this produced a nation of "Bible thumping" extremists determined to establish a theocracy.

It may be even more surprising to those concerned about religious indoctrination that the vast majority of all early education in the United States was religious education, founded by churches to train ministers. Even more shocking to those adhering to the modern myth of the separation doctrine is that many of these religious institutions were founded in partnership with the government. Harvard, for example, was established by the government of Massachusetts to train Congregationalist and Unitarian ministers. The college was named after John Harvard, a prominent minister. It no doubt is considered scandalous to the secular mind that the Harvard Student Guidelines read, "Let every student be plainly instructed and earnestly pressed to consider well the main end of his life and studies is to know God and Jesus Christ which is eternal life (John 17:3) and therefore to lay Christ in the bottom as the only foundation of all sound knowledge and learning."[22]

---

[20] Thomas Jefferson, Notes on the State of Virginia, Query XVIII5. This quotation is carved on the walls of The Jefferson Memorial in Washington, D.C. This statement comes from more complete remarks Jefferson made on the slave trade. It is especially interesting that these words come from Thomas Jefferson, who was among the *least* orthodox of the Founding Fathers.

[21] *Vidal v. Girard's Executors*, 43 U.S. 126,132 (1844).

[22] Harvard University, Rules and Precepts, Rule No. 2 (1646).

Yale, also founded to educate Congregationalist ministers, was established by the government of Connecticut. It's motto, Urim and Thummim, is Hebrew for "Light and Truth," which, according to the Old Testament, were the tools used to discern the will of God. Princeton was founded by Presbyterian ministers. Its motto was—and is—*Dei sub numine viget,* Latin for "Under God's Power She Flourishes." Columbia's motto: "In Thy light shall we see the light," and Brown's is "In God We Hope." In fact, *all* of the Ivy League colleges, save Cornell, were founded by Christian congregations with the express purpose of seeking God's truth.[23]

How times have changed.

The relegation of Christianity to the dust bin of history, regarded as irrelevant to modern man, is so absurd that it defies explanation. Christian philosophy swept the world with such rapidity and completeness that the Greek and Roman gods vanished and even the philosophical musings of Socrates, Plato, and Aristotle became matters of merely academic interest while the entire Western world embraced the teachings of a man named Jesus.

The history of Western man is inseparable from the history of Christianity. Christianity is largely responsible for the establishment of colleges and universities, including Chartres Cathedral School, the universities of Bologna, Paris, Oxford, Prague, Cracow, Wittgenstein, Georgetown, Princeton, Dartmouth, Brown, Yale, Harvard, Columbia, William and Mary, and Rutgers—not to mention the over 600 lesser-known Christian colleges in the United States alone. At the dawn of the 20th Century nearly 80% of all colleges in the United States were affiliated with Christian churches.[24]

The beginning of Western science is inseparable from Christianity. The very idea that man could understand the natural world was

---

[23] Christian clergymen of one stripe or another founded Harvard, Yale, Princeton, Dartmouth, the University of Pennsylvania, Columbia; and Brown University. Cornell, is the only secularly founded university in the Ivy League. Its motto, incidentally, is the rather uninspiring, "I would found an institution where any person can find instruction in any study."

[24] "Colleges and Universities with Religious Affiliations," https://www.encyclopedia.com/education/encyclopedias-almanacs-transcripts-and-maps/colleges-and-universities-religious-affiliations.

premised on the belief that God created in an orderly, systematic fashion. Scientific progress is unimaginable without the contributions of Nicolaus Copernicus, Francis Bacon, Johannes Kepler, Isaac Newton, Robert Boyle, Michael Faraday, Charles Babbage, Louis Pasteur, Guglielmo Marconi, Niels Bohr, Werner Heisenberg, Wernher Von Braun, John Polkinghorne, and Francis Collins, all of whom were devout and outspoken Christians.

Christianity is arguably the single greatest factor in the rise of human rights and democracy. Christian thinkers who contributed to the civil rights and liberties of their fellow humans include Augustine, Thomas Aquinas, Thomas More, Dante Alighieri, Desiderius Erasmus, Martin Luther, John Calvin, John Locke, George Berkeley, Immanuel Kant, Blaise Pascal, Gottfried Wilhelm Leibniz, Georg Wilhelm Friedrich Hegel, John Adams, James Madison, William Wilberforce, Abraham Lincoln, and Martin Luther King, Jr.

Literacy is largely a product of the publication of the Bible, which is still by far the most published, most translated, most read, and most researched book in the history of the world. Great Christian authors include Edmund Spenser, William Shakespeare, John Milton, John Bunyan, John Donne, John Dryden, Daniel Defoe, William Wordsworth, Jonathan Swift, Johann Wolfgang Goethe, Friedrich Schiller, Samuel Taylor Coleridge, Edgar Allan Poe, Matthew Arnold, Conrad Ferdinand Meyer, Theodor Fontane, Washington Irving, Robert Browning, Emily Dickinson, Emily Brontë, Charles Dickens, Nathaniel Hawthorne, Thomas Stearns Eliot, John Galsworthy, Thomas Mann, William Faulkner, John Updike, and many others.

Western art and music were influenced so profoundly by Christian thought and imagery that until the 20th Century they were almost inseparable from the faith itself. The list of great Christian composers includes such names as Brahms, Bach, Beethoven, Handel, Schubert, Vivaldi, and Mozart. Christian artists include Rembrandt, Durer, Raphael, Bernini, Botticelli, van Gogh, da Vinci, and Michelangelo. And they were not just nominal Christians, they were outspoken and devout Christians.

One could argue that these geniuses were the product of their times. That is undoubtedly true, but it does not detract from their genius. Yet even today, in a post-Christian culture, belief and intelligence are far from enemies: Sixty-five percent of Nobel Prize recipients have been Christians, including 78% of all the Nobel Prizes in Peace, 73% of Chemistry, 65% of Physics, 62% of Medicine, 54% of Economics, and 50% of all Literature awards.[25]

The relegation of religious thought as something unworthy of intellectual pursuit defies rational explanation. Imagine, for a moment, that Mark Twain's *The Adventures of Huckleberry Finn* had the same impact on the world as has Christianity. Imagine that Huck Finn had fired the imaginations of the world's greatest artists, poets, songwriters, and composers such that an enormous volume of all the great paintings, poems, songs, and music was inspired by the story of Huck Finn. Imagine that enormous strides had been made in architecture and engineering in building cathedrals devoted to the study of Huck Finn. Imagine that wars had been waged over the interpretation of one of Huck' adventures. Now, imagining all that, wouldn't it strike you as strange that *The Adventures of Huckleberry Finn* was banned from public classrooms? Wouldn't it seem odd that *The Adventures of Huckleberry Finn* were considered irrelevant to the study of academic topics because it was a fictional story? Wouldn't it seem bizarre that we didn't discuss *The Adventures of Huckleberry Finn* in school because it was controversial, we weren't really sure if Mark Twain wrote it (after all, some claim a guy named Samuel Clemens wrote it), or we couldn't completely agree on its meaning?

If *The Adventures of Huckleberry Finn* had the same impact on the world as Christianity it would be utterly ridiculous not to study the story. This is true whether Huck's adventures were real or not. It is true whether we agreed on the meaning of Huck's adventures. It is true whether we liked Mark Twain or despised him. The study of this most momentous of all books would be relevant to our world because of the unparalleled impact it had on the world—regardless of whether the story was true or false or of whether the impact was good or bad.

How did a nation that embraced faith and reason as two valued partners in the search for truth come to regard the two as separate, unequal, and in opposition? How did one of the most religious nations in the world become so thoroughly secularized? Why are the beliefs

---

[25] Baruch A. Shalev, *100 Years of Nobel Prizes* (Atlantic Publishers & Distributors, 2003), pp. 57-59.

of so many Christians indistinguishable from the beliefs of secular humanists? The secular elite have kindly provided us with an answer: modern discoveries in science and advances in human understanding have disproven the primitive beliefs of the Christian faith.

What are these alleged discoveries and advances? This is where things get a bit slippery and vague, but many are convinced that there simply exist certain self-evident truths that contradict the beliefs of the Christian faith. What, precisely these new discoveries are is hard to say. But to those predisposed to reject belief in God, it just seems *obvious* that Christianity is intellectually unsound.

This belief that Christianity is preposterous and absurd is not so much an intellectual conclusion reached after an unbiased examination of the facts as it is an article of faith itself, something that one simply must believe if one is to be taken seriously among the "right" crowd. The "right" crowd generally consists of academics, journalists, and other intellectuals and pseudo-intellectuals of whom Auberon Waugh described as the "chattering classes"—that is, those who make their living shaping, or attempting to shape, our culture. And shape our culture they have. Many Americans are convinced that one cannot be a Christian and a "serious thinker." This, as we will see, is a point of view that is not only illogical but runs counter to any study of the lives of the great thinkers throughout history. Nevertheless, such patently absurd views have become commonplace among Americans—especially (and ironically) among those who consider themselves to be good "critical thinkers."

There have been no discoveries or advances that weigh heavily upon the ultimate question of the existence of God. It does no good to say, "Well, in their day they believed in things we know are not possible." This is simply not true. When Jesus walked on water his disciples did not think it was normal. They knew, just as we know, that walking on water is impossible. Humanly impossible, that is. That is why they believed it to be a miracle and that Jesus was someone more than human. The fact that the contemporaries of Christ found his supernatural works to be miraculous is evidence that they had a firm grip on reality. They knew that people don't walk on water, turn water into wine, or come back from the dead. Those are precisely the reasons they thought Jesus' claims of deity were sound.

We, like every human before us, must answer the ultimate questions of life in our own hearts and minds, in much the same way humans have always grappled with such issues. Unfortunately, the miracles of science and technology provide little assistance in these matters. We stand no better, nor worse, prepared to answer this question than our ancestors. And yet, unlike our ancestors, many today feel certain that belief in God is somehow unscientific, irrational, unreasonable, and anti-intellectual. Why this dramatic reversal in attitude toward religious belief? The answer is that there has been a dramatic shift in worldviews. The collective worldview of a nation does not change overnight. It is a process with a cause, or more accurately with causes. We now turn to addressing the two major worldviews: Theism and Atheism.

Chapter 3

A Shift in Worldviews

The reason we harbor these malicious thoughts in our hearts against our own faith is not because of new evidence that refutes the existence of God. We doubt our faith because we have been indoctrinated with a worldview that is hostile to belief in God. We have been taught the "truths" of Secular Materialism in our schools not because they are true, but because they are *secular*. Secular Materialism is the default position in all institutions of public education because any non-secular (i.e., religious) views are strictly forbidden. By this recent misinterpretation of the Constitution, we are left with the false impression that Secular Materialism is true—and if Secular Materialism is true—Christianity cannot be.

To understand this change in our culture one must understand the concept of a "worldview." A worldview is a comprehensive set of beliefs that form the underlying presumptions upon which one bases his view of reality. These beliefs are often so embedded in our subconscious mind that we are not even aware of their existence. They are the lenses through which we view everything and as such we don't recognize that how we view the world is shaped by the invisible lens we look through. The problem with worldviews is not that we have considered them uncritically—it is that we have not considered them at all. We do not recognize our worldview as a choice, but regard it simply as "the way things are."

For example, it is a shared worldview among most Americans that people should be treated equally, that freedom of speech should not be infringed, and that our leaders should be democratically elected. These American values are such a part of our cultural DNA that we take them for granted, as if all human beings were born knowing these "unalienable rights," as we call them.[1] Of course, a little thinking on the matter reveals that hundreds of millions of people around the globe do not share these "self-evident" beliefs and that we ourselves were not born knowing these things, but were taught them by our teachers, our parents, and the culture at large.

Often worldviews explain the state of humanity in terms of a universal problem and a solution to that problem. A communistic worldview holds that the problem is unequal distribution of wealth and that the solution is common ownership of the means of production. A capitalistic worldview posits that the problem is scarcity of resources and the solution is private ownership of those resources so they will be most efficiently used. A democratic worldview presupposes that concentrated power corrupts and resolves this problem by distributing power widely among the people. A non-democratic worldview presumes that the masses are incapable of governing themselves intelligently and solves this problem by providing centralized decision-making by those presumed to be more capable—kings, monarchs, dictators, experts, or other cultural elites.

Christianity is a worldview. It is many other things, as well. It is a religion, a historical movement, a cause, a lifestyle, an ideology. But it is Christianity as a *worldview* that has been most undermined by our current culture. Christianity as a religion is an accepted part of our culture, albeit not without some serious areas of concern. Christianity as a historical movement, a cause, or an ideology is recognized, for better or for worse, by our culture. There are those who attempt to live a Christian lifestyle in terms of their social ethics, moral codes, and interactions with their neighbors. All of those modes of Christianity are now declining, but they are declining because Christian *belief* is

---

[1] Lest we forget, Jefferson wrote that these unalienable rights were granted to us by our Creator: "We hold these truths to be self-evident, that all men are created equal, that they are endowed by their Creator with certain unalienable rights, that among these are life, liberty and the pursuit of happiness, that to secure these rights, governments are instituted among men, deriving their just powers from the consent of the governed."

under attack. After all, Christian ritual and behavior only exists because Christians believe the claims of Christianity are true. The ritual will continue out of tradition and habit once the belief is gone, but not for long. That is why church attendance did not drop dramatically until recently. For a long time, the cultural attitude has been, "It's fine to attend church out of habit, respect, or community bonding, just so long as you don't actually *believe* that stuff." Now we see that the younger generations have quite rationally decided that if one does not believe in the Christian message, then attending church is pointless.

Christianity as a religion, lifestyle, or social ethic is dependent upon the validity of Christianity as a worldview. If the fundamental principles of the Christian faith are untrue, then the faith as a religion or social ethic may limp along on the inertia of its former strength, but it will eventually be abandoned. Because the Christian worldview (i.e., the foundational beliefs of the faith) have been so successfully called into question by Secular Materialism, there are many millions of Christians who are already just barely limping along, going through the motions of a religion with no assured confidence that their faith is true.

Christianity: The World According to Christ

What is the Christian worldview? What are these foundational beliefs upon which all of Christianity rests? The Christian worldview, like other worldviews, presupposes a universal problem and provides a comprehensive solution: the problem is sin and the solution is Jesus. Christianity, when not merely thought of as a religion or label, is a belief about the world that shapes all other beliefs, thoughts, and views we hold about everything else. As C. S. Lewis wrote, "I believe in Christ as I believe the sun has risen, not only because I see it, but by it I see everything else."[2]

While thousands of books have been written describing the beliefs of Christians, the central principles of Christianity may be summarized as follows: God created and sustains the world; sin is the seminal problem

---

[2] C.S. Lewis, "They Asked For A Paper," in Is Theology Poetry? (London: Geoffrey Bless, 1962), 164-165.

of humankind; and that Jesus Christ, the Son of God, provides salvation from our sins so we may enjoy eternal life with him in heaven. In this context, "sin" is our separation from God. Sin leads to misery in this life and eternal separation from God in the next. But there is good news—we have been saved from sin by the atoning death of Jesus Christ, the Son of God. Jesus is our Lord and Savior, defeating death and providing us with eternal life. Christian salvation is a free gift offered by the grace and mercy of God. It is not earned by us. All we have to do is accept it.

For many Christians, belief is much more personal than the above description, or indeed, than any possible description. Having a relationship with Christ is, for these Christians, very much like being in love. They feel the incomprehensible and indescribable love of Jesus—a very intimate and personal love—and they often feel overwhelmed with gratitude, wonder, and awe. For Christians with a personal relationship with Christ, the reason they believe is not based on the Bible, the teachings of their church, or even the evidence they find in the material world. Although all of these things are important factors, the undeniable truth is that Jesus is alive in their hearts and souls. These Christians have experienced a personal illumination from God Himself, through the Holy Spirit, that makes all other truths pale in comparison. This experience is so profound and overwhelming that one could call it supernatural—it transcends the ordinary bounds of reason, science, and logic. In fact, it so overshadows all other human experience that reason itself is tested based upon the one true thing that these Christians know: the Gospel of Jesus Christ. Rather than measure their beliefs by man's science, logic, or reason—these Christians measure man's science, logic, and reason against God's revealed Word.

Now, three things must be said about this:

First, many Christians do not experience this sort of "born again" or revelatory phenomenon. For these Christians their belief is based on reason, logic, experience—and some amount of faith. This is certainly not irrational, as all belief systems—theistic or atheistic—rely, in part, on reasonable faith. For example, even the most scientific among us must have faith in the scientific method; in his five senses; in his ability to correctly analyze, synthesize, and reason; in the accuracy of the scientific instruments he is using; in the veracity of the scientific laws he is relying upon; and many, many other assumptions upon which his scientific conclusions rest. So, the fact that Christians rely on some measure of faith does not disqualify their conclusions any more than it disqualifies the faith of the atheist that the world is entirely natural and material. No one—Christian or atheist—can really know with absolute certainty the truth of the universe, the vast majority of which we have not even begun to explore.

Second, for a person who has experienced this illumination, it is absolutely reasonable to follow the truth of the illumination. In fact, if one believes that they have been given some kind of revealed truth by the God of the Universe, it would be the height of irrationality to disregard that truth. As Martin Luther is said to have asked, "Is it more foolish to hear thunder and think it is the voice of God, or to hear the voice of God and dismiss it as thunder?"

This feeling of a direct connection to God is a remarkable experience. Yet, we know that such experiences happen to people who are known by one and by all to be a rational, sane, mentally healthy human beings and after this experience, they remain, by all measures, rational, sane, mentally healthy human beings. Further, this experience is not especially unique or abnormal. Millions of other Christians have attested to this "awakening" or "enlightenment," and they testify to shockingly similar experiences. This would indicate the experience is not the result of some personal mental condition, but is consistent with the same phenomenon that other rational, sane, and mentally healthy people have experienced. Finally, this experience would be tested against not only the experience of other Christians but against the Scriptures to see if it conforms to the teachings of the Bible. Such experiences do.

Third, and perhaps most importantly, almost without exception the truth placed on the hearts and minds of those who have experienced such an illumination are entirely consistent with reason, logic, and experience. They may not be consistent with what the person formerly believed to be rational, but once reviewed in the new light these truths make infinitely more sense than the person's former understanding. This is not an unusual occurrence, incidentally, even in the secular world. For example, once a scientist makes a new breakthrough, he often sees things very differently. While the new breakthrough may reject his old way of thinking, it makes so much more sense and fits the world so much better that the scientist discards his old "truth" and accepts the new truth. Such things have occurred with Copernicus' heliocentric theory, Newton's theory of gravity, Einstein's theory of relativity, and countless others.

This new awakening, rebirth, or illumination is usually something so compelling that the person experiencing it cannot deny its veracity. It often leads to a much better understanding of the world for one who has been so awoken. People have described it as a key that opens every door, a puzzle piece that fits in such a way that the entire puzzle may be solved, or a sort of Rosetta Stone that unlocks a new language.

I have a friend who was a confirmed atheist. He is very rational and highly intelligent. One day he experienced such an illumination, and being a very skeptical and modern man, he tested his illumination against all the logic and experience he had at his disposal. His conclusion that Jesus Christ is indeed the Son of God was based not only upon his illumination, but upon all the evidence he saw after his illumination that he was formerly blinded to. He described it to me as being color-blind, but not knowing it, and now being able to see the world in all its true colors.

As Augustine, one of the world's greatest thinkers—and skeptics—put it: "Therefore, do not seek to understand in order to believe, but believe in order to understand."[3]

All this is to say that it is not irrational to believe what one knows to be true. There is, for example, no scientific way to "prove" that I love my children—but it would be the height of idiocy for me to believe I did not love my children simply because my love is immeasurable using man's current tools of discovery. Christian belief is similar. One knows it is true. Its transcendent and revealed truths can be tested using our tools of logic, reason, and experience. But if our poor tools do not attest to what we know in the innermost fabric of our being, it is entirely rational, sane, and logical to doubt our tools instead of the truth we hold in our hearts and souls.

Now, Secular Materialists are quite content to accept the Christianity that most resembles secular humanism—the "Christianity" that holds that Jesus was a wise moral philosopher, but no more. This anemic

---

[3] Augustine, *Gospel According to St. John*, 184.

"Christianity" is not seen as a threat from the secular culture, probably because it isn't. Christianity that is nothing more than secular humanism is not Christianity. The Christianity of the Bible holds that God created the heavens and the earth; that Jesus is the Triune Son of God; that man is sinful and needs a savior; and that that Savior is Jesus Christ. It is this Christianity—the Christianity of Christ—that is rejected by Secular Materialism. It is rejected not because the secular worldview rejects Jesus as a man, but because they reject Him as the Christ—the Risen Son of the Living God. They reject Him as the Christ because they reject all things that do not comport with their material, physical, and naturalistic view of the world.

This is the challenge to the modern secular mind. Secularists do not doubt the virtues of love, charity, and forgiveness—they doubt the veracity of sin, hell, and grace. Why love is any less supernatural than sin cannot be explained. Why heaven is any more rational than hell they cannot say. Why forgiveness is easier to accept than grace defies logic, but the modern mind is very uncomfortable with the immaterial and the transcendent. When people who identify as Christians are surveyed, one finds that the number who would be considered "Christian" falls precipitously as they are asked about their belief in the supernatural. Those who take the traditional, orthodox, historic view of Christianity and believe in such things as the Immaculate Conception, the Virgin Birth, Satan, and hell falls to under 10% according to some surveys.[4] It seems the primary stumbling block for modern Christians is the Secular Materialist belief that science has disproven the immaterial, the metaphysical, and the supernatural.

Of course, science has done no such thing. History reveals that the greatest minds of every age, including the present, find no necessary disjunction between the material and the immaterial, the physical and the metaphysical, or the natural and the supernatural. The harmony of these concepts was not considered irrational by Socrates, Plato, Aristotle, Bacon, Newton, Hobbes, Locke, or Einstein. Many of the greatest minds of our own age are in, unsurprisingly, agreement with the greatest minds

---

[4] "Barna Survey Examines Changes in Worldview Among Christians Over Past 13 Years," https://www.barna.com/research/barna-survey-examines-changes-in-worldview-among-christians-over-the-past-13-years/.

of past ages. The number of Christian astronomers, biologists, chemists, cosmologists, engineers, mathematicians, neurologists, paleontologists, philosophers, and physicists who are the leading minds in their fields is remarkably rich. The myth that modern science provides evidence for atheism is not only false, but if anything, the opposite is true. The fact that this myth persists reveals an astounding failure of both our secular educational system and our churches. Why, then, have so many of us, in our infinite wisdom, determined that rational people must reject the phenomenal?

The truth is we have not. What has happened is due to a misapplication of the separation of church and state doctrine the only worldviews permitted in public schools are those that are not religious or theistic. This leaves the secular worldview as the only option. After decades of secular teaching many Americans have come to believe that Secular Materialism is not simply an alternative worldview, but the *only rational* worldview. They believe this, not because Christianity has been discussed and rejected, but because the consideration of anything outside the secular worldview has been entirely ignored in our schools.

Secular Materialism: The World According to Freud, Marx, and Bill Nye The Science Guy

Secular Materialism adheres to a worldview that is, for all practical purposes, the same as atheism. Atheism boldly proclaims that there is no God, whereas Secular Materialism teaches propositions which, if true, make the existence of God impossible. A brief review of Secular Materialism reveals that its propositions are entirely consistent with atheism:

- *Religious Irrelevance*: Secular Materialism holds that religion is irrelevant to public policy because religious belief is based on faith, not reason, and therefore has no place in the formulation of rational policy. Further, because different people have different faith beliefs, it is the best policy to keep all mention of God out of the public sphere. Atheism holds that religious belief is

based on faith, not reason, and that religion should play no role in public affairs.
- *Scientific Materialism*: Secular Materialism, like atheism, is the belief that only the natural, material world exists. Both Secular Materialism and atheism reject the supernatural.
- *Moral Relativism*: Secular Materialism and atheism hold that morality is a social construct, created by man, and changing from time to time and culture to culture. Secular Materialism and atheism hold that morality is, at a minimum, relative. Some forms of Secular Materialism and atheism would go further and embrace nihilism, the belief that morality does not exist at all.

It is evident that the doctrines of Secular Materialism and of atheism are so similar they could be considered synonymous. What, then, is the real difference between Secular Materialism and atheism? In theory, Secular Materialism takes no position on God. Secular Materialism makes no mention of God, whereas atheism boldly proclaims there is no God. In practice there is no real difference between the beliefs of Secular Materialists and atheists. In some ways Secular Materialism is merely the inductive form of atheism. Atheism boldly proclaims there is no God, whereas Secular Materialism claims there is supernatural and that morality a construct of human cultures—and then leaves it for the student to come to the quite obvious conclusion that there is no God.

This is one of the most insidious things about teaching Secular Materialism in our schools. It is teaching atheism without using the troublesome word, "atheism." Where atheism shouts that God is dead, Secular Materialism whispers, "We take no position on the existence of God, but the facts are…" Secular Materialism has managed to teach the principles of atheism without raising the ire of parents that schools are teaching atheism.

But make no mistake: our schools are indoctrinating our children in an atheistic worldview. A comparison of the theistic worldview with the atheist worldview may be of assistance to showing just how atheistic our schools have become.

Theistic Worldview	Atheistic Worldview
God exists	God does not exist
Truth exists	Truth is a social construct
Morality is established by God	Morality is created by man
God is a supernatural being	There is no supernatural
God created man	Man evolved without any creator
God created the world	The world "popped into" existence
God determines what is good and evil	Man invents the concepts of good and evil
God is the highest good	The betterment of man is the highest good
Our purpose is to know and love God	Our purpose is to achieve self-actualization

Which of these worldviews is taught in our public schools? Which of these worldviews most closely matches the worldviews of people under 30? Which of these worldviews do most college graduates hold?

Our students are not being taught atheism *per se*. They do not even realize they are being taught atheism, and I dare say most teachers do not realize they are teaching atheism. But our students are being taught a worldview that is entirely consistent with atheism.

This explains why so many people, especially the young and college-educated, just "know" that God does not exist without actually ever being told that God does not exist. This is why so many people, especially the young and college-educated, just "know" that science is inconsistent with belief in God without ever being told that science is inconsistent with belief in God. This explains why these same people cannot explain why God does not exist or how science is inconsistent with belief in God. It is because they have never examined the relationship between God and reason or between God and science. Indeed, they have not studied the philosophical basis for belief in God at all. They have simply been indoctrinated with the beliefs of Secular Materialism and these beliefs are incompatible with the existence of God. If they were to critically examine the precepts of Secular Materialism and compare them with the precepts of Christian thought, they would find that what they think they "know" about God is not quite as simple as the dogma they have been taught, which is that Secular Materialism is based on reason and belief in God is based on faith. As we shall see as we explore these two worldviews, this conclusion is far from the truth; yet, this myth that the beliefs of Secular Materialism are based on objective facts and the beliefs of Christians are based on superstition, tradition, and blind faith is imprinted on the minds of millions of Americans as if it were an irrefutable truth about the world that no intelligent person could dare even question.

The teaching of atheism under another name explains our current cultural exodus away from belief. Consider:

- In the space of little more than a decade there has been a dramatic abandonment of belief in God. This unbelief in God has nothing to do with a disillusionment with Christianity specifically. People are not leaving Christianity to become Buddhists, Hindus, Muslims, or Jews. It is not only a rejection of *religion*—it is a rejection of *God*.
- There have been no new discoveries in science or philosophy that can explain this change in attitude toward belief. What we know of the world insofar as it regards the existence of a Creator has been unchanged from what we knew 100 years ago. Indeed, insofar as the essential philosophical questions of life, what we know now is no different than what men and woman have always known. The questions of reason, purpose, and meaning are unchanged.
- The belief that science has disproven God cannot be explained. There is no scientific evidence that God does not exist. Yet this belief is firmly planted in the minds of many as a self-evident axiomatic truth.

Add to these realities the fact that young Americans are not embracing atheism, they are embracing "nothingism." The number of atheists in the United States, while growing, does not explain the enormous decrease in belief in God. Americans are not leaving Christianity to become atheists; they are leaving Christianity to become "Nones." A large percentage of Americans under the age of 30 have embraced a sort of religious nihilism, rejecting all meta-narratives, whether those metanarratives are about God, truth, morality, or the superiority of one view over another. The intention of such teaching may have been to reduce conflict and increase tolerance; but the result has been a generation of students who feel life has no meaning, purpose, or value.

Interestingly, surveys show that while 82% of atheists do not believe in God (one wonders why it was not 100%?), only 37% of "Nones" said they do not believe in God.[5] This is good news: The majority of those claiming no religious belief still believe in God. This also confirms my theory that the reason so many Millennials identify as "Nones" is because they have been indoctrinated with the beliefs of Secular Materialism. Remember, Secular Materialism does not specifically address the issue of the existence of God. Because Secular Materialism is taught in our schools not as a religious worldview, which it certainly is, but simply as objective facts about the universe, God is never mentioned. Indeed, if God was mentioned, Secular Materialism would be exposed for what it is: atheism. In any event, the fact that a majority of Millennials self-identify as "Nones," yet 63% of this same group has not entirely given up belief in God is exactly what one would expect in the early stages of the teaching of Secular Materialism. It takes a long time for something as firmly engrained in our psyche as belief in God to go away, especially when Secular Materialism does not *directly* teach there is no God. But over time, there are only two choices: reject belief in Secular Materialism or reject belief in God.

Further evidence that the teaching of Secular Materialism is behind the dramatic decrease in the number of Christians in America is provided by a survey conducted by Pew Research in which "Nones" were asked why they left Christianity. Nearly half of the respondents said the reason they left Christianity is that they no longer believed. This is compared to only 20% who said they left Christianity for political reasons or because they disliked institutional religions. For that much

---

[5] "Why America's 'Nones' Left Religion Behind," Michael Lipka, Pew Research, August 24, 2016, https://www.pewresearch.org/fact-tank/2016/08/24/why-americas-nones-left-religion-behind/.

larger group who left because they no longer believed, respondents most often gave the following reasons:⁶

- "Learning about evolution when I went away to college."
- "Too many Christians doing un-Christian things."
- "Religion is the opiate of the people."
- "Rational thought makes religion go out the window."
- "Lack of any scientific or specific evidence of a creator."

All of these reasons, except "Too many Christians doing un-Christian things" are directly related to the teachings of Secular Materialism. In fact, the reason, "Religion is the opiate of the people," is a direct quote from Karl Marx. The works of Marx, not incidentally, are assigned to college students more than any other author save Shakespeare, Plato, Aristotle, and Foucault. If you haven't attended college recently, Foucault may be unfamiliar to you. Foucault, a social theorist, was, perhaps unsurprisingly, an outspoken atheist. Foucault is assigned more than any other author except Shakespeare, Plato, and Aristotle. The combined works of Foucault, Marx, and Freud (another militant atheist) are assigned more than the works of John Adams, Maya Angelo, Thomas Aquinas, Winston Churchill, Henry Clay, Thomas Edison, John F. Kennedy, Abraham Lincoln, James Madison, Sylvia Plath, Ronald Reagan, Henry David Thoreau, Mark Twain, and George Washington *combined*.

Indeed, a review of the coursework assigned students at most American colleges and universities reveals an enormous bias toward thinkers who are atheists. The works of Bertrand Russell, perhaps the 20th Century's most famous atheist, were assigned about as often as the writings of Abraham Lincoln. At least Russell was also a philosopher. Others, such as Richard Dawkins, Daniel Dennett, and Christopher Hitchens, who are famous for *nothing but their atheism*, are frequently assigned to students as required reading.⁷

---

[6] Ibid. See also: "Why America's 'Nones' Don't Identify with a Religion," Becka A. Alperhttps, August 24, 2016, http://www.pewresearch.org/fact-tank/2018/08/08/why-americas-nones-dont-identify-with-a-religion/.

[7] This data comes from The Open Syllabus Project, a non-profit research organization affiliated with Columbia University. The Open Syllabus Project currently has a corpus

It is not just the works of atheists such as Marx and Freud whose works permeate almost every college course, either directly or indirectly, or the rantings of famous atheists such as Richard Dawkins that are so popular among college students. The real problem is much deeper. The real problem is not that students are immersed in the work of famous atheists, but that so much of their reading is written by scholars with an atheist or Secular Materialist worldview. It is one thing to read Richard Dawkins', *The God Delusion*, or Christopher Hitchens', *God Is Not Great*. As anti-Christian as these books are at least their agenda is not hidden from the reader. It is quite another thing to read a history, psychology, or sociology book written by an author with an atheist worldview. The reader of such a book might reasonably expect the book to present an unbiased and objective view of history, psychology, or sociology when in reality the author has, either consciously or subconsciously, allowed his worldview to slip into the textbook. When this occurs teachers and students alike are usually unaware that the author is espousing an atheistic worldview. This is certainly the case with teaching the principles of Secular Materialism. While Secular Materialism is for all practical purposes indistinguishable from atheism, because it is taught not as a religion or philosophy but simply as objective truths about the world, its principles are accepted by all—teachers and students, believers and unbelievers, Christians and atheists.

Often these atheistic principles are subtle and unrecognizable. Three small examples that all college students should recognize are as follows:

- The alleged battle between sociology and biology in determining personality: Is it nature or nurture? This is a staple question among students of psychology and other disciplines. But it is a false dichotomy. It leaves out the possibility of free will. This is so because naturalists, materialists, atheists, and positivists (in other words almost all "enlightened" thinkers) reject the

---

of seven million English-language syllabi from which it compiles data. See: https://blog.opensyllabus.org/about-the-open-syllabus-project/. (Note: *The Communist Manifesto* ranks second when not counting such works as English grammar and style handbooks or mathematics textbooks. Even including such almost universally assigned works, *Manifesto* is the sixth most assigned book to college students).

concept of free will. As Freud tells us, free will is an illusion. We are merely products of our environment or our biology. This is in direct contradiction to Christian thought which tells us man, created in the image of God, has free will. Of course, the nature/nurture debate also leaves out the possibility of God's action or influence on our lives.

- The oft-repeated literary conflicts: All stories are ultimately about the struggle between man and himself; man and other men; or man and nature. These three options leave out the most compelling and original of stories: Man versus God.
- The famous Maslowvian Hierarchy of Needs that all psychology students learn: According to Dr. Maslow (an atheist) humans have a hierarchy of needs. The most necessary must be filled before one can proceed with the higher order needs. At the bottom of the pyramid are Physiological Needs, such as food and shelter. At the very top of the pyramid is Self-Actualization. Students dutifully draw this pyramid, most never realizing that it is a direct contradiction to Christian thought. Jesus does not tell us to "actualize ourselves," he tells us to "die to ourselves." At the top of the hierarchy from a Christian worldview is submission to God, not aggrandizement of self.

These are just a few of the many examples of how modern education teaches the principles of atheism. Again, there is no "Atheism 101" class or "Introduction to Secular Materialism," but there does not need to be. The principles of atheism (via Secular Materialism) are woven into the fabric of what constitutes being "educated" in the modern era.

What is particularly disturbing is that Secular Materialism has been so successfully drilled into the minds of students that *even Christians* agree with the atheistic worldview!

Ask a Christian if he believes in the supernatural and he will likely respond, "Of course not! I wasn't born in the 14th Century!" If you then ask, "Is God supernatural?" he will most likely scrunch up his face in confusion and mutter something like, "Uh...well...that's different."

Ask a Christian if she believes in moral absolutes and she will most like say, "Oh, no. Morality changes from one culture to the next and one age to the next. It even changes from one person to the next. What is right for you may not be right for me." If you then ask, "Do moral laws come from God or are they created by man?" she will probably say something like, "Well, some moral laws come from God and some are made by man." If you pursue this line of questioning, she will most likely offer some classic conversation stoppers such as, "Who knows what God's laws are, anyway? And don't we have to interpret what God said? And how do we know God said it and not just some Bronze Age chauvinist man pretending he heard the voice of God? In the end, we have to decide what our own morality is."

Ask a Christian what the purpose of life is and a majority will say, "To live a good life and be a good person." Many will go so far as to say, "To be happy."[8]

It never occurs to these Christians that their answers are entirely consistent with answers given by atheists and completely inconsistent with Christianity. When it does occur to them, as happens to many college students who, after all, are devoting most of their day to thinking about such questions (one hopes), they will often agree that their answers are indeed inconsistent with Christianity. The tragedy is that the "truths" of Secular Materialism are so deeply entrenched in their minds that many will come to the conclusion that they can no longer call themselves Christians because their secular beliefs are inconsistent with Christian thought. They are quite correct that their secular beliefs are inconsistent with Christian thought—but they never even consider that perhaps it is their secular beliefs that are wrong, not their Christianity.

But What If Secular Materialism Is Taught Because It Is *True*?

My atheist friends will not deny that modern education presumes there is no supernatural, that morality is relative, and that man and his achievement should be our major concern in life. But, they kindly point

---

[8] 84% of Americans believe the purpose of life is to "enjoy it as much as possible." 67% of practicing Christians agree with this hedonistic sentiment. See: "The End of Absolutes," ibid.

out, the reason these things are presumed is because *they are true*. It may bode ill for Christians, but the facts are the facts, so they say.

This is the ultimate question we will address: Are the teachings of Secular Materialism consistent with reason, logic, and experience? In other words, does Secular Materialism withstand critical review?

As a Christian it is entirely appropriate to simply reject Secular Materialism because it contradicts the teachings of the Bible. Even secular philosophers agree that there are certain basic beliefs, such as the belief that one is alive, that are logically permissible to assume. For Christians such a properly basic belief is that God exists. A Christian is completely justified in beginning with the presupposition that God exists and judging all else based on that presuppositional belief.[9] Note that Christianity does not *need* to withstand the test of secular reasoning—although I believe it performs quite well even under secular standards. However, Secular Materialism *must* withstand the test of secular reasoning because its truth or falsity rests entirely upon secular standards of reason, logic, and experience. In this book, we will judge Secular Materialism by its own standards: reason, logic, and experience. We will not use the Bible or personal illumination as a source of authority, although for the Christian these are the ultimate sources of authority. Instead, we will challenge Secular Materialism using only the tools of reason, logic, and experience. We will, as fairly and objectively as possible, examine the precepts of Secular Materialism to test its veracity.

This examination may prove to be an interesting journey because Secular Materialism in one form or another has been taught in our public schools as if its assertions were undisputed facts. Because most of us have been taught the principles of Secular Materialism from elementary school through college, their central principles are very hard to deny.

The central principles of Secular Materialism are hard to deny *not* because they stand up to the scrutiny of evidence, reason, logic, and

---

[9] Two brilliant philosophers who have written extensively on the concept of presuppositional belief are Alvin Plantinga and Cornelius Van Til. See: Alvin Plantinga, "Is Belief in God Properly Basic?" *Noûs*, Vol. 15, No. 1, 1981 A. P. A. Western Division Meetings (Mar., 1981), pp. 41-51 and Cornelius Van Til, *The Defense of the Faith*, (Phillipsburg, NJ: Presbyterian and Reformed Publishing Co., 1955).

experience—as we will soon discover—but merely because they are what we have been taught. Ironically, Secular Materialism has become the new national religion and its doctrines are no more provable than any other religious doctrines—and in many cases much *less* likely than other religious doctrines. The sole advantage of Secular Materialism is that its views are *secular* and therefore permitted to be taught as a worldview that is not formally religious. But make no mistake: Secular Materialism is not based on findings of science, rational conclusions of logic, or the wisdom of experience. They are merely what is left when you remove the other alternative because the other alternate worldview happens to be based on belief in God, and any worldviews based on God are not permitted in public schools.

If one removes any theistic explanations for the world, he or she is left with a secular explanation. Secular Materialism reigns supreme *not* because it is the most reasonable and logical worldview, but merely because it is *secular*! This may not have been the intended effect of our current application of the separation of church and state doctrine, but it is where we are.

Is a secular worldview the only worldview permitted by the Constitution to be discussed in public schools? Is there an alternative path that gives alternative worldviews a chance to be heard? Does the separation of church and state doctrine require that Christianity play no role in the political, academic, and policy making institutions of our nation?

We turn to these questions in the next chapter.

CHAPTER 4

SEPARATION OF CHURCH AND STATE

The Myth of a Secular America

Most students are taught, if not in high school, then certainly in college, that the United States was founded as a secular nation, upon the principle of a strict separation of church and state, and that there should be an impenetrable wall between all things religious and our public lives. Many take the separation doctrine even further. Polls show that 70% of Americans believe it is inappropriate for religious leaders to make recommendations for which candidates to vote for; 63% think leaders should not rely on their religious beliefs when making policy decisions; 62% feel a presidential candidate's religious beliefs are unimportant; 28% feel it is inappropriate for public officials to make references to God; and half of Americans believe it is inappropriate for the candidates themselves to talk about their religious beliefs.[1] When polled, over 40% of Americans say that the separation of church and state should be "absolute."[2]

Whatever else may be said of these sentiments one cannot say the

---

[1] These numbers are derived from a variety of polls taken by different polling groups. They may be found at PollingReport.com, http://www.pollingreport.com/religion2.htm.

[2] "By 41% to 34%, Americans Think Separation Of Church And State Should Be Absolute," *Economist/YouGov Poll,* March 9, 2012, https://today.yougov.com/topics/politics/articles-reports/2012/03/09/41-34-americans-think-separation-church-and-state-.

Framers shared these views. Those who believe the United States was founded as a secular nation with a strong and impenetrable wall of separation between church and state are either ignorant of the history of our nation or are purposefully ignoring it. Or, more likely, they, like myself, were taught this lie in high school and college and simply believed it to be true. If the Framers of the Constitution wanted to create a secular state where religious belief was purely a private affair, how does one explain the following facts?[3]

- In 1789 Congress set aside federal land for the building of public schools, proclaiming that "religion, morality, and knowledge are necessary to good government."
- For the first 70 years of our Republic, church services were held in the House of Representatives. James Madison, the author of the First Amendment and Thomas Jefferson, the man who penned the phrase, "separation of church and state," regularly attended services there.
- Quotations from the Bible and quotations praising God are carved into the granite of The National Archives, The Washington Monument, The Jefferson Memorial, The Lincoln Memorial, The Vietnam Veterans Memorial, The World War II Memorial, The Capitol Building, The White House, and The Supreme Court, to name only a few.
- The United States Senate and House of Representatives employ chaplains who open each session with a prayer. These chaplains have always been Christians.
- The United States Armed Forces employ over 3,000 chaplains. Over 400 of these soldiers have died in the line of duty.
- U.S. military troops have been given Bibles printed at government expense from the Revolutionary War through World War II.
- The United States Supreme Court opens with the pronouncement, "God Save the United States and this Honorable Court."

---

[3] Sources for these statements are numerous and may be found in many places. An accessible book that provides sources for many of the above facts is Newt Gingrich's *Rediscovering God in America*, (Grand Rapids, MI, Thomas Nelson, 2009). An updated and expanded edition was published by Center Street Publishing in 2016.

- Federal holidays (Holy Days) just happen to coincide with such things as the birth of Christ, the death of Christ, and a National Day of Thanksgiving to "Almighty God."
- The Bible and textbooks replete with Scriptural language and imagery were the primary books of learning in public schools for the first 200 years of education in America and prayers and Bible study were a daily part of most school curriculums until the 1960s.

Now, one may approve of all, some, or none of these things, but the fact is they reveal a separation doctrine very different from the one most of us were taught in college. There is an inconsistency here that calls for resolution. Either our understanding of the separation doctrine is not consistent with the intent of the Framers, or the very people who wrote the Constitution regularly ignored this alleged "impenetrable wall" of separation!

Part of the problem is that the words "separation of church and state" are not in the Constitution. Rather, the words "Congress shall make no law respecting an establishment of religion, or prohibiting the free exercise thereof..." is what the Constitution says about religion. Even a cursory review of history reveals that the Framers meant precisely what they said: Namely, that the Congress shall not *establish* a religion and that neither could they prohibit the free exercise of religion. By "establish" the Framers had something very specific (and obvious, when looked at through the lens of history and the context of their times) in mind. They meant that the Congress cannot declare that the United States is a formally Catholic nation or a nation under the Church of England or a Baptist nation or a Calvinist nation. That's it.

To say that the separation doctrine as taught by Secular Materialists is somewhat different than what the Framers had in mind would be a gross understatement. To understand what the Framers meant by separation of church and state, we need to unlearn much of what we think we know.

The Framers and the Constitution

Part of our modern secular myth is that the Framers were Deists and skeptics, men who tolerated religion only because the times did not allow them to express their hidden doubts. The truth is most of the Framers were devoutly religious men. They regularly attended church and wrote of their Christian faith with such intense passion that today they would be probably be considered religious zealots. A reading of their correspondence, journals, diaries, and philosophical musings makes it abundantly clear that they were very serious about their faith. The late Franklyn S. Haiman was one of the nation's leading experts on the First Amendment. He was also an outspoken atheist. Nonetheless, he acknowledged:

> It is undisputed that the creators of our federal government were believers in God and that a majority of them were, to one degree or another, adherents to a specific Protestant denomination or to Christianity in general. It is also true…that they had no hesitancy about creating sole or multiple establishments of religion in their respective colonies despite their theological belief in some sort of separation of the spiritual and material worlds and thus between church and state.[4]

The truth is the Framers were almost exclusively Christians. Their individual beliefs, like the beliefs of all individuals, vary and were not always entirely orthodox, but historians cannot find a *single* Founding Father who adhered to any religious faith outside of Christianity, with the exception of a few Deists, such as Thomas Paine.

While the Declaration of Independence refers to God several times, the United States Constitution makes no mention of God or Christianity. This, however, has nothing to do with animosity toward Christianity or any religion. Indeed, the presupposing principle as evidenced by the writings of the Founders and, perhaps as importantly, by the sources the

---

[4] Franklyn S. Haiman, *Religious Expression and the American Constitution* (Michigan State University Press, East Lansing, Michigan, 2002), 6.

Founders cited in their writings, was that the nation was deeply religious and that its religion was Christianity. A study of the documents cited by the Framers in their writings reveals that the Bible is by far the most cited of all the sources making up 34% of everything cited in their writing. Interestingly, the second most cited source were writers from the Enlightenment, but all Enlightenment writers *combined* account for only 22% of the sources cited by the Framers.[5] To say that the Framers were children of the Enlightenment is most certainly true, but it is equally true that the Framers were the children of a Christian culture. To imagine that the Founding Fathers were secularists is nothing more than wish fulfillment by Secular Materialists. There is not one shred of evidence to suggest that most of the Framers were anything less than devout Christians.

It is also true that the United States was a nation composed almost exclusively of Christians. America is a far more religiously diverse nation today than it was at the time the First Amendment was written, yet even *today*, after 250 years of immigration from all over the world, Jews, Muslims, Buddhists, Hindus and all other non-Christian faiths *combined* make up a mere 7% of the population. This is not to suggest the First Amendment was written only to protect Christians. It was not. It was written to protect people of all faiths and those few of no faith. But to imagine that the United States was a diverse "melting pot" of religious beliefs when the Constitution was written is simply untrue. Indeed, even today it is a myth that the United States is a diverse melting pot of religious belief. It may be more diverse than many other nations, but we remain (at least for the time being) an overwhelmingly Christian people.

While the First Amendment protects all religious (and non-religious) beliefs, history shows the First Amendment was written to ensure that the federal government did not favor one religious group over another. Even this statement is not quite correct. At the time of the writing of the Constitution, fewer than 1% of the nation were Catholics and fewer than that were anything other than Protestant Christians. While in theory the First Amendment protected all people

---

[5] See David Barton, *Original Intent: The Courts, the Constitution, & Religion* (Aledo, TX: WallBuilders, 2000), 226.

of all faiths, which is certainly does, the reality at the time was it was written primarily to ensure that the government did not favor or one Protestant denomination over another. The Framers had little experience outside of the Christian faith and the miniscule number of Muslims, Hindus, Buddhists, and Jews in America made it unthinkable that the government would favor any of those faiths over a Christian denomination. Hence, the distribution of Bibles or the funding of Christian schools by the federal government were not thought to violate the First Amendment because nearly everyone in the nation at that time was a Christian. What the Framers of the First Amendment were attempting to accomplish was for the *federal* government to remain neutral on matters of religion. For all practical purposes, this meant that the federal government would not establish any one of the many Protestant religions as the official national religion of the new country.

Of course, none of this is meant to imply that the United States is an exclusively Christian nation. It most certainly is not. We have been, from the beginning and are today, an exceptionally tolerant nation, open to all faiths and beliefs, and protective of the religious freedom of all people. But we were, from the beginning, a religious people deeply concerned with religious freedom. Our Constitution was explicitly designed to protect freedom of religion. The goal was to permit any and all religious beliefs—including the right to disbelieve—without showing favoritism to belief or unbelief.

This is *not* the same as establishing a *secular* state. This is critically important. A *neutral* government is not the same as a *secular* government. Neutrality, which is what Framers wanted, is to treat all religious beliefs—or unbelief—equally in the eyes of the law. The Framers meant to avoid the problems caused by nations that established official religions, as was the European model. Secular Materialism, on the other hand, is not neutrality. Secular Materialism is a rejection or exclusion of religion. It is the belief that religion should not be involved in the ordinary social and political activities of the nation.[6]

---

[6] The Merriam Webster Dictionary defines secularism as "indifference to, or rejection of, religion and religious consideration." The Cambridge Dictionary defines secularism as "the belief that religion should not be involved with the ordinary social and political activities of a country."

The Framers were most certainly not secularists. They did not want to keep religion separate from the government because they disdained religion, but because they revered religion. The Framers did not want the government to establish a national religion because they wanted to preserve the religious liberty of all people. Secularists want to keep religion from public policy because they find religion irrelevant and irrational. This was most assuredly not the view of the Framers. It is also why the phrase "separation of church and state," although pithy, was not used by the Framers when drafting the First Amendment. They chose the words, "Congress shall make no law respecting an establishment of religion, or prohibiting the free exercise thereof." It is evident that the actual words used in the Constitution are much less secular and bellicose toward religion than the "separation" phrase so often used in our current culture.

The polls cited at the beginning of this chapter reveal that Americans are becoming more and more secular. For example, today most Americans believe it is inappropriate for religious leaders to make recommendations on which candidates to vote for, while doing precisely that was commonplace in our early history. Similarly, while most Americans feel a presidential candidate's religious beliefs are unimportant, such a sentiment would have been unthinkable, not only to the Framers but also to most Americans just a few generations ago.[7] Indeed, during the lives of the Framers, Georgia, Massachusetts, New Hampshire, New Jersey, North Carolina, South Carolina, and Vermont required officeholders to be Protestants. Delaware, Maryland, and Pennsylvania were more tolerant; they required only that office holders be Christian.[8]

Of course, a nation may evolve or devolve, may become more or less religious as time goes by, but if we are going to transition to a secular state let's not do so believing that we are upholding the intent of the

---

[7] While 54% of the population says they would vote for an atheist candidate for president today, as recently as 1958 only 18% said they would support an atheist. See: "Atheists, Muslims See Most Bias as Presidential Candidates: Two-thirds would vote for gay or lesbian," Jeffrey M. Jones. June 21, 2012, https://news.gallup.com/poll/155285/atheists-muslims-bias-presidential-candidates.aspx.

[8] Derek H. Davis, "Religious Oaths," in *The First Amendment Encyclopedia*, a project of Middle Tennessee State University, *https://www.mtsu.edu/first-amendment/article/927/religious-oaths*.

Founding Fathers. It is clear by their words and actions that what the Framers meant by "separation of church and state" and what many of us understand that phrase to mean today are two very different concepts.

The Framers meant only that the *federal* government would not formally establish a religion. The state governments were free to do as they pleased and individuals, of course, were—and are—free to vote for a candidate based on his religious beliefs, political party, charisma, or any other factor one likes. It is only in a radically secular culture that one would believe the religious views of a candidate are "irrelevant." Why are one's religious views less relevant than one's political party or economic views, for example? Such a belief only makes sense if one finds religious views to be irrational or unimportant. But for millions of devout Christians a person's religious beliefs are not only important, they are the single *most* important thing about a candidate. This is neither illogical nor unconstitutional. The amount of weight a voter places on a candidate's religious views is simply a factor of how important that religion is in that particular voter's life.

Our current policy of favoring secularism is just as misguided as if we favored Catholicism, Methodism, Buddhism, Congregationalism, or atheism. In fact, it could be argued that favoring secularism *is,* for all practical purposes, favoring atheism. Prohibiting any discussion or worship of God is very hard to distinguish from supporting the position that there is no God. To prohibit any prayer, discussion, or mention of God may not be the same as endorsing atheism in theory, but it certainly is in practice. This is not what the Framers intended. In fact, to favor secularism or atheism is as much a violation of the First Amendment as if the government favored Catholicism or Protestantism. Our Founding Fathers created a government that protects religious freedom—not one that promotes secularism.

Federalism and Limited Government

To understand the separation doctrine, the Constitution, and the First Amendment, one must look at these concepts in their larger context. The Framers of the Constitution were intent on creating a national government with limited powers. This is readily evident when viewed in context of everything they did. Hence, we have a federal government and 50 separate state governments. The federal government was granted specific powers and those not specifically given to the federal government were reserved to the state governments, or to the people.[9] Within the federal government, the Framers devised three branches, the Executive, the Legislative, and the Judicial, each designed to check and balance the other branches. At the time the Constitution was written, only one of those branches (the House of Representatives) was directly elected by the people. The Senate was elected by the governments of the states and the judicial branch was, as it still is, appointed by the president with confirmation by the Senate.

The entire framework (and genius) of the Constitution was meant to limit power. The states checked the federal government, the president could veto legislation, the House needed approval of the Senate for a bill to progress, and the judiciary could declare an act of Congress to be unconstitutional, and on and on. It was a brilliant design to limit the power of any one state, of any conglomeration of states, or of any one branch of the federal government. It is within this framework that the separation doctrine was envisioned.

Consistent with the Framers' distrust of government power and promotion of individual liberty, they drafted the First Amendment, which in pertinent part reads: "Congress shall make no law respecting an establishment of religion, or prohibiting the free exercise thereof." There was to be no establishment of a national religion by the federal government and the free exercise of religion was never to be prohibited.

All of this was meant to *protect and preserve religious liberty*, not to limit it. The federal government was not permitted to establish a national religion not because the Framers were attempting to limit religious freedom, but precisely the opposite. If the federal government chose one denomination over another, that would be restricting the religious freedom of those whose denomination was not favored. The federal government was to remain neutral toward all denominations, faiths, and beliefs so all could be practiced without government favor

---

[9] The Tenth Amendment to the United States Constitution reads: The powers not delegated to the United States by the Constitution, nor prohibited by it to the States, are reserved to the States respectively, or to the people.

or hindrance; while at the same time the federal government was never to prohibit the free exercise of religion.

This critical work of creating a limited government took place in the context of a time when the federal government barely existed. At that time in the United States there was no strong federal government—indeed, there was really no "United States." The Framers were presenting the Constitution to the states for ratification and it was not an easy sell. The proposed Constitution would create a much stronger federal government than currently existed under the weak Articles of Confederation, the document that loosely held the states together. The state governments, naturally, were less than enthusiastic about releasing any power by joining this new union. In return for ratification of the Constitution the states demanded a Bill of Rights ensuring that the federal government would not infringe upon the rights of the state governments.

Among the rights that the states cherished was the right to determine their own religious destiny. Far from being disinterested, agnostic, or secular regarding religion, Christianity was extraordinarily important to citizens of the United States. The federal government promised to remain neutral regarding the various Christian denominations and beliefs not because religion was unimportant, but because it was central to the governments of most states. Every single state mentioned God in their constitutions, some several times. (The Constitution of Massachusetts mentions God no less than 12 times.) As we have seen, some states required officeholders to be Protestants, others required only that they be Christians. So, when the Framers drafted the Constitution, there was great concern among the states as to whether the federal government would favor one Christian denomination over another. To avoid this problem, the Framers of the Constitution ensured the state governments that the federal government would remain neutral as to religious preference.

A few examples: At the time of the drafting of the Constitution, New Hampshire, Massachusetts, and Connecticut required citizens to attend public worship and citizens could be fined if they did not regularly attend church. Of the first 13 states, 11 had religious requirements for office holders. Until 1799 New Jersey Constitution guaranteed religious liberty to "any Protestant"; until 1833 Massachusetts required every citizen to be a member of a church; and until 1877 New Hampshire required members of the legislature be Protestant. Until 1835, North Carolina required all office holders to be Protestant. In 1876 that was amended to "any Christian." In fact, the North Carolina Constitution still prohibits atheists from holding elected office, although that provision was held unconstitutional in 1961.

A review of the history, including the letters, speeches, proclamations, books, and debates regarding the First Amendment, reveals that the Founding Fathers wanted to assure the *state* governments that the *federal* government would not establish a national religion nor would it regulate religion at the state level in any way.[10] In fact, the religious protections of the First Amendment were not applied to the state government until 1947[11] and the Supreme Court did not strike down any state establishment of religion until 1961 when a provision of the Maryland Constitution was declared unconstitutional because it required a declaration of the belief in God to hold public office.[12] In other words, the original purpose of the establishment clause of the First Amendment was to *protect* the churches established by the states from being replaced by a national church. This is a far cry from the separation story we are told in high school, but it does explain why the Supreme Court never declared any state established churches unconstitutional and why it was not until 1961 that the Supreme Court first struck down a religious requirement in a state constitution.

While the state governments were free to treat religion in any manner they pleased, the same was not true of the federal government. The federal government was prohibited from establishing a national religion. This was radically different from the European experience. In this regard, and only in this regard, did our Constitution call for a "separation of church and state." This, the historical record reflects, is what Jefferson meant when he penned those now famous words "separation of church and state," in a letter to the Danbury Baptist

---

[10] Akhil Reed Amar, *Bill of Rights* (Yale University Press, New Haven, CT, 1998).
[11] *Everson v. Board of Education*, 330 U.S. 1 (1947).
[12] *Torcasco v. Watkins*, 367 U.S. 488 (1961).

Church. He meant that the new federal government would not choose any one denomination to be the nation's official religion.

Radical though this may have been in the 18th Century, the truth is that other than prohibiting religious tests for federal office and prohibiting the establishment of a national religion, there was very little separation of church and state in the age of the Framers, and indeed throughout the history of the United States until the 1960s. For the first 150 years after the ratification of the First Amendment it appears the amendment meant that the federal government would not establish an official national religion and meant very little more than that.

There are, of course, those who wish the above were not true or who wish to move the nation in a secular direction. Indeed, these individuals have largely succeeded in their efforts to create a secular nation. They have every right to attempt to move the country in any direction they desire. What they should not do, however, is revise the history of our country so it fits their agenda. Sadly, many Americans are so certain of the existence of the "high and impenetrable wall of separation of church and state" myth that simple logic bounces off their minds like bullets off Superman's body. But if the radical separation doctrine we have been taught was true, how does one explain the fact that President George Washington declared a national day of Thanksgiving because, as he wrote, "It is the duty of all Nations to acknowledge the Providence of Almighty God, to obey his will, to be grateful for his benefits, and humbly to implore his protection and favor..."[13] How does one explain the fact that Presidents Jefferson and Madison regularly attended church services which were held in the U.S. Capitol Building?[14] How, indeed, does one explain the words, "In God We Trust" on our currency, or the words "One nation, under God," in our National Pledge of Allegiance? As we know, the federal government's involvement in religion has been rather ubiquitous, from declaring Christian Holy Days as national holidays to engraving statements from the Bible upon the edifices of government buildings. Again, these facts conflict with what we have

---

[13] "George Washington's Thanksgiving Proclamation," October 3, 1789, *National Archives of The United States.*

[14] "Religion and the Founding of the American Republic," *The Library of Congress*, https://www.loc.gov/exhibits/religion/rel06-2.html.

been taught about the "impenetrable wall" of separation of church and state. Perhaps this is because the words "separation of church and state," ever-present though they may be in the minds of secularists, are nowhere to be found in the Constitution.

The Words Most Quoted From the Constitution Are Not In The Constitution. Oops.

We have strayed so far from the original understanding of the First Amendment that we don't even refer to it when we discuss religious freedom. When we speak of "separation of church and state" we are not using the language of the First Amendment. This is an excellent example of the result of removing any discussion of religion from our classrooms. Not only are many of us misapplying the intent of the First Amendment, but we are using words to justify our misapplication that are not even in the First Amendment. And all of this is done with the presumption that we are defending the First Amendment! What a tangled web we weave when first we practice to deceive...

This radical separation of church and state is a lie that has been indoctrinated into our collective cultural mind so thoroughly that to even dare question it is to be considered a religious zealot who is ignorant of the Constitution. Indeed, when one recent presidential candidate mentioned that the words "separation of church and state" are not in our Constitution she was viciously and almost unanimously attacked by everyone from the mainstream media to college professors —and her presidential aspirations were ended. The fact that she just happened to be right was irrelevant.

The phrase "separation of church and state," is not, and never was, in the Constitution. Those words are from a letter Thomas Jefferson (who did not draft the First Amendment, incidentally) wrote to the Danbury Baptist Church in 1802—thirteen years after the First Amendment was written. In fact, Jefferson was in France while the First Amendment was being written.

For these and other reasons, Jefferson may not be the best interpreter of the meaning of the First Amendment. Nonetheless, the metaphor of a wall of separation has become part of the cultural language when discussing the meaning of the First Amendment. Does Jefferson's famous phrase accurately capture the intent of the First Amendment? That depends, of course, on what one means by "separation of church and state." A careful review of Jefferson's writings and actions reveal that what Jefferson meant by "separation of church and state" is probably what almost everyone at that time meant by separation of church and state: namely, that the federal government should never establish a national religion.

Jefferson most assuredly did not mean that there should be the kind of separation of church and state that we misquote him for today. Indeed, there was a church in the U.S. Capitol Building and Jefferson attended services in this government supported church regularly. In fact, he attended services at the church in the Capitol Building *two days* after he penned his letter to the Danbury Baptist Church. As historian James Hutson writes:

> It is no exaggeration to say that on Sundays in Washington during the administrations of Thomas Jefferson (1801-1809) and of James Madison (1809-1817) the state became the church. Within a year of his inauguration, Jefferson began attending church services in the House of Representatives. ...Worship services in the House—a practice that continued until after the Civil War—were acceptable to Jefferson because they were nondiscriminatory and voluntary. Preachers of every Protestant denomination appeared. (Catholic priests began officiating in 1826.) As early as January 1806 a female evangelist, Dorothy Ripley, delivered a camp meeting-style exhortation in the House to Jefferson, Vice President Aaron Burr, and a "crowded audience." Throughout his administration Jefferson permitted church services in executive branch buildings. The Gospel was also preached in the Supreme Court chambers.[15]

To imagine Jefferson was some post-modern separationist is a gross misrepresentation of Jefferson's beliefs. Jefferson's religious beliefs are no mystery. He was not as orthodox in his Christianity as were most of the

---

[15] "Religion and the Founding of the American Republic," *The Library of Congress*, https://www.loc.gov/exhibits/religion/rel06-2.html.

other Founding Fathers (for example, as a child of the Enlightenment, he questioned the miracle stories reported in the Gospels), but he was, as he wrote, "A real Christian, a disciple of the doctrines of Jesus."[16] But whatever Jefferson meant by this sentence, there is little doubt among historians and legal scholars that placing so much weight on one sentence from one letter is an absurd way to interpret the Constitution, particularly when there is ample evidence detailing the intent of the Framers from the actual records of the drafting of the Bill of Rights.

Historian Stephen Mansfield concludes:

> Never before in American history had language from a private letter been elevated to such stature. Never before had a man's words been set at such odds with his life and given the authority of law. Never before had an action of State been interpreted exclusively through the words of a man who was not present at the time and who was writing more than a decade after the fact. The Court's use of Jefferson's phrase would prove to be an American tragedy, and little makes this more certain than the words and actions of Jefferson himself.[17]

The phrase "separation of church and state" was first used in any significant legal way in the 1947 case *Everson v. Board of Education—156 years after the First Amendment was ratified.* In drafting the majority opinion, Justice Hugo Black takes an obscure letter written by Jefferson and misinterprets Jefferson's words to establish a never before imagined separation of church and state that Jefferson himself—much less the actual framers of the First Amendment—would have been appalled by. Why Justice Black chose perhaps the *only* writing issued by the Framers that could even possibly be interpreted to call for a total separation of church and state is a mystery. Why Justice Black ignored the clear history of our nation's *non-separation* of church and state is equally a mystery. Why Justice Black chose to use Jefferson's letter rather than

---

[16] Edwin S. Gaustad, *Sworn on the Altar of God: A Religious Biography of Thomas Jefferson* (Grand Rapids: Eerdmans, 1996), x.

[17] Stephen Mansfield, *Ten Tortured Words*, (Nashville: Thomas Nelson, 2007), 33.

the many other documents written by the legislators who drafted the First Amendment is puzzling.[18] The fact is that Jefferson's private letter should have no bearing on how we interpret words written by James Madison—not Jefferson—particularly when there are ample words written by Madison himself that show no such meaning was contemplated. Indeed, there are words even by Jefferson that show no such meaning was to be imputed on his own words![19]

Interestingly, the Supreme Court itself has never broadly interpreted the separation doctrine. This is why religious symbolism and terminology is used so frequently in our national anthem, national currency, and national holidays. This is why it is not a violation of the Constitution for the federal government to employ military chaplains, House and Senate chaplains, provide governmental services to churches and private religious schools, and on and on. The separation doctrine is, contrary to popular myth, not a high and impenetrable wall, but a rather low shrub, quite easily climbed.

No less a constitutional expert than the former Chief Justice of the United States Supreme Court, William Rehnquist, believed that the "separation" language was so misleading that it should not be used by the Court:

> The "wall of separation between church and State" is a metaphor based on bad history, a metaphor which has proved useless as a guide to judging. It should be frankly and explicitly abandoned.[20]

---

[18] Some historians have suggested that Justice Black, who was a former member of the Ku Klux Klan, had a particular animus against the Catholic Church. The early religious liberty cases often involved taxpayer money being used to support Catholic schools. See e.g., Stephen Mansfield, *Ten Tortured Words*, (Nashville: Thomas Nelson, 2007).

[19] See: *Christianity and The Constitution*, John Eidsmoe (Grand Rapids, MI: Baker, 1987); *Original Intent: The Courts, the Constitution, & Religion,* David Barton (Aledo, TX: WallBuilders, 2000); *Ten Tortured Words,* Stephen Mansfield (Nashville: Thomas Nelson, 2007); *The Bill of Rights,* Akhil Reed Amar (New Haven: Yale University Press, 1980). Almost any history of religion in America will reveal that the nation was, by any standard, devoutly religious, even radically so by modern standards. That this truth has been lost on so many in our current culture is a shocking display of how history can be forgotten or rewritten.

[20] William H. Rehnquist in his dissent in *Wallace v. Jaffree*, 472 U.S. 38 (1985).

While our post-Christian culture has latched on to words that are of only minor importance to the interpretation of the First Amendment, and have even then grossly misinterpreted these words, let us not make that same mistake. Rather, let us look at the actual words of the First Amendment.

Chapter 5

The First Amendment: A Maligned Masterpiece

The actual language of the First Amendment is strikingly different from the "separation of church and state" mantra so loosely thrown about. The First Amendment clauses on religion read:

> "Congress shall make no law respecting an establishment of religion, or prohibiting the free exercise thereof…"

Constitutional scholars separate these 16 words into two clauses: The "Establishment Clause" and the "Free Exercise Clause." The Establishment Clause prohibits Congress from establishing a national religion and the Free Exercise Clause protects the religious freedom of individuals. Taken together, these two clauses are meant to ensure that the government will not interfere with the free exercise of religion in any way: it will not dictate to its citizens what religion they must practice nor will it prevent individuals from practicing the religion of their choice.

Further, the First Amendment should be read in context of its *entirety*. The entire First Amendment reads:

> Congress shall make no law respecting an establishment of religion, or prohibiting the free exercise thereof; or abridging the freedom of speech, or of the press, or

the right of the people peaceably to assemble, and to petition the Government for a redress of grievances.

When read in light of the other rights guaranteed in the same amendment, which is the normal way one would engage in legislative interpretation, we see that the First Amendment guaranteed the right to free speech, freedom of the press, freedom of assembly, and the right to petition the government. Each and every one of these is a positive right to *engage in expression of belief.* It would be rather odd that the First Amendment would list a panoply of rights to engage in freedom of expression and then add…except free expression of religious beliefs! It is comical to imagine the Framers drafting the very first amendment to the Constitution to say, "We Americans have the right to free speech, to a free press, to the freedom of assembly, to the freedom to petition our government—except on matters of religion, where we should just keep our beliefs to ourselves and our mouths shut!"

The religion clauses of the First Amendment have been treated in ways that none of its sister clauses have. For example, if we applied the same reasoning to the free speech clause as we do to the freedom of religion clause, we would treat all speech equally by equally prohibiting all speech! No sane person would believe that we were preserving the freedom of speech by proclaiming that no one—regardless of their political views—was allowed to speak publicly about those views. Yet, that is precisely how we have often dealt with matters of faith. Rather than permitting all religious beliefs to be explored, examined, and expressed, we have prohibited the mention of any and all faiths on the grounds that we are treating all faiths with neutrality. To equally prohibit all discussion of faith in the name of freedom of religion is bizarre and perverse.

This ridiculous outcome is the foreseeable result of moving away from the words and context of the First Amendment and interpreting its meaning by an obscure letter written 13 years after the First Amendment was written, and to make matters much worse, misinterpreting (intentionally or otherwise) the meaning of even that letter. Prior to this odd reliance on a line from a private letter, interpreting the First Amendment was unproblematic. For the first 150 years of our Republic this caused very little controversy because the Establishment Clause was interpreted in a quite literal sense: the federal government shall not formally establish any religion as the official national religion. Unfortunately, the Supreme Court began tremendously increasing the scope of the Establishment Clause by holding that such things as having a Bible in a public school classroom or saying a prayer at a graduation ceremony was somehow "establishing" a religion. Whatever one thinks of such practices, they clearly were not considered "establishing" a religion until very recently in our nation's history.

This extraordinarily broad definition of "establishment" was a stark departure from nearly two centuries of First Amendment jurisprudence. As we have observed, if this was the intent of the Establishment Clause then the government began violating the First Amendment before the ink dried and is currently violating it today! It has led to a conflict between the Establishment Clause and the Free Exercise Clause in ways that were never intended and that never occurred prior to this ill-fated interpretation.

If we are to interpret the First Amendment the way some secularists and radical separationists want, the problems raised become insurmountable. For example, if saying a short prayer at the opening of a high school football game is "establishing a religion," then is prohibiting students from engaging in this prayer violating their right to the free exercise of religion? Does it matter if the prayer is said by a teacher or a student? What about a member of the school board? Does it make a difference if the prayer is recited by a guest of the school who is not an employee of the school? Does it matter if that guest is a minister? Is it a violation of the First Amendment to give taxpayer money to Christian schools or is it a violation of religious freedom to withhold taxpayer money from schools merely because they are Christian? Does it matter what the money is used for? Does it matter if the prayer is recited at a private school or a public school? Could Congress pass a law forbidding all school prayer, whether private or public?

While most Americans are in agreement that a private school is free to engage in any religious activity it likes, the possibility of prohibiting religious freedom even in private schools, businesses, or hospitals is currently being debated. If government money is given to a Catholic hospital, for example, can the government now prohibit the Catholic hospital from hanging Crucifixes on the walls? What if the hospital accepts Medicare payments from its patients? Does that mean the federal government now must maintain a "separation of church and state" policy wherever the Medicare money is spent? What if the nation moves to a single-payer national healthcare program? Does that mean all religiously-based hospitals must now remove all indicia of their faith in order to accept *any* patients? The only reason these questions are now arising is because we strayed completely off course from what the meaning of the Establishment Clause was when we replaced its plain language with the ambiguous and misleading phrase, "separation of church and state," in *Everson v. Board of Education*.

After *Everson,* interpreting the First Amendment became very difficult. If such things as a government employee wearing a rosary is an "establishment of religion" then do all people employed by the government lose their right to the free exercise of religion while they are at work? What if these individuals are "at work" all the time, such as military personnel or police officers? Are soldiers and police officers never permitted to express their religion simply because they happen to work for the government? Is a school teacher allowed to read a Bible during her lunch break? During classroom time while students are taking a test or otherwise engaged? Aloud, at a school sponsored football game to students? Silently, to herself at a school sponsored football game? Is her mere presence *anywhere* with a Bible, whether on-duty or off-duty, whether at school or in the shopping mall, a violation of the separation doctrine by the simple fact that she is a school teacher and may be recognized as such by one of her students?

There is almost unanimous opinion among legal scholars that the Supreme Court's religious freedom jurisprudence has been irregular, inconsistent, and confusing. Many of the major cases handed down by the Court on this topic have been very narrowly decided, often 5-4 decisions, and the dissent in these cases have often been strongly critical of the majority opinion. It is exceedingly difficult to come to any conclusion about where, precisely, the Court stands on any particular case involving freedom of religion. This was decidedly not the case prior to the Court deciding they would use the nebulous phrase, "separation of church and state," as their guide rather than the actual words and history of the First Amendment.

Prior to *Everson* the conversation went something like this:

Question to the Honorable Court:	"May a school teacher wear a necklace in the shape of a cross to class?"
Answer from the Honorable Court:	"Well, is a school teacher "establishing a religion" by wearing a necklace? Let's not be ridiculous! We don't see a problem here."

Under the tortured reasoning of the Court, anyone who works for the government is an agent of the government and therefore their personal actions are the same as governmental legislation! This is ludicrous. It also leads to the very real problem of restricting the individual rights and liberties of everyone who happens to be a governmental employee. What if we lived in a society where everyone worked for the government? Would that mean that all of our individual Constitutional rights are now wiped away because we are governmental employees? What about students who receive government guaranteed student loans? What about a person who receives a Social Security check from the federal government? If that person is a Christian, is the government engaged in unconstitutional support for religion by giving taxpayer money to this person? What if he is a minister on Social Security? If one took the reasoning of some separation extremists to its logical conclusion, a private individual would not be able to say a prayer or listen to Christian music inside his own automobile if that automobile was traveling on a road paid for with taxpayer money.

These are the kinds of irresolvable cases the Supreme Court has had to dance around in an attempt to make their faulty interpretation of the Establishment Clause work. It has been, frankly, a Constitutional nightmare that even legal scholars find impossible to awake from. If any time the government is even minimally "entangled" in religion (as the Court describes it) they are "establishing" a religion, then logic would require the removal of the words "In God We Trust" from our currency, the phrase "One Nation, Under God" from our Pledge of Allegiance, as well as the removal of every white cross or Jewish Star of David placed on a soldier's grave on Normandy Beach. One might even wonder if the presidential oft used phrase, "God bless the United States of America," is an unconstitutional utterance!

The results of extending the Establishment Clause to mean that any support whatsoever from the government is a violation of the separation of church and state is simply unworkable. It is unworkable because the Framers never intended the Establishment Clause to be interpreted the way the Supreme Court has—on again, off again—interpreted it since *Everson*. The reason the Court's Establishment jurisprudence is impossible to predict is because they have attempted to create a separation doctrine that was never envisioned, intended, or enacted by the Framers of the Constitution. The Bill of Rights was written to protect states (and individuals) from an intrusive federal government. To claim that any individual who works for or receives some benefit from the government loses their rights and liberties as individuals is a perversion. It is the exact opposite of the intent of the Bill of Rights, which was to provide restrictions on the *government* and to protect the freedom of individuals.

It is so clear that such things were not originally thought of as "establishing" a religion that in *Everson v. Board of Education*, the case first annunciating this odd interpretation, the Supreme Court relies on the words "separation of church and state" to justify their new view of the Establishment Clause. Apparently, the idea that a child reciting a prayer was the equivalent of the federal government establishing a national religion was so ludicrous that a different approach was taken: *if* "separation of church and state" is very strictly and broadly interpreted, and *if* the separation of church and state in this new meaning of the phrase is what the Establishment Clause means, then any governmental involvement in any way in any religious behavior, however slight, is the establishment of a religion. To quote John Gay: "I know you lawyers can with ease, twist words and language as you please…"

First, there is no "separation" language whatsoever. While it is commonplace when discussing religion for people to use the phrase, "separation of church and state," it would be better to use the actual language of the First Amendment, as the separation language is pregnant with assumptions, meanings, and implications that are often not consistent with the actual language or intent of the First Amendment.

Second, the first word of the First Amendment is *Congress*. Today the federal government is so powerful, so intrusive, so ubiquitous, that we forget that we were originally a nation of states and that the states were the primary governing authorities, not the federal government. The Constitution limits the power of the federal government and the Bill of Rights was written to even further limit those powers. The First Amendment was to limit the *Congress*, not the states. The Supreme Court did not apply the religious clauses of the First Amendment to *any* state until 1947.[1] That explains why many states had religious laws that would be illegal if those same laws were federal laws. The states, at the time, were allowed to legislate religion, but the federal government was not. When Jefferson wrote of "separation of church and state," he meant that there should be a separation of church and the *federal* government. States can, and did, "establish" religions. Indeed, Jefferson himself, as governor of Virginia, proclaimed a day of thanksgiving and prayer, but he did not celebrate the nationally proclaimed day of Thanksgiving as President. This is because Jefferson understood the nature of our federal system of government: the states, at that time, were free to engage in religious practices but the federal government was not.[2] To pretend that the First Amendment required a strict separation of church and state that is now so popular is simply untrue.

Third, the First Amendment states that Congress shall make no law respecting the *establishment* of religion. The word "establishment" had a

---

[1] In *Everson v. Board of Education*, 330 U.S. 1 (1947) the Supreme Court applied the First Amendment to the states via the 14th Amendment, a post-Civil War amendment that applies certain due process rights to all citizens through what is referred to as the "incorporation doctrine." The intent of the 14th Amendment was to ensure that the freed slaves were not discriminated against by any state governments. Over time, the Supreme Court has used the 14th Amendment to grant most rights guaranteed by the Bill of Rights to all citizens regardless of state laws.

[2] "Thomas Jefferson's Complicated Relationship with Thanksgiving: The third president declined to participate in the tradition," Erin Blakemore, November 21, 2017, updated November 18, 2019, *History*, https://www.history.com/news/thomas-jeffersons-complicated-relationship-with-thanksgiving.

very clear and specific meaning to the Framers. It did not mean school prayers, Bible study, or religious instruction. We know this because congressionally proclaimed days of prayer, Bible study conducted within the Capitol Building, and religious instruction supported by the federal government were all seen as perfectly consistent with the words of the First Amendment. "Establishment" meant the legal preference of one denomination as a national religion as was done in so many European countries. The European experience the Framers were familiar with was the actual legal declaration that a country was a "Catholic" country or a "Lutheran" country or a "Protestant" country. That is what establishing a religion means. The Supreme Court has extended this to mean such relatively innocuous things as saying a prayer at a high school graduation ceremony. Whether a graduation prayer is an "establishment" of religion or not, one thing is certain: the Framers did not consider it so. Hence, the issuing of Bibles to federal troops, the hiring of chaplains to pray for the Congress, and all the many other religious activities the federal government engaged in—and engages in to this day.

That is why the use of the language "separation of church and state" is so inappropriate. This language is not used in the Constitution for the very sound reason that it does not describe the relationship between our government and its people. If the Framers had wanted to use the term "separation of church and state," they would have. Instead, they chose the words, "Congress shall make no law respecting the establishment of a religion." These choices of words have very different implications from the words "separation of church and state." Consider, for example, a typical case where a teacher reads her Bible during her lunch break at school. If the legal issue before the Court is, "Is this an establishment of a religion?" the answer may be quite different than if the question is, "Is this a violation of the separation of church and state doctrine?" Perhaps if the Supreme Court started asking the right *question*, it would arrive at the right *answer*. Currently, its impossibly convoluted rulings on religion are often indecipherable even to legal scholars.

Finally, and perhaps most importantly, the First Amendment not only prohibits the federal government from establishing a religion, it also protects the *free exercise* of religion. This section of the First Amendment is often overlooked in our radical "separation" culture. But it should be noted that immediately after prohibiting the creation of a national religion, the First Amendment ensures that Congress shall not prohibit the free exercise of religion.

These things—the history, culture, context, letters, writings, and the plain language of the First Amendment itself—reveal that the First Amendment was meant to protect religious freedom so that it could flourish unabated by the federal government. The clear meaning and purpose of the First Amendment is to protect religious freedom—not to keep it separated from every part of our lives.

Any unbiased review of the history of the First Amendment, whether conducted by Christian scholars or not, confirms that the original meaning of "separation of church and state" did not mean a total separation of religion and state much less a limitation upon the religious freedom of any *individual* whether that individual was employed by the government or not. Nor did it limit any private activity by any person, business, or institution—whether they were regulated, funded, or supported by the government or not. To interpret the First Amendment so that a private entity loses its religious freedom anytime it interacts with the government is to effectively eliminate religious freedom in America. As our government regulates our lives more and more with each passing year, it becomes almost impossible for any person or organization to exist without interacting with the government. If this government interaction—usually *not at the invitation* of the individual—triggers the surrender of his First Amendment right to religious freedom, then religious freedom in America is lost.

Under some interpretations of our misguided "separation" doctrine, engaging in the following activities requires the surrender of one's religious liberty:

- Receiving government financial assistance
- Admitting students to a college who receive government financial assistance
- Being employed by the government
- Working in a government owned office building
- Obtaining a license from the government

One can only pray that the United States Supreme Court realizes the error of its previous interpretation of the First Amendment and corrects this intolerable situation. It is Kafkaesque that the government could tax its citizens and then require its citizens to give up their religious freedom in order to receive some of the money back that was taken from them. It is even more ridiculous for the government to regulate a business and then by virtue of that very regulation to require the business to give up its religious freedom in order to obtain the permit or license that the government is withholding.[3] As constitutional law scholar Michael McConnell puts it: "Excluding religious institutions and individuals from government benefits to which they are entitled under neutral and secular criteria, merely because they are religious, advances secularism, not liberty."[4]

It is a sign of the triumph of Secular Materialism (and indeed, of atheism) that what is routinely taught about religion in America in our public schools is at odds, not only with the language of the First Amendment and the historical record, but even with the opinion of the former Chief Justice of the U.S. Supreme Court. One may disagree with the Founding Fathers, the intent of the First Amendment, and the Chief Justice, but one should not teach students a "history" of the separation doctrine that is almost very nearly the polar opposite of the truth. I doubt very much that most teachers are aware that what they are teaching is simply mistaken. I, myself, trained in the law and a teacher of the U.S. Constitution, was not even aware of how misguided my education was until I noticed there was an enormous chasm between what I had been taught and the religious history of our nation. We have

---

[3] This is precisely what the government threatened to do in the case of Chick-fil-A restaurants. Chick-fil-A had donated some money through its charitable organization to a Christian organization that, among other things, opposed homosexual marriage. Mayors of several cities announced that they would refuse to grant the government permits necessary for Chick-fil-A to open in those cities unless the restaurant owner cease giving money to Focus on the Family. This is an example of government suppression of religious freedom that the First Amendment was written to prohibit. Whether one supports or opposes homosexual marriage one would think that all people who believe in religious freedom and separation of church and state would be appalled by the behavior of these mayors.

[4] Michael W. McConnell, "Accommodation of Religion", 1985 Sup.Ct.Rev. 1 as quoted in *The First Amendment: A Reader*, ed. by John H. Garvey and Frederick Schauer (West, 1992), p. 409.

been taught a lie and we innocently pass that lie on to our own students. It is a tragedy, not only for Christians, but for anyone concerned with American history, religious liberty, or the Constitution.

Separation of Church and State Based on the Genius of the First Amendment

An appropriate separation of church and state is indeed a proud part of the American experiment. The European model has shown that establishing a national church is not good for the church or the state. To give any one church or religion a monopoly on how the nation defines God, limits religious freedom in a way that violates the rights of individuals and hinders the growth of churches. It is self-evident that establishing one national church would trample the religious freedom of those who do not adhere to the teachings of that particular church or religion. What is less evident is how it hurts *all* religious belief. Many theologians and historians believe that churches in America have prospered precisely because the government has not established a national religion. By keeping the government out of the religion business, the market for religion has been free to expand, experiment, and evolve. Rather than have one established, static church, the United States is home to a vibrant variety of religious beliefs and places of worship. The free market principles that apply to grocery stores or hamburger joints apply equally to religion: Let the people decide what they want through the genius of the free market. This not only permits religious liberty for individuals, but it allows places of worship to adopt to the needs of their worshippers.

The way to return to sanity is not to create a theocracy or to build an impervious wall of separation between our religious lives and our public lives. It is simply to return to the intent and language of the First Amendment. We should, as suggested by Chief Justice William Rehnquist, abandon the "separation of church and state" metaphor and instead base our constitutional jurisprudence on the Establishment Clause of the First Amendment. The question before the courts should be: Does this action create an establishment of religion? The answer to that question would sometimes be difficult to ascertain. But it would be far superior to the tangled web we have weaved when we abandoned the intent of the Framers.

The current jurisprudence is simply unworkable. It does not protect religious freedom—it *establishes the national religion of secularism*. This is a clear violation of the intent (and language) of the First Amendment. There may be times when the correct application of the law under the Establishment Clause will be disappointing to Christians and there will be times when it will be disappointing to secularists, but it will provide clear guidance and keep the government out of religion while protecting religious freedom of individuals. For example, a school teacher leading a Christian prayer in a public school may well be an establishment of religion. On the other hand, a student reciting a prayer at a graduation ceremony would certainly not be. The question the courts would ask would simply be: is the government establishing a religion by engaging in this behavior? Asking this question would lead to the desired results of prohibiting the government from establishing a religion while protecting the free exercise of religion by individuals. This is precisely what the First Amendment calls for—and says.

Separation of Church and ...Everything

It is encouraging to note that the current Supreme Court seems to be showing some signs of rectifying these past errors and returning to the original meaning of the First Amendment.[5] The bad news is that even if the Supreme Court changed its First Amendment jurisprudence tomorrow, serious damage has already been done. Fifty years of misinformed teachings on the separation of church and state has

---

[5] See, for example, *American Humanist Association v. Maryland-National Capital Park and Planning Commission*, No. 17-1717, 588 U.S. ___(2019), in which the Court held that a large cross erected on public land to honor veterans of the First World War did not have to be removed; *Trinity Lutheran Church of Columbia, Inc. v. Comer*, 582 U.S. ___(2017), in which the Court held that a Missouri program that denied a grant to a religious school for playground resurfacing, while providing similar grants to non-religious groups, violated the freedom of religion guaranteed by Free Exercise Clause; and *Town of Greece v. Galloway*, 572 U.S. 565 (2014), in which the Court decided that the town of Greece, New York may permit volunteer chaplains to open each legislative session with a prayer.

led many to believe that religious belief has no place in the public square whatsoever. A large number of Americans want not only a separation of *church and state* but a separation of *religion and society*. For these people, religious belief is to remain private, subjective, and irrelevant to anyone but the believer. To attempt to influence others based on one's religious beliefs is considered to be acting intolerantly and quite possibly immorally. For example, polls show that almost half of Millennials who are *practicing Christians* believe it is wrong to share one's faith—not impolitic, not annoying—but *wrong*. There is a growing view in our post-Christian culture that one may attempt to influence public policy based on conservative ideology, liberal ideology, socialism, communism, capitalism, feminism, utilitarianism, pragmatism, or nihilism—but not based upon one's religious beliefs:

- 55% of Americans believe there should be a "strong" separation of church and state.
- 50% believe churches should not give their opinions on political matters.
- 36% believe religious values should have less influence in our culture.
- 36% believe our current separation doctrine has not gone far enough to keep religion out of politics.
- 70% believe it is wrong for a church to suggest a candidate to their congregation.
- 48% say it is not important to them whether a candidate shares their religious beliefs.
- 41% say that it makes no difference to them if a presidential candidate is an atheist. This is up from 18% in 1958.[6]

Of course, people are free to desire more or less religious involvement in their public lives. It is not necessarily "wrong" that so many Americans want religion to play no role in the shaping of public policy. It is, however, a dramatic change from the history of our nation. There was a

---

[6] See: PollingReport.com, https://pollingreport.com/religion2.htm; and Pew Research Center, Faith and the 2016 Campaign, January 27, 2016, https://www.pewforum.org/2016/01/27/religion-and-other-candidate-traits/ and "Atheists, Muslims See Most Bias as Presidential Candidates," Jeffery M. Jones, *Gallup Polls*, June 21, 2012, http://www.news.gallup.com/poll/155285.

time, not long ago, when it was considered an appropriate role—even a duty—of the church to help shape the moral and political culture. The history of the United States includes a vibrant interaction between our religious views and our political views. Public education, the abolition of slavery, and the civil rights movements are just a few of the great national causes led by religious leaders and church congregations. This is still true today. But polls reveal that the younger one is (and not coincidentally the more they have been exposed to Secular Materialism) the more likely they are to desire a complete and total separation of not only church and state but of religion and public policy.

Many in our culture believe that the answer to any question involving the public expression of religion is simply to shout: "Separation of church and state!" and presume the argument ends there. As a former college professor, I recall listening to many conversations between students that went something like this:

Alan: "I am opposed to abortion because it conflicts with the teachings of my church."
Becky: "That is an improper argument! Separation of church and state!"

Or:

Crystal: "I am opposed to the death penalty because the Bible says, 'Thou shall not kill.'"
David: That should hold no weight in the discussion! Separation of church and state!'

Or:

Ellen: "I am voting for Smith for governor because he is a Christian."
Frank: "That is illegal! Separation of church and state!"

Not only are the positions of Becky, David, and Frank demonstrably wrong, but almost all of my students thought that Becky, David, and

Frank were simply pronouncing inalienable truths established by the First Amendment! The fact that the vast majority of my students believed that the First Amendment means the polar opposite of what it actually means is an example of how thoroughly indoctrinated our children are in the precepts of Secular Materialism.

A private individual has the right to vote for only Christian candidates, only Muslim candidates, only Jewish candidates, or only atheist candidates. A citizen has the right to inform all of his or her political decisions on the Bible, the Koran, or the wisdom of Stephen Colbert. This is what religious freedom looks like and this is what the First Amendment protects.

Harvard law professor Laurence Tribe, perhaps the nation's leading liberal constitutional scholar, believes the Constitution holds religiously held beliefs not only equal to other beliefs, but even *superior*:

> The Framers, whatever specific application they may have intended, clearly envisioned religion as something special; they enacted that vision into law by guaranteeing the free exercise of *religion*, but not, say, of philosophy or science.[7]

One may shape their political opinions by reading Sigmund Freud, Michel Foucault, Thomas Jefferson, Immanuel Kant, John Stuart Mill, Gloria Steinem, Marx (Karl or Groucho), Lenin (Vladimir or John), Oprah Winfrey, or Conan O'Brien—but not Jesus Christ. The public square, it seems is diverse, pluralistic, and open to all opinions—so long as they are not religious.

Why should religious belief be singled out as forbidden from influencing public policy? Why is it permissible for a citizen to base his vote on the advice of a friend, the recommendation of his employer, the wisdom of his spouse, an article in *The New York Times*, a conversation with a co-worker at lunch, or the sage advice given by a late-night talk show host—but it is an outrage to vote based on the teachings of the Scriptures?

---

[7] Laurence Tribe, *American Constitutional Law*, 3d ed. (Foundation Press, Mineola, N.Y., 1988), 1189.

The answers to those questions are varied and complex, but most of them are not very good. Assertions that religion is divisive and polarizing, for example, may be true, but are not good reasons to prohibit religion from the marketplace of ideas. After all, political parties and ideologies are divisive and polarizing—for that matter, so is democracy. Our solution to political factions has been to follow the advice of James Madison. In "Federalist No. 10," Madison famously wrote that there were two ways to control political factions: either eliminate factions or permit one faction to balance another. The first choice, Madison penned, was a "cure worse than the disease." Hence, our public marketplace is filled with diverse groups, ideologies, and interests all competing with each other. The genius of this democratic pluralism is that no group or interest is banned from the free market of ideas. Each faction, interest, or ideology is allowed to openly compete—and may the best policy win.

This is what real tolerance looks like. It is precisely what pluralism and diversity requires. The fact that many Americans want to prohibit religious opinions from access to the marketplace of ideas in the name of "tolerance" and "diversity" is so ironic as to be Orwellian. How did a nation that prides itself on religious freedom get to the place where religious freedom means the right to practice your faith only in the privacy of your home and the confines of your place of worship? True religious belief expresses itself as a worldview—as a way that shapes and informs everything we do. Real religious freedom is not practiced by singing a few hymns on Sunday mornings.

More importantly, many people mistakenly believe that the words religion, faith, belief, church, morality, and God are basically interchangeable and that when Jefferson wrote of a separation of *church* and state, really, he meant that all everything and anything to do with religion, faith, belief, morality, and God should be kept out of public life. Of course, nothing could be further from the truth. The church is certainly not the same as religion; which is quite different than faith; which is itself different than belief; which is distinct from morality; none of which are quite the same thing as God. Today, a large percentage of Americans believe that not only should there be no formally recognized national church, but that there should be a complete and total separation of God from our public lives!

That is the 800-pound silent gorilla in the room. The truth is secularists are not only opposed to the public expression of "religion." They are equally opposed to the public expression of God. Is there really a fight waging over the particular beliefs of, say, Baptists versus Congregationalists? No. The problem secularists have is with any "God talk." The particular beliefs of different denominations being discussed in a school classroom is not what is at issue in our nation. It is the mention of God in any way, shape or form. We are not arguing about whether the host is physically the body of Christ or only represents the body of Christ. Our secular culture has moved far beyond those arguments. We are now at the stage that even a moment of silent prayer to any god of one's choosing, or to no god at all, is thought to be an egregious violation of the separation doctrine! The unspoken truth is, secularists in our society want to stamp out any and all discussion—or even *silent thought*—about God.[8]

Of course, no law or Supreme Court decision requires that God, or even religious belief, be irrelevant to our public lives. What has occurred has not been legal, but cultural. There has been a massive cultural shift in our attitudes and beliefs about the role of faith and religion in our society. Such rapid and enormous shifts do not take place in a vacuum nor are they accidents of nature. There has been an intentional dismantling of the role of religion in our culture and that dismantling has largely taken place in our public high schools, colleges, and universities. To say it was intentional is not to say it was necessarily nefarious. It may be that most of the removal of religious influence from our educational institutions has been done with good intentions. But you know what they say about some roads that are paved with good intentions…

---

[8] A woman was recently arrested in England for *silently* praying outside an abortion clinic. The police asked her if she was praying. When she answered, "Yes," she was promptly arrested and hauled to jail.

CHAPTER 6

THE ACADEMIC ASSAULT ON EDUCATION: REMOVING GOD FROM THE CLASSROOM

We revere teachers in our nation, which is generally appropriate and commendable. Most of our educators are people of high principles who work hard helping our children become better thinkers and better citizens. Most teachers—like most Americans—are Christians. So it is with some trepidation that I must now turn our attention to public schools as one of the leading causes of the decline of Christianity in America. The ignominious role public schools have played is certainly not because the typical elementary or high school teacher is in any way anti-Christian. Rather, it is due to a variety of factors almost all of which have been imposed on school teachers, often against their will. Unfortunately, the same cannot be said of college professors, who have much more academic freedom than do high school teachers. The role of college professors is more complicated, and, we will explore it separately as the problem in our colleges and universities is somewhat different than it is in elementary and secondary schools.

I have spent most of my adult life deeply entrenched in the halls of higher education, either as a student or a teacher. I hold a bachelor's degree, a master's degree, and a law degree. I have attended or taught at 10 different colleges or universities. I taught for 17 years to undergraduates, graduate students, and law students. I love teaching and I love students.

Spending most of my adult life as a teacher has taught me that schools are not without deep failures, flaws, and faults, and among their greatest is their transition from citadels of moral learning to cubicles of secular indoctrination.

A Brief Primer on American Education

Education in America has changed dramatically in the last several decades. To even discuss such things as "separation of church and state" in regard to schools, we first need to understand that our forefathers (and mothers) would find our current school system nearly incomprehensible. Our schools today are in almost every measure the polar opposite of what schools were like for the first 150 years of our Republic. Our Founders lived in a world where schools were generally private, supplemental to a child's education, voluntary, not regularly attended, and devoutly Christian. Today, almost all schools are public, central to our lives, mandatory, and militantly secular. What began as private, voluntary associations established primarily to provide a Christian education have become government mandated institutions where our children are subjected to 12,000 hours of entirely secular education. What began as local, voluntary, and small efforts to supplement our children's educations is now an enormous enterprise manned by over 1,000,000 employees—*not including teachers*—where we place our children for almost every waking moment of their lives.

Until the 20th Century, schools in America were primarily private and devoutly Christian. This was true not only of colleges, but also of public elementary and high schools. Almost all of the schools in our country were founded by churches, administered by clergymen, and established to teach Christian virtues. This was the case from colonial times well into the late 1800s. In fact, as late as 1900, about 30% of children in America did not even attend school and those who did engaged in Bible study, Scripture memorization, and school prayer along with secular academic topics until the 1960s. Few thought this was an affront to the Constitution. As discussed in Chapter 3, the separation of religious study—namely, Christian study—from schools is a relatively recent event that most anyone living prior to the 20th

Century would find as perverse. Perverse, because until not too long ago it was thought that the primary purpose of education was to instill moral values and civic duty in young people and these moral values and civic duties were taught almost exclusively through the study of the Bible.

What is important is not that children recite a routine daily prayer, but that the history of Christianity—and other religions—with all their richness of literature, philosophy, poetry, and wisdom be a part of a child's education. That our children have the benefit of the greatest minds of the world as they pondered the greatest questions in life. That the Bible, the most influential book in the world (by any measure—including secular measures), be offered as a course of study. The Bible is not only a "religious" book, it is a book containing some of the world's greatest poetry and most profound philosophy. The study of Western philosophy, art, music, and literature is greatly diminished without understanding the Christian influence on these subjects. Indeed, up until the 20th Century it is no exaggeration to say that Western art and music were largely expressions of Christianity—along with much of Western architecture, philosophy, history, and literature.

Our schools have been deprived of much more than prayer. They have been deprived of the Christian worldview in its entirety. Christianity has been stripped from our schools—and our culture—not just as a faith or a religion, but as a worldview. As a way of explaining and understanding purpose, meaning, and existence. The loss has been enormous. And this loss would be enormous even if Christianity were not true! To deprive students the study of Christianity is to deprive them of an education. This is so even if the students are atheists.

It is utterly impossible to understand the history of the Western world without understanding the history of Christianity. This was true as early as the First Century and it is just as true today. How, for example, could one understand the death of all of the Greek and Roman mythological gods without studying Christianity? How could one begin to comprehend the Middle Ages and the Holy Roman Empire? How could one appreciate the works of Da Vinci, Michelangelo, Dante, Bach, or Beethoven without a knowledge of Christianity? How does one appreciate the Reformation, the Renaissance, and the Enlightenment without first understanding Christianity? And how, today, could one truly grasp the struggle between the West and radical Islam without understanding Christianity?

These are the reasons to study Christian history and Christian thought—not to proselytize or preach or convert; but to familiarize students with the single most significant movement in the history of Western man. To ignore Christianity as a philosophy, worldview, and historical force is an affront to education. It is to intentionally choose ignorance over truth about a topic that is not only important—but that is by far the most important phenomenon in the history of the Western world. And this is true whether Christianity is true or not. To utterly disregard the Christian worldview (or even prohibit its mention) because some people think its claims may not be true is entirely irrelevant. Christianity should not be taught in public schools as *the truth*, but as an undeniable historical event, a philosophy, and a worldview. Its truth is no more relevant in this regard than the "truth" of Greek mythology, Platonic forms, or the Marxist Dialectic.

Replacing Christianity With Secular Materialism

The trajectory of education in America has gone from almost no one attending school to mandatory school attendance; from almost all students attending private schools to almost all students attending public schools; from virtually all schools, including public schools, being founded and governed by Christian churches, to almost all schools being governed by the state; from the curriculum being primarily focused on Bible study and building Christian character to the curriculum prohibiting the teaching of anything related to Christianity; from daily Scripture reading and communal praying to the enactment of policies that make such activities terminable offenses.

Children spend more time in schools than doing anything else, except sleeping. (Incidentally, the least amount of time spent per day is on "religious, spiritual, or voluntary activities," coming in dead last at 0.2 hours per day versus 6.5 hours per day for school). For better and for worse, our children spend the vast majority of their waking hours being taught about life not by their parents or their churches, but by employees of the government.[1]

In a total reversal of what public education was like for the first 150 years of our Republic, children now attend school 8 hours a day, 180 days a year, for a period 13 years—and during this long period of time they will hear almost nothing about God, faith, Christianity, Jesus, church, or the Bible. This is tragic not only for Christians, but also for anyone interested in exploring religion, faith, or even the possibility of God. Not only will our children learn little or nothing about Christianity, but also in most schools, they will hear almost nothing about *any* faith or religious belief or about anything related to the spiritual or metaphysical. This entire aspect of human existence, which carries with it such things as morality, purpose, and meaning has largely been eliminated from the lives of our children. While these changes have occurred over time and often with the best of intentions, our current educational system would have been accepted by our forefathers only at the point of a bayonet. And for good reason: one need not be a Christian to believe that the study of morality, purpose, and meaning are essential to developing healthy humans and productive citizens. One need not be a Christian to believe that the study of the existence—or non-existence—of God is central to a person's life. One need not be a Christian to believe that the spiritual, the metaphysical, and the transcendent are topics worthy of contemplation.

The dramatic change in education in America took place incrementally. The first major transition was requiring children to attend school. In 1918, the federal government made education of children compulsory, and since it was compulsory, it was also free. Because public schools charged no tuition, parents began removing their children from private, mostly Christian schools, and enrolling them in the free public schools. At this time, and until the middle of the 20th Century, there was no real separation of church and state in public school classrooms. Prayers were recited, Bible study was common, and the teaching of Christian values was considered entirely appropriate.

---

[1] U.S. Department of Labor, Bureau of Labor Statistics, *American Time Use Survey*, 2017.

It was not until 1947 that the Supreme Court applied the separation doctrine to schools, and in that case they *upheld* a New Jersey law that provided public transportation for schoolchildren to attend public and parochial schools.² The first real separation cases did not arise until the 1960's, nearly 200 years after the writing of the First Amendment: and in *School District of Abington Township v. Schempp* (1963), the Court struck down a school requirement that students participate in daily Bible verse reading and in *Epperson v. Arkansas* (1968), the Supreme Court struck down a law that made it a crime to teach evolution

But it wasn't until 1971, in *Lemon v. Kurtzman*, that the Supreme Court made their colossal blunder. In *Lemon*, the Court determined that a state could not reimburse the costs of teachers of secular subjects in private religious schools. It was not the decision itself that is so troubling about the *Lemon* case, but the test fashioned by the Court to resolve all future separation cases. The Court developed a 3-pronged test, referred to as the Lemon Test, that would become the official test in separation jurisprudence for the next several decades. In determining whether an action by the government is permissible under the First Amendment, the Court looks at the following factors:

1. The statute must have a secular legislative purpose.
2. Its principal or primary effect must be one that neither advances nor inhibits religion.
3. The statute must not foster an excessive government entanglement with religion.³

The test is flawed in many ways, including the fact that the third prong is so vague as to give the Court no real guidance, leaving the Court with unbridled discretion in each and every case. Much more problematic, however, are the test's first two prongs. By requiring that the action taken must have a *secular* legislative purpose and that it neither "advances nor inhibits" religion, is to rewrite the language and intent of the First Amendment. The history of the First Amendment prior to *Lemon* is absolutely clear: religion, the advancement of religion,

---

[2] *Everson v. Board of Education*, 347 U.S. 1 (1947).
[3] *Lemon v. Kurtzman*, 403 U.S. 602 (1971).

and legislative religious purposes were not only permitted, they were considered virtues of government and were regular occurrences.

We have already seen how the government was, and is, "entangled" with religious proclamations, from Washington's declaring a day of National Thanksgiving to the invocation of God at the opening proceedings of the Supreme Court. Ironically, when the federal government first set aside land to provide for public education, they rather explicitly stated their legislative purpose:

> Religion, morality, and knowledge, being necessary to good government and the happiness of mankind, schools and the means of education shall forever be encouraged.[4]

The examples are so many and the "entanglement" and "advancement" of religion so extensive that the authors of the Lemon Test surely knew they were moving the nation in a new direction. The animus toward religious belief, particularly Catholic belief, is shockingly clear in *Lemon*. Justice Douglas, in the opinion for the Court, wrote:

> In the parochial schools Roman Catholic indoctrination is included in every subject. History, literature, geography, civics and science are given a Roman Catholic slant. The whole education of the child is filled with propaganda. That, of course, is the very purpose of such schools [...] That purpose is not so much to educate, but to indoctrinate and train, not to teach Scripture truths and Americanism, but to make loyal Roman Catholics.[5]

From the enacting of the First Amendment until the 1970s, the commonly recognized understanding of the role between government and religion was that the government was supportive of the many

---

[4] See: "An Ordinance for the Government of the Territory of the United States, North-West of the River Ohio," Library of Congress.
[5] *Lemon v. Kurtzman*, 403 U.S. 602 (1971), p. 635 (note 20).

benefits of a religious people, but would not support one religious denomination over another. When compulsory education became the law, religion was still very much a part of the curriculum. If the Supreme Court had simply ordered the schools not to proselytize and to present all religious viewpoints in a fair and balanced manner, this would have had the distinct advantages of being true to the Constitution, consistent with religious freedom, and supportive of a full and complete education. Instead, the Court infamously decided to abandon the neutrality of the Constitution and the deeply held religious beliefs of the vast majority of citizens, and declare that all public education must have a "secular purpose" that does not "advance religion." This is not only inconsistent with the history of the country and the clear language of the First Amendment, but even with the Court's prior judicial rulings. As Charles C. Haynes, a senior scholar at The First Amendment Center, writes:

> For James Madison, Thomas Jefferson and other early supporters of church-state separation, authentic religious liberty requires that government remain neutral toward religion while simultaneously upholding the right of religious people and institutions to participate fully in the public square of America. Ignoring the role of religion ... is hardly "neutral." On the contrary, such exclusion sends a message of government hostility to the religious. The First Amendment does not guarantee atheists or anyone else "freedom from religion."[6]

The movement from government neutrality to government promotion of secularism has resulted in decisions that have been polarizing and impossible to harmonize—not only with the First Amendment, but also with the Court's own decisions on the same topic. In *Stone v. Graham* (1980), the Court ruled that a display of the Ten Commandments in public school classrooms violated the Establishment Clause of the First Amendment; in *Wallace v. Jaffree*, 472 U.S. 38 (1985), the Court

---

[6] Charles C. Haynes, "Ground Zero Cross: A Display Is Not a Shrine," April 4, 2013, *Freedom Forum Institute*, https://www.freedomforuminstitute.org/2013/04/04/ground-zero-cross-a-display-is-not-a-shrine/.

struck down a moment of meditation or voluntary prayer by students; in *Edwards v. Aguillard* (1987), the Court struck down a law requiring the teaching of creation science alongside the teaching of evolution in schools; in *Lee v. Weisman* (1992), the Court determined that a clergy-led prayer at a graduation ceremony was a violation of the Constitution; and in *Santa Fe Independent School District v. Doe, 530 U.S. 290* (2000), the Court struck down a student-led, student-initiated prayer at school football games.

On the other hand, in *Board of Education of Westside Community Schools v. Mergens* (1990), the Court ruled that it was unconstitutional for a school to prohibit a student religious group from meeting on school premises during non-instructional time; in *Zobrest v. Catalina Foothills School District* (1993), the Court held that the government may provide sign-language interpreters for deaf students at religious schools, but a year later in *Kiryas Joel School District v. Grumet*, the Court disallowed the creation of a special school district to benefit disabled children in an Hasidic Jewish neighborhood; in *Mitchell v. Helms* (2000), the Court allowed the funding of educational materials and equipment to private, Christian schools; in *Good News Club v. Milford Central School* (2001), the Court ruled that Milford Central School violated the First Amendment by prohibiting a private Christian organization for children from meeting after hours in the school; and in *Zelman v. Simmons-Harris* (2002), the Court upheld an Ohio law that provided tuition vouchers for public school children who chose to attend certain classes at Christian schools.

To say that these decisions, not to mention other equally convoluted decisions involving public manger scenes—the singing of Christmas carols, the practice of opening legislative sessions with a prayer, and other cases—are confusing, is an understatement. As one studies the separation doctrine cases, the confusion transitions to frustration and eventually to outright resignation of even the slightest hope of untangling the separation knot. Why, for example, is it a violation of the separation doctrine for someone to recite a prayer at a graduation ceremony but not for the Congress to open its sessions with a prayer? Why is it impermissible for a football coach to say a prayer with his team, but perfectly fine for the government to print, "In God We Trust," on our national currency? Supreme Court Justice Antonin Scalia, lamenting the misguided separation doctrine, wrote of the Lemon Test:

> Like some ghoul in a late-night horror movie that repeatedly sits up in its grave and shuffles abroad, after being repeatedly killed and buried, Lemon stalks our Establishment Clause jurisprudence once again, frightening the little children and school attorneys...[7]

While it is impossible to know, the Supreme Court may finally be recognizing the error of their ways and returning to the intention of the Framers, the words of the First Amendment, and their own jurisprudence for the first 189 years of Constitutional interpretation. Some of the most recent decisions of the Court seem to be abandoning the "secular purpose" criteria and returning to a more neutral view that permits religious advancement so long as there is no "establishment" of religion. Unfortunately, it may be too late.

Public Schools: What We Do...and What We *Should* Do

Because the jurisprudence regarding religion and public schools is complex, confusing, and changing, many school administrators have adopted a rather simplistic view: "Don't ever mention Christianity, God, or religion in the classroom under any circumstances—ever!"

This is unfortunate, because it is *not* the position of the Supreme Court, and because it leads to a wholesale abandonment of all things spiritual, religious, or metaphysical. In other words, it results in the teaching of a secular worldview. And as we have seen, the secular worldview is, for all practical purposes, indistinguishable from the atheist worldview.

The problem is not that children are being taught that Christianity is wrong—it is that they are not being taught anything about Christianity at all. They are, however, spending literally years in the classroom

---

[7] *Lamb's Chapel v. Center Moriches Union Free School District*, 508 U.S. 384, 398–99 (1993).

learning the "truth" about Secular Materialism. As William Barr, the former Attorney General of the United States, puts it:

> The problem is not that religion is being forced on others. The problem is that irreligion and secular values are being forced on people of faith.[8]

The result is that the only worldview public school students are made familiar with is Secular Materialism. Because Secular Materialism is the polar opposite of the Christian worldview, one does not need to attack Christianity. The indoctrination of Secular Materialism into the minds of students without mentioning that there is another worldview is the equivalent of telling our students that Christianity is wrong. In fact, it is worse. By not mentioning Christianity in public schools, it is informing our students that Christianity does not matter, or at the very least, that it is irrelevant to education and relegated only to church. It is implied, however inadvertently, that schools are places of "fact" and churches are places of "faith," and never the two shall meet.

Again, this may not have been what our educational leaders and Supreme Court justices had in mind, but the consequences of our separation of church and state policies have been to teach the subjective worldview of Secular Materialism as if it were the only possible explanation of reality. Because of our misguided ban on any religious talk in public schools, the Christian worldview is not criticized—it is non-existent! That is why most teachers, parents, and students are unaware that Christianity is under such vehement attack. There is no acknowledged attack on Christianity because in the public school system there is no Christianity. Our school system treats Christianity the way the former Soviet Union treated political leaders who fell from favor: Trotsky was not compared unfavorably to Stalin; Trotsky was simply not mentioned as someone who ever existed. We have effectively eliminated Christian thought from public schools and the winner by default is Secular Materialism.

Rather than pretending that faith and religion have no place in our public schools, it would be far better to recognize the unsurpassed

---

[8] William Barr, Speech Delivered at Notre Dame University Law School, November 11, 2019.

impact religion has had on humankind. The wholesale banning of all things religious from our classrooms is not required by the Constitution. It is perfectly legal to discuss religion in a wide variety of ways. What is not permissible is to preach, proselytize, or worship. Aside from those activities, religion may be taught as history, literature, poetry, or philosophy. Religion may be mentioned in classes on history, government, art, literature, and others. Entire courses may be taught on comparative religion, the history of religion, religion as literature, religion and art, religion in modern culture, or religion in politics, to name just a few.

Even better than teaching specific courses on religion would be to integrate a theistic worldview into classes where an atheistic worldview is currently present—and this includes courses ranging from biology to psychology. Teachers would not teach an exclusively theistic view, they would simply note that a theistic view exists that may or may not be consistent with the current atheistic view, and that both the theistic and atheistic views are possibilities open to reasoned analysis. For example, in a psychology course the teacher would not only present Maslow's Hierarchy of Needs to explain human desire and purpose, but would also present the theistic worldview on this matter. To do anything less (as is current practice) is to indirectly teach students that the topic of human needs has only been seriously addressed by secular psychology. Of course, nothing could be further from the truth.

This would be entirely consistent with the First Amendment and it would have the enormous advantage of actually educating students rather than throwing our arms up in despair and simply ignoring the topic. Incidentally, religion is the *only* topic that we have ripped from the curriculum to be treated with intentional and deliberate ignorance. Teachers do not ignore different economic systems—they compare and contrast them. It would be an act of utter ignorance to order teachers to never discuss capitalism, socialism, or communism. The same is true of family units (traditional, blended, two-parent, one-parent, gay and straight parents, etc.); types of governments (democracy, monarchy, dictatorship, etc.); personalities (introverted, extroverted, sanguine, melancholy, Type A, Type B, etc.); gender (male, female, androgynous, bi-gender, cis-gender, pangender, transgender, etc.); sexuality (heterosexual, homosexual, LBGTQ, etc.) Our schools have proven themselves to be quite capable of discussing events in history with great nuance, whether the topic be slavery, the Industrial Revolution, the causes of World War II, the Civil Rights Movement or the war in Vietnam.

Indeed, the only subject our schools seem unwilling to discuss is religion. Religion alone has been singled out as a topic that is *verboten* from the classroom. Is the discussion of Christianity, Islam, Judaism, and other world religions any less important than discussions about economics, government, or gender? Is it really so fraught with disagreement that a reasonable discussion is impossible? Is it any more controversial than human sexuality, civil rights, family structure, gender, or dropping atomic bombs on Hiroshima and Nagasaki? No. Religion has been relegated to a very special place in our educational system—a place of non-existence. This ridiculous approach toward the treatment of religious belief in public schools has resulted in an educational system that, regarding the topic of God, is indistinguishable from those in North Korea, China, and the former Soviet Union! This is most certainly not what the Framers envisioned, or more importantly, what most Americans want.

Completely removing all discussion of the possibility of God from the classroom is not consistent with an unbiased, neutral state—it is consistent with atheism. Then again, to say it is consistent with atheism is not entirely true. The truth is worse. Teaching that God does not exist would be teaching atheism. Not mentioning God at all is not *teaching* atheism, it is *confirming* atheism. It is sending a message, intentionally or otherwise, to our children that the existence—or even the *possible* existence—of God is irrelevant to our intellectual lives. It is promoting the belief, intentionally or otherwise, that God's existence is irrelevant to mathematics, physics, biology, chemistry, history, literature, economics, and government. It is teaching that *even if* God exists His presence has no impact on the "real" world. This, of course, is not a scientific fact, but a mere dogmatic belief. And it is a certain kind of dogmatic belief. *It is a faith-based statement about God*. It is a worldview based on a certain philosophy that cannot be proven or disproven. It is, in other words, a kind of *religious* belief, no different than a belief that God is the creator and sustainer of everything in the universe and that all truth is God's truth—including truths about math, science, and the human condition. To assert that God is relevant to everything is Christianity. To say that God is not relevant to anything aside from religious belief is Secular Materialism. Both the Christian view and the Secular Materialist view are inherently philosophical views. Neither can be objectively proven beyond all doubt. Either is possibly true. In other words, both are at heart religious assertions. But only one of these religious views is taught in our public schools, and it is taught not as the subjective philosophy that it is, but as objective truth.

To prohibit the discussion of even the *possibility* of God is to promote atheism in the classroom. And it is to do it in a way that is far worse than simply presenting the case for atheism. Public schoolteachers do not discuss religion, God, or atheism at all. So, instead, what is an essentially atheistic worldview is taught as if it were an objective, scientific fact. Students do not know they are being taught a view entirely consistent with atheism and diametrically opposed to theism. Instead, they understandably presume they are merely being taught "scientific facts." That "science" happens to refute Christian teachings is just an unfortunate fact of life, or so the students conclude. The truth, as we have seen even in the example of something as objective as biology, is much more complicated. In topics such as history, English, or the social sciences, the "objective facts" are even more difficult to ascertain. Yet, because of our misunderstanding of the separation doctrine, all of these topics are taught either as if there is no God, or that His existence is irrelevant. This is far worse than having an open and honest discussion about theism versus atheism and how they offer two opposing worldviews. Because of our fear of any "God-talk" in the classroom, our students end up being taught an atheistic worldview masquerading as objective truth.

Reaping The Whirlwind

The damage to our culture, not only religiously, but morally, ethically, and spiritually, has been immense. What has been removed from our schools is far more than daily prayer. After 50 years of keeping almost all conversations about the existence of God, religion, and faith out of the classroom, many Americans feel that religious belief is not a topic that is appropriate to public conversations, academic inquiry, or public policy. While it is difficult to imagine a topic *more* relevant to our lives, it is understandable that people could reach the rather bizarre conclusion that religious belief is something unworthy of intellectual pursuit.

After all, if the study of faith in God was a matter of academic interest, why is there almost no discussion of this topic in high school or college? Why is the study of faith, religion, or the existence of God not a required course? Why is this particular topic not included in the panoply of subjects that academics deem important to study, such as history, geography, art, music, mathematics, literature, biology, chemistry, and the social sciences?

We may not consciously ponder these thoughts, but surely in our subconscious mind the utter absence of the study of religion in our schools tells us something. For many Americans the fact that religion is disregarded in academic institutions tells them that religion is irrelevant to the real, material world. For others, it suggests that religion, while important, is based entirely on faith and is therefore not susceptible to the rigors of intellectual analysis. For still others, it indicates that religion is a purely private matter and therefore illegitimate as a source of public influence. For some, this combination of presumptions leads them to the conclusion that religious belief is irrational, illogical, and irrelevant.

This may not have been what the Supreme Court had in mind when it set out to remove religion from our schools, but this is one of the results. The great harm done to our culture was not in the removal of *prayer* from our schools but in the removal of any discussion of faith, religion, the metaphysical, and God. This not only had the rather foreseeable consequence of making Americans less interested and informed about Christianity, but also had the less foreseeable consequences of removing from the classroom discussions about morality, meaning, and purpose.

The history of education in the United States tells the story of a Christian tragedy. Schools in America were founded almost exclusively by Christian churches for the purpose of teaching a Christian worldview. This was as true of the local one room schoolhouse to Harvard, Yale, and Princeton universities. The idea that religious belief and education should—or even *could* be separated—was unthinkable. Today, even among devout Christians, the suggestion that schools should discuss the concept of God (much less Christianity!) is considered radical and dangerous. We have been fully indoctrinated with the lie that religious belief poisons the free and open search for truth; that the church will impose its "anti-intellectual" views on teachers and students alike. The truth is that education and religion coexisted in this nation until very recently and there has been no history of anything even remotely approaching a theocratic dictatorship of thought in American education. Furthermore, any attempt at a serious education is doomed to failure without considering the greatest questions of humanity—those of meaning, purpose, existence, morality, justice, and death.

Where academia has failed miserably is precisely at this juncture. Students from elementary school through graduate school are bored. *Bored!* How can an educational system that is functioning properly so thoroughly bore its students? What could be less boring than discussing and learning about life's great issues, mysteries, and questions? Students are regularly bored precisely because they are *not* discussing and learning about life's great issues, mysteries, and questions. Those topics, which invariably lead to the discussion of the possibility of God or a god or the gods have been entirely eliminated from our educational system. And so, students are left wondering, "Why am I here? What is this all about? Who *cares* about this stuff?"

And these questions are not asked only by the immature or the apathetic student. They are asked by almost all students, and often by the very best students. They are, in truth, excellent questions. Students know, deep in the core of their beings, that there must be something more worthy of study—more significant to their lives—than *Moby Dick* or the Periodic Table of the Elements. I am a fan of both great literature and scientific discovery—but day after day after day for year after year after year of studying fractions and the conjugation of verbs leaves the thoughtful student feeling a bit cheated. Then, this poor lass or lad moves on to college hoping they will finally get to discuss "real" things and "adult" topics only to be taught more of the same, with occasional ramblings on the Oedipus Complex and the Marxist

Dialectic. They feel—rightly so—somehow deprived of learning anything of importance.

The problem may have originated with the idea that open academic inquiry should not be controlled by the church. And, indeed, it should not. But this fear of some all-powerful, authoritative church has never been a reasonable fear in America. It has not even been a reasonable fear in Europe since the fall of the Holy Roman Empire! And to compound this error, we have extended a fear of the church into the fear of religion generally. Even at this juncture all was not lost. We could certainly keep the church and even religion out of the classroom and still provide a quality education. Where we have gone horribly wrong is to assume that the church, religion, and God are one and the same thing. They are most assuredly not.

God can be discussed in schools without imposing any particular religious beliefs on anyone. Will such study be easy? No. Will it be fraught with difficulties of bias, prejudice, and favoritism? Perhaps. But surely no more than the study of sexuality, gender, race, and politics—yet all of these topics are discussed, particularly at the college level, and it would be unimaginable to ban those topics from the classroom because they are "controversial." Indeed, if one is earning a liberal arts degree, it seems these topics are the *only* things discussed. The study of God, of the existence or non-existence of God, is at the core of humanity and is a question of the greatest importance and intellectual contemplation. No conclusion about these most momentous questions need be reached by the student, but the inquiry is essential. Without pondering these questions, one cannot be considered truly educated. The study of purpose, meaning, and existence should be a required part of a student's education—not a prohibited topic of discussion!

On a less broadly philosophical level, the study of Christianity is essential to the understanding of human history. No serious study of art, music, or literature would be complete without a knowledge of the impact of Christianity on these disciplines. We lie to ourselves if we believe we can remove all traces of Christianity from our schools and still understand Western man. Yet this is precisely what we have done and it has been to our detriment. We are now graduating students who have been inadequately educated—they themselves feel this, but they know not why. They know something is amiss. They know they have been in school for 12 or 16 or 20 years and yet seem to have an incomplete education. They do not know what is missing, but they know something is wrong. This is the result of ripping out all vestiges of Christianity in a culture that has been shaped by Christianity for two millennia. It can be done—indeed, secularists have been enormously successful at doing it—but we are left with a gnawing feeling that much of what we have spent studying is meaningless. That great philosopher Bruce Springsteen puts this sentiment best: "We learned more in a three-minute record, baby, then we ever did in school."[9]

This is where we find ourselves at the beginning of the 21st century. We have several generations of people educated entirely in Secular Materialist dogma. Tens of millions of these people have not even been introduced to the opposing worldview in any serious fashion. They have been inculcated with at least 12 years of secular education and exposed to thousands of hours of secular television. Things only get worse when our children attend secular colleges and universities. Unlike public high schools, many of their teachers at the university level are antagonistic to religion in general and to Christianity in particular. Our children are first exposed to a world that seldom if ever mentions God when they are in elementary and high school and then spend the next four years in a world that often aggressively attacks Christianity. Further, in all likelihood their parents, their teachers, and their teachers' teachers were taught the Secular Materialist worldview. Because of this, most of them do not feel they are being overly antagonistic toward Christianity—they simply feel they are passing on "truths" to their children.

We live and have lived for many decades in a culture where the separation of church and state is almost absolute. And with each passing

---

[9] I think Mr. Springsteen's line is not meant as hyperbole. Of course, he did not learn more in a three-minute record about math, science, or history than he learned in school. But no doubt means he learned more about life, spirituality, love, meaning, etc. in a song than he did in school. This is the tragic result of schools removing all traces of the spiritual, metaphysical, and religious. Mr. Springsteen is not the only poet-philosopher critical of modern education. Paul Simon penned a song that expressed the opinion that after years of high school it was a "wonder I can think at all." Pink Floyd devoted an entire album to repressive education called, *The Wall*; and Bob Dylan, who dropped out of college, wrote of his experience, "I'm lucky I got out alive."

year more and more of our culture is managed by the state. Our public school system is the perfect example. We have entrusted the education of our children to the government—a government that is, by law, entirely secular. In light of this it is astonishing that Christianity is as strong as it is in America. But with each generation we become less and less Christian.

While it is evident based on the historical record that our current separation policy is not required by the Constitution, this does not mean that our nation cannot choose to embrace secularism. While we should disabuse ourselves of the myth that the Constitution *requires* a secular culture, it is true that the Constitution does not *prohibit* a secular culture. There are those who are fully aware that they are not *required* to keep their religious views to themselves, but they simply *prefer* to do so. What, such people may ask, is the harm in that?

Actually, there is a great deal of harm in voluntarily relegating one's religious beliefs to the purely private and, therefore, the culturally irrelevant. Some of the harm by this privatization is limited to Christianity, but some of it is visited upon our culture and even upon democracy itself. When one's religious faith is pushed out of the public square and restricted to one's home and one's church, we are all the worse for it. This hurts not only individuals and institutions but the very concept of freedom of speech. For Christians to have their faith silenced, whether by law or cultural coercion, is an affront to people of all faiths *and* to people of no faith. The silencing of any voice is an injury to all voices. The protection of one voice ensures the protection of all voices. This is precisely the theory upon which the First Amendment was written and it is the freedom of speech and the freedom of religion that are both protected by that very same amendment. The Framers wisely understood that freedom of religion and freedom of speech were two forms of freedom of expression and that this freedom is among the foremost of human civil liberties. It should be shocking to the conscience that the First Amendment through the so-called "separation doctrine," has led to the suppression of the very thing it was written to protect.

All of us—Christians, Jews, Muslims, and atheists alike—should be appalled at the suppression of religious speech we find in our public schools, our common media, and the public square. And now, like clockwork, we see this suppression resulting in the belief that even a *private individual* has no right to consider his religious beliefs in the voting booth. This is the all too predictable result of the public school system treating religious belief as if it were something unworthy of classroom discussion. One could say that for 50 years our schools have treated religious belief like sexual deviance—something one may have the right to think about or even engage in, but not an appropriate topic for public conversation. One could say that but it would be untrue. Sexual deviance is discussed openly in our schools, on our televisions, and in our culture generally. It is only religion that has been shunned from our public conversation.

When a culture, either formally by law or informally by custom, prohibits any speech, that prohibited topic soon fades into insignificance. That is, after all, the very purpose of prohibiting the specific speech to begin with. In totalitarian states speech criticizing the government is prohibited with the intent that this will make it difficult to oppose or change the government in power. Whether a stifling of speech comes from the dictates of a totalitarian regime or is caused by ridicule, derision, or a mistaken understanding of the separation of church and state—the result is the same. When Christian conversation is eliminated as a meaningful part of the culture this leads to misunderstandings, misconceptions, and ignorance about Christianity which leads to the near elimination of any serious or meaningful Christian thought which leads to the perfunctory performance of religious ritual without any cognizant purpose. Eventually this results in the abandonment of a faith that is already dead.

This is the harm to Christians and Christianity by this purportedly "neutral" policy imposed by a clearly mistaken application of the separation doctrine. But, as mentioned, there is harm that extends to all people regardless of faith, and indeed to the very heart of our democracy.

The removal of religion from our public schools is not simply about the elimination of school prayer. It is about the elimination of discussing and wondering about who we are in this world—to ourselves, to each other, and to our Creator. It is about the elimination of pondering and debating the meaning of life, the purpose of our existence, and the possibility of life after this existence. This is what we have lost in our schools and in our culture—and the results are evident in each evening news broadcast.

The prohibition of all discussions pertaining to faith leaves an unmistakable impression on students: Faith is separate from and irrelevant to the real, material world. We do not discuss faith in school for the same reason we do not discuss unicorns and Bigfoot. These are not topics to which reason, logic, and science may be applied. God is a topic that is subjective, supernatural, unprovable, and unscientific, and therefore has no place in the classroom—or in the formation of public policy.

But is a philosophical discussion of God subjective, irrational, and illogical? The world's greatest philosophers most certainly did not think so. Indeed, pondering our creation, existence, purpose, and eternal destiny have been considered by both Eastern and Western philosophers to be the only questions really worth pursuing. Why has our culture taken a position counter to the combined wisdom of the greatest minds the world has known?

To answer these questions, we must turn to a study of our colleges and universities.

CHAPTER 7

THE FALL OF CHRISTIAN THOUGHT

If one is searching for the reason the United States is becoming a post-Christian nation, one need look no further than our public colleges and universities. Each year nearly 15 million men and women enter the hallowed halls of higher education. The vast majority of them will enter college as practicing Christians. Four years later the vast majority will leave college with their faith in God greatly reduced and their commitment to religion almost gone.[1] This is not simply the result of going off to college and learning new ideas. In 1980, students went to college and learned new ideas, too, but today *three times* as many of them reject religious belief as in 1980.[2] Nor is it simply a function of them being young. College graduates today are significantly less religious than previous generations were at that same age.[3] There is a real, measurable decline in faith among college students that is much greater than in any previous generation.

College, we hear, is a time when students will be exposed to a wide-variety of disciplines, lifestyles, and worldviews. This exposure to new ideas is not, however, quite as diverse as it appears. With few exceptions, nearly all of the myriad theories, doctrines, and dogmas taught will be entirely

---

[1] "Students Abandoning the Faith: Why It Happens and What We Can Do," March 2, 2010, *Summit Ministries*, https://www.summit.org/resources/articles/students-abandoning-the-faith/.

[2] "The Real Reason Religion is Declining: Why The U.S. Will Eventually Resemble Europe," Jean M. Twenge, May 27, 2015, *Psychology Today*.

[3] Generational and Time Period Differences in American Adolescents' Religious Orientation, 1966–2014, Jean M. Twenge, *et al.*

consistent with atheism and completely inconsistent with a Christian worldview. They will not be promoted or discussed *as* atheism or even as Secular Materialism (a term I coined) but merely as "simple facts" about the nature of the world. Nonetheless, nearly all of the "diverse" philosophies studied in college will be consistent with an atheistic worldview.

Something has occurred in our hallowed halls and ivory towers of education that has resulted in a wholesale purge of any and all things religious. While Christianity has had an unsurpassed—indeed, almost immeasurable—impact on Western architecture, art, music, literature, philosophy, government, and history, it is almost entirely ignored at our colleges and universities. The entirety of what is taught about Christianity at many universities amounts to little more than a brief and biased commentary on the Crusades, the Inquisition, the persecution of Galileo, and the Salem Witch Trials. Some professors openly express their contempt for Christianity; most simply ignore it entirely.

The Christian worldview did not lose to the secular worldview in the battlefield of ideas. While it may come as a surprise to many, Christianity is a robustly intellectual religion. The great philosophers of the faith are far too many to mention, but include such intellectual giants as Paul, Augustine, Anselm, Aquinas, Bacon, Descartes, Erasmus, Locke, Newton, and Pascal. Their work on Christian thought was not disproven, it has simply been ignored. For example, it is little-known that Newton wrote more on Christianity than he did on science; that Descartes was not only a philosopher, but a staunch defender of the faith; or that Locke was a Christian apologist as well as a political philosopher. Their thoughts on God and Christianity are works of intellectual genius, but are almost never assigned reading in public colleges and universities. Their thoughts on Christianity have been ignored because, and only because, they are thoughts on Christianity.

Why is the study of God, or even the mention of the possible existence of a god, so roundly rejected at most colleges and universities? This question is not easily answered. The presuppositions, assumptions, and worldviews upon which the answer is based take a bit of unraveling. The effort is necessary, however, because it is in this unveiling that we find the key to the current crisis. The removal of all things related to

God from our educational institutions is perhaps the primary reason for the triumph of secularism over Christian thought.

While college professors are not shouting at their students, "There is no God! Write that down—it will be on the test!" Secular Materialism is the prevailing worldview in American higher education. This is not to say that colleges are intentionally teaching atheism. The truth is a little more nuanced.

Much of modern education has been greatly influenced by atheist thinkers and atheist thought. The typical college professor may not be aware of this anymore than is the typical student or parent, but a study of the books assigned and the theories taught reveals an undeniable atheist bias. This is not to be confused with the acceptance of atheism as a *religious* view. Religious views, *qua* religious views, are almost entirely ignored in higher education. A professor may be Christian or may be atheist, but one thing is almost certain: he or she will find it inappropriate to discuss religious belief in the classroom. A survey of professors at leading research universities found that 92% believed religious belief has no place in the rarefied air of academia.[4]

Our current educational system is not formerly atheistic, but it is (a) theistic. What I mean is that while educators are not promoting atheism—the belief that there is no God—modern education is systematically *a*-theist—meaning "without God." Almost everything that is taught in schools—whether high school or college—is taught with the *presumption* that God does not exist or that God is irrelevant to the material. The relationship to God and modern education may best be described in an exchange that is said to have taken place between Napoleon and the noted scholar, Pierre-Simon Laplace. Napoleon, after reviewing a theory of the universe written by Laplace, mentioned that Laplace never mentioned the Creator in his theory. Laplace answered bluntly, "I had no need of that hypothesis."[5] This arrogant and anthropocentric view is firmly entrenched in our colleges and universities.

By not discussing religion, educators incorrectly assume that their

---

[4] "How Religious are America's College and University Professors?" Neil Gross and Solon Simmons, Feb 06, 2007, *Social Science Research Council*, http://religion.ssrc.org/reforum/Gross_Simmons.pdf.

[5] *Mémoires du docteur F. Antommarchi, ou les derniers momens de Napoléon*, vol. 1, 1825, Paris: Barrois L'Aîné, p.282. Others claim, that while Laplace did say these words,

teaching is neutral as to religious viewpoints. Nothing could be further from the truth. While atheism *as a religious belief* is not discussed, the atheistic *worldview* is simply an unnoticed and accepted part of academic thought. Refusing to discuss religious worldviews, all *theistic* views are treated with equal dismissal, leaving atheism as the default worldview.

Secular Materialism is the dominant—indeed, almost the *only*—worldview among academics. The principles of Secular Materialism originated at colleges and universities, and it is here that they are taught to students, and eventually passed on to the larger culture through these students. Most professors probably do not think they are teaching atheism, and most students are certainly unaware that they are being taught atheism, but the principles of Secular Materialism are identical to the principles of atheism with the exception that Secular Materialism makes no mention of God's existence or non-existence.

Of course, to hold that the supernatural does not exist; that religious belief is entirely irrelevant to intellectual pursuits; and that morality is relative, is to deny the existence of God. Similarly, to teach that free will is an illusion; that man originated from unguided, random mutation; that we are products of our biology and our environment; and that truth is either unknowable or non-existent, is also counter to Christian teaching and entirely consistent with atheistic teaching. The mere fact that Christianity, God, and atheism are never mentioned hardly makes a difference. It may come as a surprise to many professors, but they are teaching their students atheism by another name.

Worse, there is no mention that Secular Materialism is a worldview—indeed a worldview that contradicts the Christian worldview: Rather, students presume what they are learning are objective, scientific facts. It would be far better if students were told that the theories they are being taught are merely a set of beliefs that presume a secular or atheist worldview. Instead, instructors are teaching atheistic beliefs as if they were simply objective facts. For example, not one of the principles of Secular Materialism is an objective fact. Whether religion should be separated from the public square, is an opinion, not a fact; whether scientific materialism

---

they were in response to a specific part of the Laplace's theory, and not meant as a general refutation of God.

is the only, or even best, way to ascertain the truth about the world, is an opinion, not a fact; whether morality is relative, is an opinion, not a fact.

When students are taught atheistic beliefs as if they were facts, they will naturally come to the conclusion that atheism is the truth. This is the reason so many students have given up their Christian faith and why so many others who remain Christians do so in spite of what they think is the "evidence." The attitude, even among Christian graduates, seems to be: "Well, I am a believer based on my faith in the Bible, even though I know it contradicts everything science tells us."

This is a tragic thing for anyone to believe—Christian or otherwise—because it is simply a lie. Science has not proven that the supernatural does not exist; that morality is relative; that the universe was created by fortunate, random happenstance; or that man evolved through unguided, blind genetic mutation. In fact, there is a great deal of scientific evidence that the supernatural *does* exist, that the universe was designed, and that human evolution was not unguided. (More on these fascinating scientific discoveries in Chapter 11).

Atheism, as a religious belief, is not being taught in college. But atheism, as a worldview, is taught in college as if there were no other logical alternative. To better explain what is meant by that, we need to look more closely at the world of higher education. We will examine the scholars and books students are assigned to study, the religious beliefs of their college professors, and the worldview prevalent in the philosophy of education. We will find that by these measurements, college students spend four very influential years of their lives being indoctrinated with atheist thought.

The Course Material: Who and What Students Study

If you have attended college in the last 20 years, the following list of scholars should be familiar to you. These scholars are among the most studied in universities across the nation.[6] Reading their works is, in large part, what constitutes a liberal education: Isaac Asimov,

---

[6] While there are several sources that list which books and scholars are most assigned in colleges and universities, an excellent source is The Open Syllabus Project found at: https://blog.opensyllabus.org/. The Open Syllabus Project is located at Columbia University and is supported by the The Sloan Foundation, The Hewlett Foundation,

Simone de Beauvoir, Jeremy Bentham, Albert Camus, Rachel Carson, Noam Chomsky, Daniel Dennett, John Dewey, Emile Durkheim, Umberto Eco, Barbara Ehrenreich, Bart Ehrman, Hans Eysenck, Michel Foucault, Sigmund Freud, Betty Friedan, Erich Fromm, Stephen Hawking, Martin Heidegger, Christopher Hitchens, David Hume, Franz Kafka, John Maynard Keynes, Jean-Francois Lyotard, Karl Marx, Abraham Maslow, Frederick Nietzsche, Ivan Pavlov, Marcel Proust, Ayn Rand, John Rawls, Phillip Roth, Bertrand Russell, Carl Sagan, Margaret Sanger, Jean Paul Sartre, Peter Singer, B.F. Skinner, Kurt Vonnegut, and E.O. Wilson.

Some of these scholars will be remembered in 100 years, some not in a decade. Some have made meaningful and lasting contributions to their disciplines; others were simply loud voices that gained great attention by being controversial. But they all have one thing in common: Every one of these scholars are agnostics or atheists, many of them militantly so. Some of them, such as Dawkins, Dennett, Harris, and Hitchens, are assigned specifically *because* they are atheists. They have nothing to contribute to their respective fields *but their atheism*.

It is impossible to make a list of similarly influential Christian scholars whose works and thoughts are studied at public colleges and universities. This is not because Christian scholars are not turning out excellent scholarship. Quite the opposite. The majority of Nobel Prize winners, as just one measurement, are Christian.[7] The reason atheist scholars are selected is because atheist thought is the dominant worldview among American academics.

As just one example of this extraordinary bias, Francis Collins, one of the world's leading genetic biologists and Director of the Human Genome Project, has no doubt that humans evolved over time through genetic mutations. However, he strongly disagrees that these genetic mutations are "blind and random," as is generally taught in our public schools. Collins, who won a Nobel Prize in Medicine for his genetic

---

The Arcadia Fund, and The Templeton Foundation. It is a repository of the syllabi from over 6,000,000 courses at 4,700 schools.

[7] Baruch A. Shalev, *100 Years of Nobel Prizes* (Atlantic Publishers & Distributors, 2003), pp. 57-59.

research, believes the evidence strongly points to an intelligent design, not random mutation.⁸

Richard Dawkins, an accomplished biologist more famous for his atheism than his biology, believes evolution is entirely blind and random. In his book, *The Blind Watchmaker*, Dawkins writes as if it is a scientific fact that the evolutionary process is unguided, whereas Collins, in his book, *The Language of God*, rather more objectively, explains the scientific fact that no one knows why cells mutate or whether evolution is blind or guided at the molecular level.⁹ Collins points out that the odds that genetic evolution is random are so astronomical as to defy both science and common sense. Collins makes this assessment not as a Christian, but as a scientist. In fact, scientists estimate that there is less than 1 chance in 10 to the 40,000 power that life could have originated by random trials.¹⁰ Ten to the 40,000 power is a 1 with 40,000 zeros after it! Dawkins does not deny this, but simply replies that we know God does not exist, so life *must have* originated by chance—no matter how ridiculously unlikely!¹¹

Yet, in a large sample of college syllabi, reveals that Dawkins' book was assigned to students 1,932 times while Collins' book was assigned 8 times.¹² The discrepancy is stark—especially considering that Collins was the Director of the National Institutes of Health and the leader of the Human Genome Project, and Dawkins is…a famous atheist.

Unlike Dawkins, most of the atheist scholars assigned to students are not writing about religion nor are they directly promoting atheism. Rather, they are writing about their respective disciplines from an atheistic worldview. Some of them are very aware of the influence their worldview has on their work, others less so. But just as a devout Christian psychologist or sociologist cannot help but be influenced in

---

8   Francis Collins, *The Language of God: A Scientist Presents Evidence for Belief* (New York: Simon & Schuster, 2006).
9   Francis Collins, *The Language of God*; Richard Dawkins, *The Blind Watchmaker*
10   Stephen Meyer, *Signature in the Cell: DNA and the Evidence for Intelligent Design*, (HarperCollins, New York, 2009); and for a short summary of Dr. Meyer's book see: The Odds of a Cell Forming Randomly by Chance Alone, *Cyber Penance*, August 20, 2018, https://cyberpenance.wordpress.com/2018/08/20/the-odds-of-a-cell-forming-randomly-by-chance-alone/.
11   Richard Dawkins, *The Blind Watchmaker*
12   See: The Open Syllabus Project: https://blog.opensyllabus.org/.

his or her views on psychology or sociology by his or her Christianity, so too, a committed atheist will take a view of psychology or sociology that is atheistic in its premises.

For example, a Christian psychologist will think of human behavior in light of such things as the Fall, Original Sin, and the concept of the soul. For the Christian psychologist, God and His relationship with man will be at the center of his psychological presumptions. For the atheist psychologist, such things as the id, the ego, and the super ego; determinism, and biological predisposition, will be central. If God is considered at all, He will be considered a negative imaginary source, responsible for such things as the desire for a father figure and the cause of human guilt. This is not to say that all of these things (or none of these things) help explain human behavior, but it most certainly biases a student's thinking if every psychological theory studied presumes an agnostic or atheist worldview and no psychological theory studied is based on a Christian worldview. It leads the student to believe not that Christian psychology is wrong—but that Christian psychology is *nonexistent*. I have known many psychologists who, after years of practicing secular psychology, came to the realization that many of the problems their patients encountered where best described by biblical concepts of the human condition. It is a shame these psychologists and their patients were deprived of that source of assistance for so long.[13]

The concept that colleges teach atheism without directly teaching atheism is a difficult concept to understand and so perhaps an example would be of assistance. I will use the famous psychologist Abraham Maslow and his oft-studied "Hierarchy of Needs." If you have attended college and taken a course in psychology, you are probably familiar with Maslow's Hierarchy of Needs. The textbook usually provides a helpful pyramid showing the most basic human needs on the wide bottom of the triangle (security, food, etc.) which, the theory goes, must be met before we can move on to the higher human needs. At the very top of the triangle in the narrowest block is the highest human need: self-actualization. On the face of it, Maslow's Hierarchy of Needs pyramid is neutral as to religious belief. However, it is a good example of how

---

[13] Dr. Karl Menninger addresses this issue admirably in his book, *Whatever Became of Sin?* (New York: Hawthorn Books, 1973).

Secular Materialism is benignly and perhaps inadvertently taught in our colleges and universities.

First, Maslow, like so many of the psychologists studied in colleges, was an atheist. His atheism was not an incidental part of who Maslow was but shaped his thinking about meaning, purpose, and truth. He rejected the existence of God, founded the *Journal of Humanist Psychology*, and was awarded "Humanist of the Year" in 1967.

In his celebrated pyramid of needs, Maslow's places "Self-Actualization" at the top, representing the greatest of human psychological achievement. Because we live in a post-Christian culture most of us would probably not recognize this as an affront to Christian thought. However, "Self-Actualization" as the greatest human achievement is in direct conflict with the Christian view. Christian thought holds that the greatest human achievement is dying to oneself and accepting Jesus as one's Lord and Savior. A less Christian and more theistic view would hold the greatest human achievement is transcending self and becoming aware of God. In either case, Maslow's seemingly innocuous hierarchy of needs is a confirmation of the atheist worldview and a contradiction of the theistic worldview. Although not obvious, it is a denial of what is taught by Christians, Muslims, Jews, Buddhists, and Hindus. It is an inherently *religious* worldview disguised as some sort of "scientific" truth.

Of course, Maslow's rather arbitrary list of needs is hardly scientific. It is, in fact, simply a list of human needs entirely consistent with an atheist worldview and ultimately inconsistent with a theistic worldview. It is one of those small things that when combined with other similar advancements of an atheistic worldview, over a four-year college program, contributes mightily to the belief that Christianity either has nothing to say on psychology or that Christianity is wrong. The truth is that Christianity has a great deal to say about the human psychological condition and what it has to say is often, but not always, in contrast with what students are taught in college. The fact that students never get to benefit from reading what great Christian psychologists and philosophers have to say on this topic is an educational tragedy.

One final word on Dr. Maslow and his hierarchy of needs. In

his later years, he modified his theory and created a new level on his pyramid: at the very top of the pyramid, above Self-Actualization, was "Transcendence." For Maslow, Transcendence was not necessarily a theistic transcendence—Maslow remained a secular humanist and atheist throughout his life. However, even this small concession to the spiritual side of a human's psychological needs was too much for most academics. In the vast majority of textbooks, Maslow's pyramid remains capped with Self-Actualization. Maslow's addition of Transcendence was just a little too spiritual for the academic community to embrace— even if it came from the author of the theory himself!

Maslow's example is not an exception, but the rule.

We Three Kings of Atheism Are...

The three men who have had perhaps the greatest influence on modern higher education are Auguste Comte, Sigmund Freud, and Karl Marx. All three thinkers were not merely atheists who happened to be scholars, rather, their atheism informed their work and often provided the essential foundation of their philosophy. All three wrote extensively on the "fact" that religion was a primitive way of explaining the unknown and of providing comfort in a frightening world, and that as science resolved the mysteries of the universe religious belief would fade away.[14] While they wrote in great depth on this topic, their general sentiments about religion may be summarized as follows:

> Religion is an illusion of childhood, outgrown under proper education.
> —Auguste Comte, *The Positive Philosophy*

> [R]eligion is comparable to a childhood neurosis, and I am optimistic enough to suppose that mankind will

---

[14] Poor Karl Marx had a penchant for thinking that things would "fade away" that have remained. Marx predicted that not only religion would fade away, but also capitalism and the "temporary" apparatus of the communist bureaucratic state. He was, one might kindly put it, a bit off in all of these predictions.

surmount this neurotic phase, just as so many children grow out of their similar neurosis.
—Sigmund Freud, *The Future of An Illusion*

Religion is the sigh of the oppressed creature, the heart of a heartless world, and the soul of soulless conditions. It is the opium of the people. The abolition of religion as the illusory happiness of the people is the demand for their real happiness.
—Karl Marx, *A Contribution to the Critique of Hegel's Philosophy of Right*

While the work of Marx and Freud are generally well-known, it was Comte's Positivism that may have had the greatest impact on modern education. Positivism holds that the highest and most advanced stage is the "scientific." Prior to the scientific age we lived in the dark and superstitious world of religion. According to Comte, as man evolved, he would cast off the chains of religion and be liberated by the Age of Science. In anticipation of this new advanced age, Comte, ironically, even developed a new religion. With Comte's new "Religion of Humanity" came the elimination of belief in God, but in exchange at least we got a new calendar, each month being renamed for a great secular scholar. Apparently the "old" calendar, which divides the world into everything that happened prior to the birth of Christ (BC) and everything that happened after the birth of Christ (AD) is a tad offensive to those who would like to rewrite history so as to reduce the impact of Jesus on the Western world.

While Comte's calendar never caught on, the influence of Positivism has been profound. Comte's preference for scientific analysis over other kinds of knowledge became more than a preference—it became a form of religion in itself. Comte, the father of modern social science, held that society evolved in progressive stages from the theological, to the metaphysical, and finally, to the scientific. Karl Marx, not to be outdone, developed an economic theory of history which claimed humankind was evolving from capitalism to socialism, and finally to communism. Evolution and science were where it was at for all "enlightened" thinkers, and so we are told that not only do animals evolve, but so does economics, politics, law, and society. Never mind that history shows that human progress is rather subjective, advancing in fits and starts, sometimes taking giant steps backwards, and always being defined by the particular culture that fancies itself the most "advanced."

Nonetheless, the scientific method was so successful that entire academic disciplines changed their names to get in on the action and be taken seriously. Academic disciplines are categorized as natural sciences, applied sciences, formal sciences, and social sciences. Hence, instead of the government and the humanities, we now have political science and the social sciences. Everyone wants their discipline to be a "science" because to be a "science" means the discipline is objective, subject to empirical testing, reason, and logic. Presumably the opposite is to be a discipline based on emotion, intuition, and faith—although one imagines that musicians, artists, and writers might disagree.

Science and the scientific method became so dominant that it became oppressive itself with no tolerance for any ideas that were not "scientific." As Kieran Egan writes in *The Educated Mind*:

> Positivism is marked by the final recognition that science provides the only valid form of knowledge and that facts are the only possible objects of knowledge; philosophy is thus recognized as essentially no different from science [...] Ethics, politics, social interactions, and all other forms of human life about which knowledge was possible would eventually be drawn into the orbit of science [...][15]

This radical reliance on science and science alone has led many modern academics to believe that the only valid form of knowledge is scientific—that sensory experience is the exclusive source of knowledge. Sources of knowledge outside of the orbit of science, some argued, were not even wrong—they were simply meaningless. All knowledge,

---

[15] Egan, Kieran. *The Educated Mind*: University of Chicago Press. pp. 115–116. ISBN 978-0-226-19036-5.

they argued, is based on empirical knowledge—that is, knowledge susceptible to sensory perception and measurement. Non-empirical knowledge is nonsensical. It is an impossibility. If one cannot test, measure, and quantify some phenomenon then we can speak nothing of it. Theology, some presume, falls into the category of the "meaningless."

Of course, such extreme views were not accepted by all. The great physicist, Werner Heisenberg, who won the Nobel Prize for his pioneering work in quantum mechanics remarked:

> The positivists have a simple solution: the world must be divided into that which we can say clearly and the rest, which we had better pass over in silence. But can anyone conceive of a more pointless philosophy, seeing that what we can say clearly amounts to next to nothing? If we omitted all that is unclear we would probably be left with completely uninteresting and trivial tautologies.[16]

Heisenberg has been joined in his criticism of Positivism by other philosophers and scientists, including Max Weber, Karl Popper, Thomas Khun, and Friedrich Hayek. Nonetheless, it has been Comte, Marx, and Freud who have most influenced educators and education in the 20th Century.[17]

A nationwide survey conducted by The Open Syllabus Project at Columbia University reveals that Karl Marx was required reading in over 16,607 syllabi, placing Marx in 6th place of all authors.[18] Freud was

---

[16] Heisenberg, Werner (1971). "Positivism, Metaphysics and Religion". In Ruth Nanda Nanshen (ed.). Werner Heisenberg - Physics and Beyond - Encounters and Conversations. World Perspectives. 42. Translator: Arnold J. Pomerans. New York: Harper and Row. p. 213. LCCN 78095963. OCLC 15379872.

[17] A review of academic articles reveals that the vast majority of published articles in scholarly journals rely explicitly or implicitly on Positivist thought. See: Brett, Paul. 1994. "A genre analysis of the results section of sociology articles." English For Specific Purposes. Vol 13, Num 1:47–59 and Holmes, Richard. 1997. "Genre analysis, and the social sciences: An investigation of the structure of research article discussion sections in three disciplines". English For Specific Purposes, vol. 16, num. 4:321–337.

[18] The five assigned authors ahead of Marx are Shakespeare, Plato, Diana Hacker, Aristotle, and Michel Foucault. Hacker is the author of books on English grammar and writing. Foucault was an atheist, a Marxist, and a Maoist whose work was greatly

required reading in 12,000 syllabi. As a comparison, Thomas Jefferson came in at 144th place, being required reading on 4,793 syllabi. Marx' *Communist Manifesto* was listed on 7,057 syllabi compared with the 877 professors who assigned Lincoln's "Emancipation Proclamation" and 1,359 who assigned his "Gettysburg Address." More professors assigned writing from Sigmund Freud than *To Kill A Mockingbird, The Declaration of Independence, The Federalist Papers, The Constitution, Romeo and Juliet,* and *The Autobiography of Benjamin Franklin* combined. Marx' *Das Kapital* alone was assigned twice as often as Plato's *Dialogues.*

Whether Marx and Freud have been more significant to Western thought than all of the works of Washington, Madison, Jefferson, Franklin, Lincoln, Martin Luther King, John Maynard Keynes, Dietrich Bonhoeffer, and Dante combined is, let us say, questionable. Nevertheless, the thoughts of these men are required reading for almost every person who graduates from college.

Marx and Freud are regularly assigned as required reading in the fields of psychology, history, political science, sociology, and economics. Marx's *The Communist Manifesto,* for example, is the most assigned book in sociology classes and the third most assigned in history classes. Further, Marxist thought is discussed in many classes that do not actually assign his work. For example, as a professor of criminal justice I discussed Marxist theories of crime. The same is true of the works of Sigmund Freud. The dominance of Marxist and Freudian thought on college campuses is, if anything, probably underestimated.[19]

---

influenced by Freud and Nietzsche. So naturally he is assigned by college professors more than any but the above four listed writers. Richard Dawkins, incidentally, who is famous only for his militant atheist diatribes, is assigned more often than James Madison, George Washington, Winston Churchill, or Dante, Jack London, George Bernard Shaw, Ray Bradbury, Eugene O'Neill, or Maya Angelou, among others. The date used in calculating the number of times a specific book was assigned is found at: The Open Syllabus Project: https://blog.opensyllabus.org/.

[19] This is another major problem with modern higher education. The doctrines accepted by most scholars are ubiquitous and imagined to be applicable to all areas and disciplines. Students have to suffer through the Marxist Dialectic whether they are taking a course on history, philosophy, or English. The unfortunate students image a course on literature might be somewhat different from a course on economics, and instead find the same Marxist dogma being forced upon them regardless of the discipline. This is what indoctrination looks like. And it is one of the reasons so many students find their college experience less than meaningful. It is one course

But it is not only Comte, Marx, and Freud who so dominate college classrooms. After all, one might argue, these three men may have been atheists, but they were also of great historical significance to the shaping of the modern mind. Let's leave aside the rather circular reasoning that atheist intellectuals in colleges and universities decided that the work of these men would be required reading is in large part what made them so influential. Let's presume that they are worthy of the enormous place they have been given in modern education. How, then, does one explain that Michel Foucault, a French social theorist who died in 1984, is the *fourth* most assigned author at our institutions of higher education.[20] Foucault is too recent a scholar to be given the excuse that time has judged him a genius. Foucault, unlike Marx and Freud, cannot be said to have had any enormous influence on the history of the world, or even a single discipline. I am not opposed to students reading the works of Mr. Foucault, but are his views really so important as to be assigned to students more than any other author save Plato, Shakespeare, and Aristotle?[21] What is it about Foucault that makes him the darling of academics? Well, he fits quite well into the prevailing worldview: he is a leftist and an atheist.

Any objective review of the scholars, theories, and books studied at most colleges and universities reveals that atheists and atheist thought dominate the curriculum. A comparison of books and theories assigned to students that promote a Christian worldview versus books and theories that promote an atheist worldview is almost not possible, because there are almost no books assigned promoting a Christian worldview. When one compiles a list of the top five assigned authors at colleges and universities, excluding those who are pre-Christian (i.e., Plato) and those who are writing study guides, books on math or grammar, etc., the clear bias in favor of atheist thought is revealed:[22]

---

after another of repeating what the professor wants to hear, which almost inevitably is something about the Marxist Dialectic.

[20] See: The Open Syllabus Project, footnote 65, *infra*.
[21] Ibid.
[22] Data compiled from The Open Syllabus Project: https://blog.opensyllabus.org/.

Top Five Assigned Authors

	Atheists			Christians	
Rank	Author	Times Assigned	Rank	Author	Times Assigned
1	Michel Foucault	16,893	4	Immanuel Kant	10,301
2	Karl Marx	16,607	5	Martin Luther King	9,930
3	Sigmund Freud	11,114			20,231
		44,614			

Even this comparison is misleading. Students will usually only read Martin Luther King's very short writings, such as "Letter From a Birmingham Jail," or his speech, "I Have A Dream," while they are inundated with the entire philosophies of Marx and Freud in class after class. Further, King's letter and speech do not generally inform other disciplines, whereas Marx and Freud are mentioned in nearly every social science course. In my own experience, for example, when I taught criminology, I did not assign King, but I spent a good deal of time discussing Marxist criminology and Freudian criminology, both of which were, upon later reflection, vehemently atheist in their description of human behavior.

Further, as one examines the list of books assigned in college, the Christian worldview diminishes sharply. As one moves down the list of books assigned, the number of Christian authors actually decreases. With the exception of Immanuel Kant, Martin Luther King, and Augustine, there are almost no other books from the required reading list that are written by Christians, whereas the books written by atheists increases. Meaning the number of Christian authors assigned in any appreciable number amount to very few, while the number of atheist authors assigned is enormous. Please note that I am not suggesting that books should be assigned that promote Christianity in secular institutions. Nor am I counting only books written with overtly Christian or atheist messages. Rather, I am simply counting books written by Christians and books written by atheists. And I am including such authors as Kant and King, although none of their assigned reading is directly about Christianity. The overwhelming number of atheists assigned to students is even more odd considering that Christian authors outnumber atheist authors roughly 10 to 1.

Atheism, as a religious belief, is not taught directly and overtly. However, most of the scholars studied are atheists, and almost all of the theories studied presume an atheist or Secular Materialist view. We will address that worldview and its implications shortly, but first let's address the professors themselves. Are American college and university professors *themselves* atheists?

Atheism Among Academics

Much ink has been spilled about the faith—or lack thereof—of college professors. To a large degree the religious beliefs of professors is irrelevant. Not so much because professors are careful about not revealing their personal religious beliefs, although most are, but because almost all professors—believers and otherwise—are teaching theories that presume an atheist worldview. If a professor is teaching a worldview that presupposes atheism, it makes no difference whether the professor is an atheist or a believer. He or she is teaching atheist thought, even if unknowingly.

Nonetheless, recent research suggests that college professors are much more likely to be atheists or agnostics than the general population. While the majority of college professors believe in God, the percentage who believe is strikingly less than the percentage of the general public who believe. While 51% of professors say they believe in God, this is much smaller than the 87% of Americans who are believers. Similarly, while 7% of Americans are atheists or agnostics, a full 23% of college professors say they are atheist or agnostic.[23] This means college professors are *three times* more likely to be atheists or agnostics than the general public.

The numbers are much worse at elite research institutions, where

---

[23] See: "How Religious are America's College and University Professors?" Neil Gross and Solon Simmons, Feb 06, 2007, http://religion.ssrc.org/reforum/Gross_Simmons.pdf. for the data on professors. For the data on the general public see: "How Many Americans Believe in God?" Zach Hrynowski, November 8, 2019, *Gallup Polls*, https://news.gallup.com/poll/268205/americans-believe-god.aspx.

many of the textbooks used at all colleges and universities are written. At these elite institutions, the numbers of atheists among the faculty are an astounding 37%—a number *5 times* greater than the general public.[24] The fact that 37% are avowed atheists does not mean the other 63% are Christians. Nearly 20% believe in a "higher power, but not a personal God," leaving just 17% who have faith in the God of the Bible. While approximately 25% of Americans consider themselves evangelical Christians, at elite research institutions evangelicals constitute a whopping 1% of the faculty.[25]

It gets worse. The number of atheists among college instructors is misleadingly low in an important way: they show the *averages* across all disciplines, not in specific disciplines. This is significant because in those disciplines where students would be discussing and thinking about issues most pertinent to the possibility of God, such as human behavior, creation theories, and theories of the origin of life, the number of atheists is much higher. For example, in biology and psychology, two disciplines where belief in God could be discussed, a full 61% of the professors are atheists.[26] This compares to 63% of accounting professors who have "no doubt" that God exists.[27] Accounting is a class where God is probably not particularly pertinent to the discipline (except, perhaps, during time of prayer before exams). Biology, psychology, and other related fields, are disciplines ripe for a discussion of the role of God, and it is these disciplines where atheist professors are most likely to be found. That means the majority of professors in the disciplines where students might believe God is at work (creation, origins, free will, human behavior, moral formation) are atheists.

Having an atheist instructor, or being taught an atheist worldview,

---

[24] "Faculty Faith," Katherine Dunn, July-August 2007, *Harvard Magazine*, https://harvardmagazine.com/2007/07/faculty-faith.html.
[25] The number of evangelicals in America may be found at: "America's Changing Religious Landscape," Pew Research Center May 12, 2015. The number of evangelicals at elite research universities comes from: "How Religious are America's College and University Professors?" Neil Gross and Solon Simmons, Feb 06, 2007, http://religion.ssrc.org/reforum/Gross_Simmons.pdf.
[26] Ibid.
[27] Ibid.

can have an extremely important impact in how the material is discussed. But even if one's professor is a Christian, it is just as likely that they are social Christians as they are Scriptural Christians. By that, I mean that the average college professor's view of Christianity is quite different than that of the general public. Here are the results, for example, of a survey asking people about their view of the Bible:

I Believe The Bible Is…	General Public	Professors
Actual Word of God	30%	6%
Inspired Word of God	49%	42%
Ancient Book of Fables	17%	52%

Again, professors at elite doctoral granting institutions showed the greatest discrepancy from the average: 73% believed the Bible is a book of ancient fables.[28]

Although the evidence suggests that only about half of all professors are Christians, and far fewer at Ivy League colleges and research institutions—which have an enormous influence on academics at all colleges and universities—Christian thought is almost never discussed in higher education because there is near unanimous agreement among *all* professors that religion has no place in the classroom.[29]

This, not atheism, is the primary problem. I know from personal experience that for most of my academic career, I blindly accepted the nearly universal view that religious belief has no place in an academic classroom. Like all beliefs accepted on blind faith, I never asked myself,

---

[28] "How Religious are America's College and University Professors?" Neil Gross and Solon Simmons, Feb 06, 2007, http://religion.ssrc.org/reforum/Gross_Simmons.pdf. Note: Do not be fooled into thinking that the reason 73% of professors at elite universities believe the Bible is a book of fables is because those highly intelligent men and women simply know more about the Bible than the average American. Not so. Almost all serious theologians, historians, and professors of literature would agree that the Bible is not "primarily a book of ancient fables." There are many literary genres in the Bible, including myth, fable, prophecy, revelation, history, law, parables, poetry, and wisdom literature. An objective assessment of the Bible does not support the assertion that it is primarily a book of ancient fables. This view held by 73% of professors at elite universities tells us much more about the anti-religious bias of the professors than it does about the Bible.

[29] Ibid.

"Why?" When I did ask this question, I found the answers were mostly incoherent, illogical, and irrational. There are excellent reasons to prohibit the *promotion* or *proselytization* of religious belief from the classroom, but the wholesale exclusion of religious thought, history, and philosophy from academics is a colossal educational mistake, and one that can be justified only by bias, prejudice, and ignorance.

Be that as it may, there is an almost total absence of any discussion of religious philosophy, thought, or history at our colleges and universities. This complete silence on such matters is truly baffling. While there is *no other topic* that has so shaped the history of the world—for better or for worse—than religious belief, a visitor from Mars would assume we were a people who had no history of—nor even curiosity about—spiritual matters. It should be shocking to any person, especially any educator—whether believer or unbeliever—that the philosophy of God; the spirituality of the human psyche; the unmatched influence of religious belief on world history; and the questions of purpose, meaning, and existence so essential to what it means to be human, are utterly ignored in our nation's institutions of higher learning.

We will now turn to an examination of the reason that such an overwhelmingly important topic is treated as if it does not exist in our nation's colleges and universities.

Chapter 8

The Academic Worldview: I Am An Atheist; Therefore, I Am An Intellectual

It is hardly an exaggeration to say that Christianity invented higher education. In 1079, Pope Gregory VII issued a Papal Decree to establish Cathedral schools to train priests. The first such university was established at Bologna, Spain, in 1088, and by the middle of the 12th Century, universities had been established at Oxford and Paris. The mission of early universities was to ensure that the clergy would be well-educated, literate, and experts in Catholic theology. The first teachers were priests and the teaching of Christian doctrine was of primary importance. The study of Christianity remained an important, if not primary, focus of university education for the first 800 years of the history of higher education. It was not until the 19th Century that the secular state and its interests began to supplant Christianity in colleges and universities. Even then, religious study and worship was an important part of the educational experience at most colleges and universities. Required chapel attendance, for example, was not stopped at Yale until 1927, and then only because the chapel was too small to accommodate all the students.

Today, at almost all schools, from elementary school through post-doctoral education, the study of God *or anything remotely related to the possibility of a god*, has been torn from our schools root and branch as if some sort of Soviet style purge occurred. This radical elimination of any discussion of a divine being is a relatively new phenomenon. Few people prior to the 1950s would have imagined that the study of God, creation, and meaning was inappropriate or irrelevant to one's education. Indeed, the very proposition that such matters are "irrelevant" is mind-boggling, even if one is an atheist.

The fact is that no serious thinker, believer or otherwise, could hold that the questions of creation, existence, and purpose are in any way inappropriate or irrelevant to academic inquiry. The only person who would want to eliminate such timeless and essential topics would be a militant and intolerant atheist. That we have allowed such a totalitarian position to dominate our public schools is an outrage—not only to believers, but to any person who believes in tolerance, freedom of thought, and a search for the truth.

In my experience as a college professor, there are two reasons given for the near total exclusion of religious thought from colleges and universities. First, instructors fear that students might simply resort to "God" as an answer to any question about creation, the universe, the origin of life, morality, or most any other question. This is, of course, preposterous. If a student wanted to suggest God was the answer to the question, his or her answer would need to be explained in a plausible and rational way—just as if a student answered "Marxism" to every political or economic question or "evolution," to every scientific or biological question. One would expect the professor would require a somewhat more robust and detailed explanation to any student who simply answered, "God," "Marxism," or "Evolution," in reply to a question.[1] Rather than

---

[1] At least one would expect. Unfortunately, while the "God" answer is flatly ridiculed and rejected, students answering "Marxism," or "Evolution," are often rewarded for saying so. I have spoken with many students who have told me that no matter the question, an answer including the Marxist Dialectic is sure to impress. I have also been told and know of many cases where mentioning God will almost certainly result in a scathing comment by the instructor. A personal example: A colleague of mine, when working on her doctorate in Victorian Literature, cited the Bible on a few occasions in her dissertation because Victorian authors were strongly influenced by, and often referenced, biblical passages and themes in their works. My colleague was not preaching or proselyting in her work, but briefly pointing out the influence of the King James Bible on the work of many Victorian authors. Her dissertation advisor recommended that she remove any references to the Bible in her work. (In

an outright rejection of any discussion or defense of the idea of God that may be pertinent to a topic, wouldn't a true academic search for the truth be open to all responses, and then each response would be assessed on its own merits? If, for example, if a student is asked what causes criminal behavior, almost *any* response is acceptable except anything related to the Fall or sin. If a student attempted to make a case for the concept of sin, he could expect to be roundly ridiculed by professors and students alike. Why is a criminological theory based on racism or the ownership of private property a better answer than the human propensity to sin? Any of those answers could be a perfectly good or perfectly bad answer to the question, depending how well the student develops and defends his or her position.

The second reason is simply a tautology: God is not discussed in schools because His existence is not relevant to the subject matter. As Laplace said, "We have no need of that hypothesis." But this reply begs the question. If one *assumes* at the outset that God is irrelevant to the subject, then of course it makes no sense to discuss God's possible relevance to the subject! God's relevance to the subject depends entirely on one's view of God. Just as Laplace had no need for God in his assessment of how the universe was created, neither does a Creationist have the need for Laplace in his assessment of how the universe was created. Just as a perfectly good Marxist answer on the causes of crime has no need for God, a perfectly good Christian answer has no need for Marx. Neither has a need for the other because each has excluded even the possibility of the other's hypothesis. Laplace has a theory that explains the creation of the universe without God, but that does not mean that is actually how the universe was created—and the Creationist has a theory that explains the creation of the universe by God, but that does not mean that it is actually is how the universe was created. To reject all God-based theories is irrational, unless one has *predetermined* that God does not exist.

Similarly, if one presumes that God has nothing to do with physics because physics can be explained without God, this does not mean that God has nothing to do with physics. It only means we have explained

---

fact, she was advised that if she wanted to land a job in academia to focus on the Marxist influence on Victorian writers).

physics *as if* God has nothing to do with physics. It is a self-fulfilling prophesy. Explaining physics with the presumption that time, space, and energy are simply "brute facts," just things that happen to exist, is no more (and probably a good deal less) true than explaining physics by saying God created time, space, and energy. Either explanation will suffice and neither has been proven or disproven. To teach physics as if God did not exist is not the same as proving that God is irrelevant to physics. It is simply making a choice—in this case, as with all courses taught in public schools—that we will teach the subject *as if* God did not exist. The subject could just as reasonably have been taught as if God did exist. After all, in our above example, the physicist has absolutely no answer to the question: Where did the laws of physics come from? The response, "they just exist," is no different than someone saying that God "just exists." Other than, the answer that God exists ("I Am") is entirely consistent with the concept of the eternal and the premises of the Bible, whereas the answer that the law of physics "just exist" is entirely inconsistent with everything we know about physics!

The truth is we have been teaching all disciplines *as if* God did not exist for so long that we presume that we have *proven that God actually does not exist*—or at a minimum is irrelevant to our academic study. We simply never consider the implications to the study of history, biology, physics, poetry, or any other discipline if we taught them as if God actually did exist. What different insights would a theistic worldview offer to the study of psychology, for example? Would we think differently about human desire, motivation, and deviance if we examined those topics from a theistic worldview?

For most academics these questions are never even considered. Most academics, myself included, were taught that even the consideration of the possibility of God is something that "serious thinkers" simply do not engage in. It is not that academics, intellectuals, professors, and teachers have explored the God argument and found it unconvincing and unworthy of debate. Hardly. It is something that is simply not considered. It is engrained into the very fiber of most professors that the academic world and the religious world are two very separate spheres of thought and discussions of religious matters simply have no place in the classroom.

Again, this is not a conclusion reached after a careful assessment of the facts—it is simply a belief that has been accepted without question. Few academics struggle with the issue of whether the possibility of God or the Christian worldview should be addressed—it just isn't considered. The Christian worldview is rejected without thought. If asked to explain why the Christian worldview is summarily rejected, that usual answer is, "Because it's *religious*," as if that explained everything. Of course it's "religious,' just as a secular worldview is "secular," and a Marxist worldview is "Marxist." So what? This is not an explanation; it is a tautology.

Christianity as a religion or as a private, personal belief is, of course, recognized. One is free to worship or pray to the god of one's choice and God may be a very important part of one's life—no doubt even the lives of many professors. But the idea that God is an active, relevant part of the material world—that the Christian worldview has implications in history, social sciences, or even mathematics—this concept does not occur to the typical professor. The standard view is that God is fine and has His place in our lives, but is irrelevant to the study of history, math, science, music, or literature, with the possible exception of the historical impact religion has had on these topics. To consider that God might have actually invented music, directed historical events, or created the elegance of mathematical proofs, are thoughts that are simply unthought.

A Bias Observed

My 17 years as an instructor of criminal justice are illustrative of the problem. As a college professor, I had some liberties that perhaps my colleagues who teach high school do not enjoy. I was never once told not to mention religion. Nonetheless, for most of my teaching career I never once mentioned religion. Why? I incorrectly assumed that religion had nothing to do with the discipline of criminal justice. Now, any reader with common sense might presume that criminal justice and religious beliefs are closely related topics. After all, they both address morality, law enforcement, crime and justice, good and evil. What, after all, is much of the Old Testament but an ancient code of criminal law? Aren't the issues of morality, law, justice, and punishment inextricably linked with faith and religion? Well, one would think so. But rest assured, after many years of secular indoctrination in law and graduate school, most graduates—myself included, leave these institutions with an entirely secular worldview. No self-respecting graduate student would even consider the possibility that something as "archaic" and "unscientific" as the Bible could possibly shed any wisdom on the modern issues in criminology.[2]

For example, as an instructor lecturing on the causes of crime, I regularly taught biological theories, psychological theories, sociological theories, Marxist theories, and feminist theories never realizing that a more complete and historically accurate teaching would include theories based on the concepts of sin and alienation from God as causes of human criminality. But until very late in my career I never mentioned any theistic, deistic, religious, biblical, or even spiritual theories on criminology. Indeed, as a professor of criminal justice I have reviewed hundreds of books on the topic and I have never seen a textbook that even mentions a biblical view of criminology. This is rather shocking seeing as theistic theories were the first theories and they were the theories all other theories sprang from—either in agreement, modification, or rejection of the Judeo-Christian view on criminal behavior.

Now, some would reply that this is because Christian theories of criminality have been disproven or are in some way inferior to other more "scientific" theories. This is simply not so. Presuming this is merely evidence of our indoctrination that secular theories are based on established facts, whereas Christian theories have been disproven. This is not true. The Christian worldview has not been disproven—it has been summarily rejected for the simple reason that it is a Christian theory and for that reason alone. The anti-Christian animus among academics is deep and profound, so much so that even many Christian academics agree that their "faith" life has nothing to do with their "academic" life. They incorrectly assume that their Christian beliefs

---

[2] There are some exceptions. See Baylor University Professor Byron R. Johnson's book, *More God, Less Crime: Why Faith Matters and How It Could Matter More* (West Conshohoken, PA: Templeton Press, 2011).

are based entirely on faith whereas their academic beliefs are based on hard science and proven concepts. As we will see, this is simply not true.

Let's look at the Freudian psychological theory of criminal behavior as an example because it is one many people are familiar with: This theory, in brief, holds that the human psyche has three components: The inner child (the id), the inner adult (the ego), and the inner parent (the superego). Crime is the result of an overdeveloped id or superego which overrides the ego, resulting in crime. There are many problems with this "scientific" theory, but perhaps the most obvious is that there is absolutely no material evidence for the existence of the id, the ego, the superego—or the "human psyche," for that matter. That does not mean the theory is wrong or unhelpful. But the psychological presumptions of the id, the ego, and the superego are no more valid or scientific than the Christian presumptions of sin, repentance, and redemption. After all, none of these things is material or measurable in a laboratory. If a doctor did an autopsy on a person, they would not find a "conscience" or "sin" the same way he would find a heart or a kidney. But neither would our doctor find an id, an ego, or a superego. That is not to say that the conscience or sin or the ego is non-existent. It is simply to say that they are on the same level from a "scientific" perspective. That does not mean psychological theories of criminal behavior should not be taught. They should. But so should theistic theories. Teaching Judeo-Christian theories of criminology is not promoting religion—it is educating students about the history of criminological theory. To hide a widely accepted, philosophically profound, intellectually rigorous, and entirely plausible theory from our students is not to protect them from religion—it is to lie to them about criminology.

One might argue that Freudian psychological theory is taught because this theory has been studied by serious academics for almost 100 years. That is, indeed, a good reason to include psychological theories of crime in a course on criminology. However, the Judeo-Christian theory of crime has been studied by serious academics for over 2,000 years! For every Freud, Jung, and Skinner, there is an Augustine, Aquinas, and Pascal. If we are being unbiased and objective, we would have to conclude that the great minds who have attributed criminal behavior to sin far outweigh the great minds who attribute criminal behavior to an overdeveloped id. Not to mention, that the biblical theory of criminal behavior has lasted thousands of years. One wonders if Freud will be taught in 2,000 years from now.

Which is not to say that the psychological theory is wrong and the Judeo-Christian theory is correct. It is simply to point out that both of these theories are interesting, legitimate, and useful in understanding human behavior. Either or neither may be correct or both may have some validity. But one of them is taught as a "legitimate academic subject" and the other is entirely ignored. It is not even raised as a historical relic or given the dignity of a former theory that has been disproven (which, incidentally, it hasn't been). It is simply treated as if it never existed.

This should strike an objective intellectual as extraordinarily curious. After all, the theory of sin as a cause of crime was the first theory of criminal behavior. It was the theory accepted by the greatest minds of the Renaissance, the Reformation, and the Enlightenment. It is still the accepted theory of Christian intellectuals and theologians, priests, pastors, and rabbis. It is also still the world's most popular theory of criminality outside the secular halls of academia. For any one of these reasons, much less the combined weight of all of these reasons, the biblical view of crime is worth mentioning in our colleges and universities. And yet it is not. This is not an accident. It is the result of an intentional effort to eliminate all vestiges of religious belief from our institutions of education. Such an agenda is not what education looks like. This secular and atheist agenda is not a search for the truth—it is religious censorship and secular indoctrination.

I know this from personal experience. I am a Christian. One of my graduate degrees is even in theology. And yet, in teaching courses in the discipline of criminal justice for over 17 years it occurred to me only in my last two years of teaching that what I was teaching was entirely secular and that I had never once lectured on criminology from a Judeo-Christian perspective. It occurred to me that I was depriving my students of a full and complete education by pretending Christianity had nothing valuable to contribute to the discipline of criminal justice. And here is the really shocking part: Separation of church and state concerns had nothing to do with my failure to give even one lecture on Christian criminology. The reason I did not lecture on a Christian view of criminology was because it never occurred to me that there was a Christian view. I had been taught nothing but secular views of criminology and so I was just as indoctrinated in Secular Materialism as my students were! None of us in the classroom—neither teacher nor student—knew what we were missing. It never occurred to me, nor to a single student, to suggest that maybe sin was the cause of human criminality. To even think such a thing was impossible. Sin, after all, is not a scientific concept—like the id, the ego, and the superego. Blaming crime on sin sounds so—well—religious...whereas mumbling something about sociopathic tendencies, subconscious Oedipal desires, and overdeveloped superegos sounds so much more scientific. I had seen the emperor and agreed his new clothes were magnificent.

Let me make myself clear: I am not suggesting that the Christian view on criminology is correct and that it is the only criminological theory that should be taught. Far from it. I am not saying that Freud is wrong. He could be right. But Jesus could be right, too! One view we teach, the other we ignore. We do so not only to the detriment of Christianity, but to the detriment of education. I am not suggesting that we proselytize or sing hymns or evangelize in public schools. I am saying that in order to provide a complete education our schools should at least acknowledge that there are worldviews aside from atheism. In fact, it is impossible to fully understand Freud without knowing the context from which his work sprung. Freud can be better appreciated knowing, for example, that much of what he theorized was in reaction to the biblical view of human behavior.

I use criminal justice as an example only because it is the discipline I taught, but the same could be said of understanding history, literature, music, art, and philosophy. It is impossible to truly appreciate the Renaissance, the Reformation, or the Enlightenment without understanding their Christian contexts. In fact, much of the post-Reformation history of the world has been a reaction to the worldview of the church and its influence, as is much of modernism and postmodernism. We do believers and unbelievers a great disservice when we ignore this truth. It is like teaching Russian history without mentioning Joseph Stalin. It matters not a bit whether one holds positive or negative views of Stalin. To pretend he never existed is a perversion and a lie and will leave any student of Russian history impoverished.

Our suppression of all things Christian in our schools, colleges, and universities is one of the reasons students find education boring, confusing, and pointless. To presume the supernatural does not exist is to presume something we do not know. To presume that morality is relative without discussing the troubling logical conclusions of this belief is to take a topic filled with endless potential for intellectual inquiry and turn it into a dull, depressing, and nihilistic lesson. Four years of college education can now be reduced to the lyrics of John Lennon's song, "Imagine."

Imagine, instead, the excitement in the classroom if high school students explored the possibilities of the supernatural and its implications. Envision the depth of critical thinking if college students gave serious thought to the wellspring of moral truth. Think of the value of a class that explored human meaning and purpose in all its varied possibilities. But none of these things can be discussed without including 2,000 years of robust and intellectual Christian thought on these topics. After all, it was Christian thought on these matters that has shaped Western history since before the fall of Rome. We should include other views on these most important matters as well—Jewish, Hindu, Buddhist, and Muslim views would all contribute to a richer, deeper, more exciting educational experience. To deny all of these extraordinary teachings under the guise of "religious tolerance" is an irony too sad to contemplate. Yet this is where we find ourselves as our culture limps along, wondering where we went wrong and why so many students graduate from college having learned little more than how to be politically correct.

Questioning The Emperor's New Clothes

There is no getting around the simple fact that over the past 50 years or so the worldview of many academics, intellectuals, and nearly all pseudo-intellectuals has become increasingly atheistic. To deny the existence of God is the sign that one is a member of the intelligentsia. Because the existence of God is, of course, far from a settled matter—the intelligentsia protect their view by prohibiting any discussion of it. When one's position is weak, it is best to scoff at your opponent rather than engage with him in an open discussion.

We have reached a point in our culture where there is an absolute prohibition of the discussion of God in our public schools. The prohibition is sometimes a legal one, but more often a cultural one: we have been convinced that a discussion of God is inappropriate and irrelevant to academic matters. Because this view is on its face ridiculous and counterintuitive, we must ask ourselves: how did we come to accept such a ludicrous idea? How is it that the elimination of any discussion of the most important questions of humankind are viewed as entirely sensible and the suggestion that we might ponder these deepest of questions in our schools is viewed as radical, extreme, and backwards? This is a question that calls for an explanation.

Unfortunately, the most plausible explanation is simply the intentional promotion of Secular Materialism, which is, for all practical purposes, an atheist worldview. The only real difference between Secular Materialism and atheism is that atheists declare there is no God, whereas Secular Materialists believe, to paraphrase Laplace, that they have no need for that hypothesis.

For many academics, whether God exists or not is a debate not worth having. The worldview of many academics is one ruled by the theories of determinism and positivism. Auguste Comte, the father of positivism and sociology, held that free will is an illusion and the only way to ascertain the truth is through empirical measurement.[3] Comte's views were accepted and promoted by Sigmund Freud, Emile Durkheim, and Karl Marx, three individuals who had an enormous impact on academic thought. This is the world of blind evolution, spontaneous creation, moral relativism, scientific materialism, and naturalism. These philosophies have in common the rejection of any *a priori* sources of knowledge, including superstition, the supernatural, intuition, revelation, and religious authority. Indeed, for many intellectuals the rejection of these things is *what makes one an intellectual*. Rejecting these sources of knowledge means, to many, the rejection of

---

[3] Auguste Comte, *A General View of Positivism* (George Routledge & Sons, London, 1848).

all religious thought. Rejecting religious thought is not considered a bias or prejudice against religion, it is simply presumed that religious thought is irrational, illogical, and unreasonable. (Well, at least it's good to know religious thought wasn't rejected out of bias or prejudice!)

Their reasoning is that while the likelihood of the existence of God may be remote, it is impossible to prove either way, and in any event, it is irrelevant. If God exists, our lives continue as if He did not. The existence or non-existence of God has no impact upon our mathematical equations, chemical compounds, or Marxist Dialectic. God, if He exists, seems to be irrelevant to the material world.

This position holds a great deal of merit for many people, including believers. The fact that even believers have conceded to this view tells us nothing about God—but it tells us a great deal about how secular our culture has become. Many of us, as evidenced by the growing number of former Christians who now describe themselves as "Nones," have been so indoctrinated with the dogma of Secular Materialism that we have succumbed to the "fact" that our religious beliefs have been disproven. We cling to our faith by faith alone, but intellectually, we "know" that science has provided a far better explanation of the world than has our faith.

What is tragic is that the "truths" of Secular Materialism do not withstand even the slightest amount of scrutiny. We have been taught the doctrines of Secular Materialism as if they were self-evident truths, something that science has proven beyond any reasonable doubt, something our teachers told us and we dutifully recorded in our high school and college notebooks—and in our hearts and minds.

The Secular Materialist worldview begins with the almost insurmountable advantage of having been taught in our public schools as truth, with almost no criticism, and with the counter worldview being legally prohibited from the classroom. This is why otherwise intelligent people can explain, for example, the existence of the universe with the wholly unscientific view that it simply "popped" into existence as a spontaneous "singularity." Excuse my mentioning that the Emperor has no clothes, but this statement is entirely incoherent and completely unscientific—not to mention there is *not one shred of evidence* for this "scientific fact." It is simply a belief held by secularists and atheists who take the view that the universe *must* have created itself out of nothing with no direction because *there is no God*, so what other explanation is there? It is a view entirely unsupported by evidence. It is a view that defies all logic. It is a view that defies what we know about science. It is a view that defies everything we know about how anything that was ever created was created.

People, dogs, cars, viruses, hammers, books, computers, mountains, cakes, and lakes do not simply "pop" into existence; yet, we have been told that an entire universe, including such "little" things as *time and space themselves* just "popped" from absolute nothingness into an absolute empty space (that was not even space) all on its own, as if it had mind, purpose, and direction. This is not a scientific view. It is the opposite of a scientific view. It is a *religious belief.* It is an assertion about the world that runs counter to everything we know about the world. It is not a view we hold because of the *result* of the evidence; it is a view we hold *in spite* of the evidence. It is not a view we have concluded after looking at the facts. It is a *presumption* we made because of a preconceived belief that there is no God. It is a conclusion in a vain search for evidence.

Any objective person who had no view on whether God existed or not would never logically conclude that all of time, space, and matter simply appeared in an absolute void of nothingness one day. Of course, we cannot really say that because *time* did not exist. Nor did space. So, the entire universe supposedly "popped into" existence not at any given moment or in any given space, because neither time nor space existed. An objective observer may not believe in God, but he or she certainly could not accept the theory of the spontaneous creation of the universe. The only way to believe such rot is if one desperately wants to believe it because the alternative seems to suggest a Creator. Or—sadly, if one has been told such things by authority figures and has never really taken the time to think it through for themselves.

It is time we approach this stronghold of anti-Christian doctrine and challenge its walls using the weapons of reason, logic, and experience. Are the truths of Secular Materialism rational? Do they, upon examination, withstand the rigors of reason and logic—or is Secular Materialism really nothing more than atheism masquerading as enlightened truth?

We will now turn to the remaining two underlying principles of Secular Materialism discussed above, namely **scientific materialism and moral relativism.** It is these two beliefs, more than anything else, that justify the exclusion of religious thought from our public lives. But can these tenets of Secular Materialism withstand the scrutiny of critical examination? We will look at each of these concepts in turn throughout the remainder of the book. We will see, once the unquestionable secular dogma has been questioned, whether its walls remain standing or, like the walls of Jericho, they come tumbling down.

CHAPTER 9

A Scientific Assessment of Scientific Materialism

The Age of Faith and The Age of Reason

Millions of Christians find themselves torn between two worlds: the modern world, heralded in by the Enlightenment, and the world of Christianity. This bipolar worldview presents a false dichotomy. In one corner stands the World of Reason and everything it purportedly represents: logic, the scientific method, positivism, determinism, objectivism, materialism, and reason. In the other corner is the World of Faith and everything it *purportedly* represents: dogma, doctrine, subjectivism, superstition, and irrationality. The Christian faces a dilemma posed by this false representation of the world. She desperately wants to be thoroughly modern. Modernity, after all, has given us advancements in science and medicine formerly unimaginable. Modernity has created a large and prosperous middle class. Modernity has liberated the minds (and bodies) of untold millions of men and women formerly living under the repression of ancient doctrines and dogma that fostered prejudice, discrimination, and war. The old order, the World of Faith, gave us the endless wars over arcane religious doctrine, the Crusades, the Inquisition, and the Salem Witch Trials. Or so the story goes.

Of course, this version of the world of faith versus the world of reason is inaccurate in many respects. It is clear, upon reflection, that there is no bright line between faith and reason. They are not two enemies, but two friends, walking side-by-side. One does not have reasonable faith in something if there are not good reasons to have faith. If your son told you he would be home by 10 p.m. on seven different occasions, and on all seven occasions he was home by 10 p.m., your faith that he would be home when he promised would be based on good reason. Similarly, when a scientist believes that a certain amount of chloride combined with a certain amount of sodium will create salt, she has faith that the container labeled salt, actually contains salt; that the chemical properties of sodium have not changed; that the reaction when combining the sodium with chloride has not changed; and that the tools she uses to measure these amounts are accurate. These are very reasonable things for her to have faith in, but they require faith, nonetheless. Faith and reason are not two different ways to reach conclusions—they work together to reach the most rational conclusion.

Further, the myth that the Age of Faith (which itself, is misleading in its description of an entire era, as if there was no reason during that age) was filled with superstition, irrationality, and violence, and that the Age of Reason (again, a misnomer) opened man's eyes to the wonders of science, peace, and prosperity. These are hardly accurate depictions of these times. After all, the 20th Century was—by far—the bloodiest 100 years in the history of the world. World War I and World War II were waged not by "primitive" religious states, but by thoroughly modern, secular nations. Mao and Stalin oversaw the deaths of millions of their own people in China and the USSR, and both of these nations were officially and thoroughly atheist states. It seems the elimination of religion did not lead to world peace.[1]

It is a story, repeated so often most of us believe it without question, that during the Age of Faith, the church was repressive, controlling, and totalitarian. We also are told, and believe, the corollary, that when the church ended its dominance, humankind was liberated, freedom reigned, and the world awoke from its religiously mandated intellectual slumber. This myth is so contradicted by historical truth that it is shocking we believe it. When Christianity reigned in Europe, we were blessed with

---

[1] *See* The Devil's Delusion: Atheism and Its Scientific Pretensions, David Berlinski, Crown Forum, 2008 (New York).

many of the greatest artistic and scientific achievements of humankind. It was during the era of the authoritarian church that the world's first great universities were created. It was during the Age of Faith that Copernicus and Newton astounded the world with their discoveries. It was during the high age of Christianity when Michelangelo, Donatello, and Bernini turned marble into living works of art, and Handel and Bach filled the soul with musical delight.

Was this golden age of faith perfect? Of course not. Did repression, censorship, and indoctrination exist? Certainly, there were instances of this. But to find the most brutal repression, the greatest censorship, and the most totalitarian indoctrination one needs to fast-forward from the Age of Faith to the glorious 20th Century—to the age of science, secularism, and atheism. One can point to the house arrest of Galileo, but for real terror one needs to look to the atheist regimes of Stalin and Mao. One can (and should) bemoan the church refusing to commission a painting, but this pales in comparison to the burning of books, villages, and people that occurred by the tens of millions under secular and atheist regimes.

In spite of these historical facts, we all "know" that during the age of religious belief, there was horrible repression, but after the "liberation" of humankind from religious superstition all has been well. This is one of the core beliefs our children are taught in school: religion equals oppression and war; secularism equals freedom and prosperity. To point out that history would suggest *the exact opposite* is unfathomable for those indoctrinated with the belief that the church is oppressive and the state is our savior. Ask most any schoolchild, or college student, "What has been the greatest cause of war and death?" and the usual reply is, "Religion." The fact that this is *not even remotely* close to the truth is of no matter—it has been etched into the minds of our schoolchildren.[2] This is one of the results of secular education. When schools are controlled

---

[2] It is estimated that approximately 1.7 million people perished in the Crusades whereas World War II took an astonishing 70 million lives. Indeed, the common myth that religion is the cause of more bloodshed than other human atrocities is completely unfounded. The atheist regimes of Stalin and Mao, alone, were responsible for over 60 million deaths. Not that anyone is counting, but the fact is that atheism has caused far more deaths than Christianity. For someone who *is* counting, see: David Berlinski, *The Devil's Delusion* (Crown Forum, 2008), 24-28.

by the church, the history of the church is aggrandized. When schools are controlled by the state, the history of the state is aggrandized.

The core beliefs of a secular education consist of what I have labeled, Secular Materialism. One of the major doctrines of Secular Materialism is scientific materialism. Scientific materialism is closely associated with naturalism and positivism. Scientific materialism, naturalism, and positivism all adhere to the belief that everything arises from natural causes; all spiritual or supernatural explanations are rejected.

While these belief systems pretend to be based on objective, scientific facts, the truth is that their underlying principles are based not on science but on atheism. Scientific materialism does not gather facts about the world and then reach the conclusion that there is no supernatural. Rather, it begins with the presupposition that there is no supernatural and then arrives at its conclusions based upon that presupposition. There is no compelling scientific reason to reject the existence of the supernatural, but there is a philosophical reason to: to deny the supernatural is to deny the existence of God. It is less offensive to claim to be a naturalist, a materialist, or a scientific materialist than to proclaim that you are an atheist—and it sounds so much more scientific—but in reality, scientific materialism is not an objective scientific endeavor, but merely adherence to an atheistic worldview.

The fact that scientific materialism is atheistic is not, in itself, an objective reason to reject it. Instead, we will examine scientific materialism using the tests of reason, logic, and experience to see if it withstands rational scrutiny.

Scientific Materialism: Atheistic Belief Masquerading as Scientific Fact

Scientific materialism is the belief that all reality is found in the material world alone and that any explanation of reality must be subject to the scientific method for it to be considered legitimate. Conversely, anything that is not material and not subject to scientific testing under the method is presumptively not real. If it cannot be measured, it does not exist. This worldview is sometimes referred to as "naturalism," and has been extraordinarily influential on Western thought. Scientific materialism, or naturalism, shares much with positivism, determinism, and atheism. These philosophies are complex, but their basic presumption is that the only things we can know objectively are those things that are measurable. Things that are not measurable are either non-existent (hard materialism) or things we cannot know anything about (soft materialism). For most scientific materialists, if something is not objectively measurable then any comments, thoughts, or beliefs about such a thing is meaningless. All meaning is reserved only to the material, physical, and natural. All else is theoretical at best and non-existent at worst.

Scientific materialism walks hand-in-hand with the ideas that man is merely an animal, controlled largely by his biology; that he has no real free will; and that nothing outside the natural world exists. Concepts such as "beauty" and "truth" are entirely subjective, if they exist at all, and belief in such things as the soul, eternity, and God are rejected.

In any discussion of scientific materialism, we must be very careful not to confuse scientific *materialism* with the scientific *method*. Scientific materialism is a *philosophy* or *worldview*, whereas the scientific method is simply a means of gathering data and reaching conclusions. All scientists use the scientific method, but not all scientists are scientific materialists. Indeed, most scientists are not scientific materialists.

Unfortunately, many people wrongly presume that scientific materialism is synonymous with science, reason, and the scientific method. Nothing could be further from the truth. Science, reason, and the scientific method are simply objective ways to discover facts. Scientific materialism is a worldview that asserts subjective conclusions from those facts. For example, it would be an objective scientific fact that DNA mutates; it is a subjective belief that this mutation is unguided and random. Similarly, most scientists believe that the universe came into existence approximately 14 billion years ago. However, it is a subjective belief that the universe simply "popped" into existence in a blind, random, and spontaneous act of nature. (Indeed, this latter view is not only a subjective belief, but a rather irrational one, as prior to the creation of the universe there was *no* time, space, or matter for something to "spontaneously" pop into. More on this in Chapter 11).

An example of a belief based on scientific materialism is a statement made famous by Carl Sagan. Sagan, a gifted scientist and even more gifted spokesperson, looked solemnly into the camera and told millions of viewers of the PBS documentary series, *Cosmos*: "The cosmos is all that is or ever was or ever will be."[3] The words seem like a statement of scientific fact, especially when delivered by a popular scientist like Carl Sagan. However, these words are no more based on scientific fact than the words, "In the beginning God created the heavens and the earth." Either statement may be true, but neither is more "scientific" than the other. The words of Sagan represent a secular worldview—the words of Moses a theistic worldview—but neither are objectively provable. If one were to ask a Christian how the universe came to be, the Christian might answer, "God created the universe." If one were to ask a scientific materialist how the universe came to be, he might answer, "The cosmos is all there is or ever was or ever will be." Both the Christian and the scientific materialist are making subjective, faith-based claims—but the scientific materialist believes he has said something that is objective and scientific. He has not. There is no imaginable way that the scientific materialist could provide empirical evidence supporting his claim because his claim is not a scientific claim, but a quasi-religious claim. How could one ever prove that "the cosmos is all that there is or ever was or ever will be?" To do so would require an omniscient knowledge of both the past and the future! It is a subjective worldview masquerading as objective fact. By uttering such foolishness, Sagan told us nothing of the nature of the universe, but a great deal about his own hubris.

Unfortunately, in a world enamored by anything pretending to be "scientific," the Christian will be at a distinct disadvantage in a debate over the origins of the universe because the Christian's statement is obviously faith-based whereas the scientific materialist's statement appears to be a statement of scientific fact. Christians, or, for that matter, any good thinker, should not let people get away with making such dogmatic value statements under the guise of "science."

Because people often confuse scientific materialism with science itself, many people believe there is a conflict between science and

---

[3] Sagan was quoting from his book, *Cosmos* (Random House, 1980), 4.

religion. To be sure, there exist some conflicts between the scientific beliefs of some people and the religious beliefs of some people, but for the most part there is no real conflict between science and religion. There is, however, a conflict between science and scientific materialism, or naturalism.

Science, when done properly, uses the scientific method of observation and experimentation to attempt to determine objective facts. Scientific materialism makes subjective conclusions based on the rather unscientific view that all reality consists of material things. This is not science; it is atheism dressed up in scientific clothing.

The scientific method can tell us much, but it is only one tool in our evidentiary toolkit that we use to determine the truth about our world—and about ourselves. To presume the scientific method is the *only* measure of the truth is wrong. This is precisely the error scientific materialists make. Scientific materialists compound this mistake by holding that anything that is not material is not real. For such persons, if something cannot be measured then *it does not exist*.[4] There are several problems with this worldview.

First, even if something were not objectively measurable, that does not mean that any comments made regarding immeasurable thing are "meaningless." One can make innumerable comments about Pikes Peak. One can say it is 14,115 feet tall, that it is in El Paso County in the state of Colorado, and that it was named in honor of the explorer, Zebulon Pike. One could also say that it is majestic, beautiful, and inspiring. While the latter comments are not objective and measurable, they are hardly "meaningless" utterances. Indeed, they may tell us much more about Pikes Peak than the rather mundane fact that it is in El Paso County.

---

[4] Auguste Comte, the father of sociology, had an enormous influence on how we teach the social sciences. Comte was a scientific materialist. Ironically, his writings make it clear that he rejected any non-empirical evidence was not based on Comte's love of science, but on his hatred for religion. His goal was to reject any religious influence or any possibility of using God to explain human behavior. To add to the irony, Comte's theory of Positivism, which is holds that only empirical evidence should be used in the study of human behavior, is itself not subject to empirical testing, but is a theory based on the *a prior* belief that empirical evidence is the only reliable evidence. The ironies never end: Comte, a militant opponent of religion, created his *own religion* based on reason and humanism. It included its own rituals, priests, and buildings of worship.

Second, it is ironically *unscientific*. Notice that scientific materialism is not *scientifically provable*. It is a worldview—a presupposed condition about the way things are. In other words, it is not a scientific fact; it is a dogmatic belief. Scientific materialism is itself not an empirical, measurable, provable thing. It is, like capitalism or Marxism, a belief.

Because scientific materialism is a philosophical belief and not a scientific fact, it is *self-refuting*. A self-refuting statement is one that could not possibly be true. An example of such a statement is, "There is no truth." If this statement is true, then it is not true. It refutes itself. Scientific materialism refutes itself in the same way. It holds that there are no truths that cannot be verified by the scientific method, yet this statement *itself* cannot be verified by the scientific method. If one were to assess the philosophy of scientific materialism using its own standards, one would have to conclude that the beliefs of scientific materialists are meaningless! They are, after all, subjective opinions, not subject to scientific measurement or analysis. The irony of this logical conclusion is apparently lost on scientific materialists.

Similarly, scientific materialism relies upon certain presuppositions that are themselves not provable by the scientific method. In other words, the very foundations of scientific materialism are built upon beliefs in things that are not real according to scientific materialism. These "non-scientific" presuppositions include:

- the existence of a theory of an independent, external world
- the orderly nature of the external world
- the knowability of the external world
- the existence of truth
- the existence of the laws of logic
- the reliability of our cognitive and sensory faculties to serve as truth gatherers and as a source of justified beliefs in our intellectual environment
- the adequacy of language used to describe the world
- the existence of values used in science (e.g., "Test theories fairly and report test results honestly")[5]

---

[5] This list comes from J.P. Moreland, "How Should A Christian Relate to a Scientific Naturalist?" The Apologetics Study Bible (Holman, Nashville, 2007), 946-47.

Finally, scientific materialism commits the logical fallacy of circular reasoning. Because it is not possible to measure God—or at least God is unwilling to subject Himself to man's measurements—scientific materialists conclude He does not exist. God, by definition, is supernatural—existing eternally outside of time, space, and matter—and is therefore not a physical, material thing subject to empirical study. Because God is not a material being, subject to empirical study, scientific materialists conclude God is not real. Notice, they do not make this conclusion based on the *results* of scientific study, but rather based on the fact that it is *impossible* to conduct such studies. In other words, scientific materialists have not concluded after examination of scientific evidence that God does not exist. They determined that God did not exist *a priori* to any study precisely because they do not have any way to measure God. They hold that if something is immeasurable it is not real. This is not a logical conclusion—it is a tautology.

This may explain why most scientists are not scientific materialists. In fact, most scientists believe in God. One can hardly be a scientific materialist and believe in God. God, after all, is not a physical being subject to measurement. It is perhaps a sign of the dominance of Secular Materialism in our culture that while 59% of the public at large believe there is a conflict between science and religion, the majority of actual *scientists* believe in God. We have arrived at a very odd place where the majority of Americans believe science conflicts with God, but the majority of *actual scientists* are believers.[6]

In spite of the rhetoric to the contrary, there is no real conflict between science and religion. Alvin Plantinga, one of our nation's foremost philosophers, has painstakingly researched the perceived conflict between science and religion, and concluded:

> If there were serious conflicts between religion and current science, that would be very significant; initially, at least, it would cast doubt on those beliefs inconsistent with current science. But in fact... there is no such

---

[6] See: pewresearch.org/science/2015/10/22/perception-of-conflict/.

conflict between religion and science, while there *is* conflict between naturalism and science.[7]

The major mistake made by scientific materialists is that they believe the scientific method is the *only* method of ascertaining facts about reality. There is nothing wrong with the scientific method when properly used. It is not of any use when measuring things that are not susceptible to the scientific method.

The Scientific Method and its Limits

While scientific materialism is not particularly scientific, the scientific method is. However, even the scientific method is not without its limitations. The scientific method is a process of gathering evidence and reaching conclusions based on empirical, repeatable experimentation. For instance, if Sue has a hypothesis that mammals need oxygen to survive, one could design a rather cruel experiment wherein she placed a rat in a container and then removed the oxygen from the container. When the rat meets its untimely demise, Sue may presume that the rat died due to lack of oxygen. However, it is possible that the rat had a heart attack when it was placed in the container, or simply died of natural causes coincidental but unrelated to the depravation of oxygen. To be sure the rat's death was really caused by a lack of oxygen, Sue might repeat this experiment several times, trying to control for any unwanted variables, thereby isolating the cause of the death of the rat to one and only one possible source: the lack of oxygen.

The scientific method is extraordinarily good at measuring things that are subject to empirical study, namely, physical properties and natural objects. It is, in fact, so useful at measuring material things, that some have concluded that it is either the preferred method of proof or even the *only* method of proof. Of course, such a conclusion is demonstrably wrong.

Some even mistakenly confuse the scientific method with the

---

[7] Alvin Plantinga, *Where The Conflict Really Lies: Science, Religion, & Naturalism* (Oxford University Press, New York, 2011), p. xii.

concepts of reason, logic, and critical analysis themselves. In reality, the scientific method is one subset of the far wider categories we call reason, logic, and critical analysis—but it is not the *same thing* as reason, logic, and critical analysis. If something is not subject to the scientific method this does not mean the thing being studied is, therefore, *disproven*. It only means that the scientific method is not the best tool in our search for such evidence.

Take our courts of law as an example. The judicial system, not the scientific community, has been entrusted with determining some of the most important issues facing men and women: the constitutionality of a law, the guilt or innocence of an accused man, the distribution of a family's estate, contractual disputes between major corporations, the determination of custody of children, and countless other matters. The most pressing matters of criminal, civil, and social justice with our fellow man are determined not in a scientific laboratory but in a courtroom. While our judicial system is not a perfect way to dispense justice, it is the best method we have. Jurists have established time-tested rules of evidence over centuries of trial and error and have concluded that justice is generally best served by assessing *all* the evidence, not just evidence of the scientific variety.

In a courtroom, a judge will permit any reliable evidence to help the jury reach a just conclusion. This includes the scientific method only in those rare cases where DNA or other such scientific evidence is available. Most often, scientific evidence is unavailable or unhelpful. For example, the presence of the defendant's DNA on a victim of sexual assault only proves that the defendant and the victim engaged in sexual activity. It tells us nothing about *consent*. If the defendant and victim know each other (as is true in many sexual assault cases) the DNA is meaningless. The defendant may openly admit he had sex with the victim, but his defense will be that it was consensual sex—not rape. Science is of no use in proving or disproving this claim. For that, other kinds of evidence will be necessary. Similarly, scientific evidence can help determine the cause of death or the time of death, but it is generally unhelpful in determining whether the defendant killed the deceased intentionally or accidentally. Knowing the caliber of the weapon used and the medical damage done to the deceased by the firing of the weapon—or even knowing *who* fired the weapon—tells us nothing of whether the weapon was fired in an act of murderous rage, in a moment of recklessness, or in justified self-defense. To determine these questions the jury must look at all kinds of other, "non-scientific" evidence.

In a court of law, many types of evidence are admissible. Scientific evidence, direct evidence, eye-witness evidence, circumstantial evidence, testimonial evidence, and sometimes even hearsay evidence. None of this evidence is legally given any more weight by the court than any other. It is entirely up to the jury how much weight to assign to any evidence admitted. The jury might, after listening to the witnesses, decide that the circumstantial evidence in the case is more reliable than the eye-witness testimony or that the scientific evidence provided by the crime lab is more compelling than the direct testimony of the victim. Sometimes a jury's *disregard* of scientific evidence may even result in the right outcome. We are all aware of cases where even DNA evidence was wrong.

The point is there are many types of evidence, most of it not formally scientific. For example, if you have dinner this evening at your favorite restaurant with your spouse, you will likely leave a large evidence trail: your testimony, your spouse's testimony, the credit card receipt from the restaurant, the testimony of the waitress or anyone else who saw you in the restaurant. None of that evidence, compelling though it is, is technically scientific evidence. None of it is subject to repeated experiment under laboratory conditions. Nonetheless, the evidence that you had dinner at that specific restaurant on that specific evening is strong and compelling.

A mere moment of reflection will confirm that most of the time we base our conclusions and judgments on evidence not based on the scientific method. Very little of what we deduce about life around us is the result of a controlled experiment where we gather empirical evidence and subject it to repeated testing. Social scientists, for example, cannot operate in the conveniently controlled environments that biologists and chemists work in. Try as we may to "scientifically" measure human behavior, we often fail. Human beings are notoriously difficult to predict and the environment in which they are studied is impossibly complex. It is one thing to determine the caliber of the murder weapon. It is entirely something else to answer *why* people commit murder.

Indeed, many of our most pressing questions about life are probably not capable of being answered using the scientific method. Questions about purpose, meaning, love, and beauty are better answered by the fields of theology, philosophy, psychology, and poetry than by science. What is love? What is beauty? What is the purpose of life? Do we have free will? What is the nature of evil? Does God exist? The answers to these questions, and hundreds of others like them, inhabit the world of the physical and the metaphysical, mingling on gossamer wings between the natural and the supernatural. Love and hate, good and evil, and right and wrong may be matters that transcend the material world—but only a fool would deny their existence.

Some may argue that these things are measurable in some manner or degree. Perhaps love for one's spouse can be measured by observing if the person is kind, generous, and protective of one's spouse. But these things cannot really be measured in any objective way. Because they are so subjective and so difficult to measure, experiments that measure love cannot really be subjected to the scientific method.

For example, how would one objectively determine what measurements are to be used in our love experiment? Who is to say that love is always determined by the kindness, generosity, and protectiveness one shows toward his or her beloved? Perhaps Bob shows his love to Jennifer not by being particularly kind, generous, or protective, but by being thoughtful, sensitive, and understanding. Who can objectively determine the descriptors of love? What Bob considers being protective, Jennifer might consider being controlling. When Bob feels he is being sensitive, Jennifer may find Bob's behavior to be appallingly weak and unmanly. Or imagine that Carl deeply loves his wife, Elizabeth. Unfortunately, Carl was injured in an automobile accident and is unable to move his arms or legs. He is not physically able to do much for Elizabeth—except love her. Because Carl cannot express his love by "doing" things for Elizabeth, does this mean his love for her is non-existent? Of course not.

Further, even if a list of love descriptors could be arrived at, how are we to measure those traits? If DeShawn is rich and can afford to shower Shanice with more material goods than Jake can afford, does this prove DeShawn is more generous than Jake? Or should we measure this by determining what *percentage* of DeShawn's income he spends on Shanice versus the *percentage* of Jake's income that Jake spends on Shanice? Imagine Matt deeply loves Becky and attempts to radiate his love for her through a certain "look" in his eye. Becky, unfortunately for Matt, finds this certain "look" to be psychotic! However, when Carlos gives Becky the exact same "look," Becky finds it irresistibly attractive. How can we measure the twinkle of an eye? Measuring love is hopelessly unscientific. It cannot be done in any objective manner.

And that is OK. As long as the scientific method stays in its proper place, measures what is measurable, and keeps quiet on what it cannot measure, there is no problem. The problem arises when we become so enamored with the scientific method and all its glory that we make an idol of it. As Apollo 14 astronaut Ed Mitchell said, "Science is a methodology. As a belief system it is disastrous."[8]

We badly err when we come to the conclusion that if something cannot be measured, that means it *does not exist*. This, of course, is lunacy. It is relegating something into non-existence simply because we are not advanced enough to measure it. This is a bit like saying because my microscope is too weak to observe DNA, DNA does not exist!

Does Scientific Materialism Survive Rational Scrutiny?

Scientific materialism is one of the major tenets of Secular Materialism. Along with its philosophical siblings, naturalism and positivism, it has captured the hearts and minds of millions. It is one of the things that our educational system simply *presumes* to be true without question. It is the rare academic who will even entertain the possibility that God, the spiritual, or the supernatural might play a role in the natural world.

But is scientific materialism consistent with reason, logic, and experience? Scientific materialism holds that only the material, the physical, and the natural exist. Christianity holds that the material, the metaphysical, and the supernatural exist. Each view is at least plausible

---

[8] Quoted on BBC TV October 11, 1981 and taken from *The Harper Religious & Inspirational Quotation Companion*, Margaret Pepper, ed.

and intelligent arguments may be made for either case. But in this particular comparison Christianity is at a distinct advantage when all the evidence is considered. While no one of the pieces of evidence is necessarily conclusive by itself, taken in totality the evidence favoring the Christian worldview is overwhelming.

First, the vast majority of the world's greatest philosophers *and scientists* have supported the existence of the metaphysical. While this is, of course, not absolute proof that the metaphysical exists, it is certainly worth noting. The common myth that Christianity is a view held by the uninformed or the unscientific is itself uninformed and unscientific. Even a cursory review of the writings of men such as Bacon, Newton, Galileo, Copernicus, da Vinci, Leibniz, Descartes, and Pascal reveals that these great scientific thinkers accepted that the physical and the metaphysical exist. And this list of such thinkers is grossly incomplete. It is much easier to compile a list of great thinkers who reject the metaphysical because there are so few of them. To presume that the world's greatest minds support an atheistic or materialistic view of the world is the polar opposite of the truth. Why so many in our culture believe this ridiculous assertion is a testament to the biased conclusions that result when the secular worldview is the only worldview taught in our classrooms.

Second, scientific materialism has a very difficult, if not impossible task, explaining such things as the mind, the conscience, the imagination, and love. Scientific materialism struggles with the phenomenon of self-awareness, intuition, and *a priori* knowledge. To deny the existence of the mind, the conscience, imagination, and love runs counter to common experience and to explain them as purely material manifestations stretches credulity.

Finally, adherents of the scientific materialism give almost no weight to any other forms of evidence, such as circumstantial evidence, personal experience, emotional evidence, intuition, and testimonial evidence. Because these things are not "scientifically measurable," scientific materialists discount them. To presume something does not exist, or that we can know nothing about a phenomenon we cannot measure, is an obvious error. It leads to the ridiculous conclusion that all immaterial, immeasurable things do not exist—such as love, happiness, and beauty—things most of us know to be very real.

One recalls the whimsical Dr. Seuss story, *Horton Hears a Who*. In the story, an entire village, Whoville, existed on the head of a flower. The town was so small no one could see it. The voices of its inhabitants, the Whos, were so tiny that no one could hear them. No one save Horton, the elephant, who had very large ears and could hear the Whos down in Whoville. Scientific materialists are so self-centered that, like the citizens of the jungle, they presume anything *they* cannot measure, does not exist. Apparently, it has never occurred to them that the fault may be in their measuring devices. For Robert to conclude that God must not exist because Robert cannot see Him, says much about Robert and very little about God. It is a bit like covering my eyes to pretend that you are not in the room. If I cannot see you—you must not exist!

But What About the Supernatural?

Scientific materialism, as a worldview, does not withstand serious rational scrutiny. There is, however, one tenant of scientific materialism that has widespread support: the disbelief in the supernatural. While it may seem irrational to discount every type of evidence but the purely material, it seems equally irrational to admit supernatural phenomenon into the realm of reason. The rejection of the supernatural is such a part of our cultural worldview that many people believe the supernatural has been *scientifically* disproven. It has not, but its rejection by nearly all who consider themselves rational thinkers has led to a great dilemma for believers. The reasoning goes like this:

1. Supernatural things do not exist.
2. God is supernatural.
3. Therefore, God does not exist.

God is most certainly supernatural. There is no denying that. The Christian cannot wish away the supernatural elements of his faith. The supernatural is inextricably intertwined throughout the Christian faith, from the very existence of God Himself, to the belief in life after death. Fortunately, there is no need to re-create Christianity to eliminate its supernatural elements because the first prong of the above syllogism is false: we do not know that supernatural things do not exist. Further, even if supernatural things do not normally exist, it is quite logical to make an exception for an exceptional being—namely, God—who is, by definition supernatural.

Nevertheless, Secular Materialism is so dominant in our culture, the mere mention of the supernatural causes many people to roll their eyes in derision, as if only a fool would believe in anything that is not part of the material world. The cultural disdain for anything outside the realm of the physical means Christians will have to fight an uphill battle when they attempt to defend the existence of the supernatural. Of course, fighting uphill battles has never stopped Christians before. Calvary, after all, was a hill.

Chapter 10

A Rational Discussion of the Supernatural

We live in a time where the predominant worldview is that the supernatural is not only irrational, but has been disproven. In fact, the supernatural is neither irrational nor has it been disproven, but it is a word loaded with such negative baggage that a good deal of unpacking must be done if we are to have a rational discussion of the supernatural.

Reason, Superstition, and The Supernatural

All of us want to be considered educated, sophisticated, and enlightened, and one of the surest signs of such esteemed status is to reject the "medieval" world of ignorance, simple-minded faith, and thoughtless superstition. Among the tell-tale signs of such backwardness (which is to be avoided at all costs) is the belief in the supernatural.

Therein lies the problem for Christians. Christianity is a religion replete with supernatural occurrences, beings, and places. The Bible is a story filled with angels and demons, miracles and curses, heaven and hell. What is a self-respecting modern Christian to do?

The first step is by explaining what is meant by "supernatural." The Christian meaning of "supernatural" is a thing or being outside or above the natural world. It is something non-material or metaphysical. The supernatural is something that transcends the natural, the physical, and the material. Scientists might say that if anything existed prior to the Big Bang, it was supernatural, meaning prior to the existence of time, space, and matter. Philosophers might regard metaphysical realms, such as Platonic forms or concepts such as "truth," to be supernatural, or outside of the physical world. Poets might consider "love" to be a supernatural phenomenon, something outside of our material, measurable world.

The supernatural is not to be confused with the irrational or superstitious. Superstition, such as the belief that black cats cause bad luck, is an irrational belief caused by fear or ignorance. While the supernatural may not be currently measurable, to believe that supernatural things exist is not irrational. It is not irrational to believe that certain things exist that are not part of the material or physical world. Love, truth, honor, and morality may be such things. Magnetism, gravity, quarks, and light may be such things as well, although because they are discussed by scientists instead of poets, we tend to think of them as material, physical objects. Another way to describe the supernatural is something outside, above, or beyond the "material" world. The supernatural is something that transcends the natural, the physical, and the material.

This is not to say that the supernatural cannot act upon the natural, physical, and material worlds. Christian doctrine holds that the supernatural *does* act upon the natural, the physical, and the material—sometimes indirectly and sometimes directly. Nor is it to say that all things that are of the natural, physical, and material world are entirely separate from the supernatural world. The two worlds can interact at both the personal level and the cosmic level. For example, at the personal level, there is comingling of the natural and the supernatural within each individual body. Christianity holds that a person has a body (as part of the natural world) and a soul (as part of the supernatural world). Furthermore, a thing or being that once was natural can become supernatural. Christians hold that we will pass from this life (the natural) into the next life (the supernatural) after our deaths.

It would be a mistake, then, to think of the natural world and the supernatural world as two entirely distinct, completely separate realms. Christians believe that we are currently part natural and part supernatural. For example, we communicate with the supernatural when we pray to God. The existence and continuation of the universe is also both a natural and supernatural event in that God, both *created* and *sustains* it. Christians in our secular society often hold a non-Christian view of God and his interaction with the world. Some erroneously believe that God created the world then walked away. But that is not the biblical view of God. The Bible tells us that God created and sustains the world by continual interaction with His creation. In this sense, creation is not a one-time event, but an ongoing activity of God. God is continually acting in supernatural ways in the natural world. The two are inextricably intertwined and to imagine them as distinct and separate is artificial.

Because the natural world and the supernatural world co-exist, comingle, and interact, it would also be a mistake to believe that it is impossible to measure the supernatural or to have any knowledge of the supernatural. This is a common misperception that exists because of the influence of scientific materialism on our worldview. Recall that scientific materialism holds that the only thing we can have any knowledge of are empirical things—things we can measure using the scientific method. It may be true that the supernatural cannot be measured in the same way that material things are measured, but that does *not* mean they are immeasurable.

For example, most sane people would agree that love exists. However, it may be difficult or impossible to measure love using a purely material, scientific method. That is not to say love is entirely immeasurable. It may be that we can, in some ways, measure—or at least detect—love. Similarly, even though love seems to belong to the supernatural realm, we can know that love exists and we can even have an excellent understanding of what love is like. Anyone who has ever been in love has intimate knowledge of this mysterious force—even if such knowledge was not obtained using the scientific method.

There is, then, evidence for the supernatural, and we can have knowledge of it; perhaps not empirical knowledge, but knowledge. Again, we must put aside our biased and preconceived notions that empirical, scientific evidence is the *only* evidence or even the *best* evidence. In gathering evidence of the supernatural, the scientific method may, in fact, be utterly useless. This is because using a purely material method to measure the immaterial is futile.

Scientific Materialism and The Supernatural

There is no conflict between science and the supernatural. Science, for the most part, studies the natural world, whereas the supernatural is by definition, outside of the natural world. Science and religion are two different disciplines that study two different things. Science is primarily interested in the "how" questions, where religion is primarily interested in the "why" questions. The supernatural is something that science normally is silent on.

There is, however, a conflict between scientific materialism and the supernatural. This conflict is easily resolved: scientific materialism is wrong. Sadly, the allure of anything even remotely scientific, or *pretending* to be scientific, is given great deference in our materialistic culture. The result is that instead of rejecting scientific materialism, many Christians attempt to resolve the conflict between scientific materialism and Christianity. For some, this results in the removal of most of the supernatural elements of Christianity. Of course, unless one is an atheist, God Himself must stay, but all other supernatural matters must be jettisoned if the ship of Christianity is to stay afloat as a rational choice in the minds of many modern Christians. This is why 80% of mainstream Protestants reject the existence of Satan.[1] It explains why former Episcopalian Bishop John Shelby Spong's book, *Christianity Must Change or Die* was an effusively praised *New York Times* bestseller. In this book, Spong expresses the view of much of the American cultural elite when he writes:

> The theistic God has no work to do. The power once assigned to this God is now explained in countless other ways. The theistic God is all but unemployed. …Human beings have evolved to the point where the theistic God concept can and must be cast aside. …The most obvious

---
[1] George Barna, "Religious Beliefs Vary," June 25, 2001.

candidate for dismissal in my mind is . . . that image of Jesus as "the divine rescuer."[2]

Spong's declaration that God is dead and Jesus is merely a wise moral sage is the common wisdom of much of our intellectual elite and of even more of our pseudo-intellectual teachers and social commentators. What is perhaps more surprising is that Spong was a Bishop of the Episcopalian Church and his book received rave reviews from many high-ranking members of the clergy as well as esteemed professors of theology across the nation.[3]

Our rejection of the supernatural may also help explain why Deepak Chopra, whom *Time* magazine calls one of the "top 100 heroes and icons of the century," has become somewhat of a cult leader to his millions of readers. In *The Third Jesus*, a book that pretends to praise Christ by misquoting His words and rejecting His teachings, writes:

> I want to offer the possibility that Jesus was truly, as he proclaimed, a savior. Not *the* savior, not the one and only Son of God. Rather, Jesus embodied the highest level of enlightenment. ...*Jesus intended to save the world by showing others the path to God-consciousness.* ...[F]aith in God becomes the same as faith in yourself.[4]

Never mind that Jesus repeatedly tells His listeners to *die to themselves* and to live in Him, Chopra illogically decides that faith in Christ really means faith in *yourself.* George Orwell's brave new world is upon us: black is white, up is down.

John Dominic Crossan, another widely-respected theologian whose scholarly books sell almost as fast as *The Da Vinci Code,* has spent a career proclaiming that the Resurrection was a myth—that Jesus' body was likely thrown in a ditch and eaten by dogs. Why does this man, a

---

[2] John Shelby Spong, *Christianity Must Change or Die*, 54; 83; and 176.
[3] Glowing praise for Spong's book was given by the director of Pastoral Studies at St. John's College, the Bishop of Ludlow, the Bishop of Worcester, and theologians at Oxford, Cambridge, and Harvard universities.
[4] Deepak Chopra, *The Third Jesus*, (New York: Harmony, 2008) pp. 9-10; 62 (emphasis in original).

distinguished Christian theologian, want to deny the Resurrection? Has he found compelling new evidence? Have we discovered new early stories of Jesus that give no record of the Resurrection? Have we unearthed the bones of Christ? No. Crossan's denial of one of the foundational beliefs of Christians is entirely based on what he thinks is self-evident: we all "know" that dead men don't rise from the grave.[5] Apparently, Dr. Crossan, acclaimed theologian though he may be, is so completely a product of Secular Materialism that he rejects—without one shred of evidence—the essential belief of his proclaimed faith. And what is more shocking is that he is viewed as an authority in many seminaries across the nation—and tragically—his completely unsupported, entirely subjective belief is accepted as fact by thousands of his readers.

It is one thing when avowed atheists such as Richard Dawkins, Sam Harris, and Christopher Hitchens attack Christianity. They are, after all, atheists. It is more disturbing when people like Deepak Chopra, John Dominic Crossan, and John Shelby Spong make equally outrageous attacks on Christianity in the guise of *Christian* scholarship. Why do Chopra, Crossan, and Spong feel compelled to "defend" Jesus while denying his deity? Because Jesus still remains one of our favorite characters and they kindly want to save Jesus from Himself. The reasoning of these celebrated and popular "defenders of modern Christianity" goes something like this: We can't possibly take seriously Jesus' claims that he is the divine Son of God—the savior of the world. Not literally. We can't really accept that He performed miracles and rose from the dead. Modern, enlightened man, "knows better." We have a choice: accept Jesus as He was and reject Him, or re-create Jesus, updating Him to an "enlightened man of reason."

These purveyors of revisionist Christianity sell millions of books because there is a huge demand to resolve the cognitive dissonance we feel between our desire to have Jesus and keep our materialistic

---

[5] Crossan gives the following "evidence" for his position: "I do not think anyone, anywhere, at any time brings dead people back to life." *See*, John Dominic Crossan, *Jesus: A Revolutionary Biography*, (New York: HarperCollins, 2009) p. 95. Taking Crossan at his word would mean he also rejects the Christian belief in eternal life. I might also add that Crossan's belief is simply that—a belief he holds. By simply stating that he does not believe in the resurrection of the dead is not offering any evidence for his belief. He simply, as a matter of *faith*, does not believe in the Resurrection.

worldview, too. Of course, this re-creation of Jesus in our own image does not work. It is historically bankrupt. It is spiritually empty. It is an attempt to have something that never was and never can be: it is Christianity without Christ.

The desire for modern men to reconcile Jesus with Secular Materialism is understandable, but not particularly new. Man has created idols from the beginning—and often those idols come in the form of "knowledge." Since Adam and Eve desired to eat from the "tree of knowledge," men have desired knowledge and power more than they have desired God. The Serpent's promise to Eve is that if she ate from the tree of knowledge her "eyes will be opened, and you will be like God, knowing good and evil" (Genesis. 3:5). The conceit that ancient people were more gullible and moderns are more sophisticated is a rather silly form of patting ourselves on the back. Any person who has read Plato, Aristotle, Paul, or Augustine knows that these men were at least our equals in intellect, skepticism, and doubt. The belief that knowledge is the only virtue and ignorance the only vice is not new. From time immemorial there have been those who would worship Man and his glory, and those who would worship God and His glory.

Indeed, one of the first heretical groups in early Christianity was the Gnostics. They believed Jesus was a mystical scholar who revealed hidden secrets to the elect. The problem, according to Gnostics was not sin, but ignorance. The solution was not salvation through Christ, but knowledge. Unsurprisingly, this group has regained widespread favor among intellectuals and scholars and the "Gnostic gospels" resurface on occasion as rival gospels to the gospels of the four evangelists.

A Rational Explanation of the Supernatural

The supernatural events of the Bible cause perhaps the greatest difficulty for modern man. We are faced with an intractable dilemma: the Bible is a book replete with supernatural events, telling a supernatural story about a supernatural being; scientific materialism teaches that there is no such thing as the supernatural.

Many Americans, Christians included, believe science has disproven the supernatural. In fact, this opinion is so strong that discussions of even the *possibility* of the supernatural are met not with reasoned analysis, but with derision and ridicule.

But fear not: It has been my experience that when one's opponent resorts to the weaponry of derision and ridicule, it means his arsenal of logic and reason is bare. The truth is that science has not disproven the existence of the supernatural, nor for that matter, has any other method of evidentiary collection and proof.

Let's use love, again, as an example. Most would agree that love is—at least in part—not a physical or material thing. Yes, there may well be physical components (change in heart rate, raised endorphin level, increased pheromone production, etc.) but what *causes* such biological reactions? After all, a *reaction* has a *cause*. We don't fall in love *because* our heart rate changes—our heart rate changes *because* we fall in love. Why does seeing Betsy not make my heart beat faster, but seeing April does? Why is it that when Gary misplaces his car keys it is annoying, but when Michael does it, it's cute? How is it that the same facial feature on Chloe is an ugly mole, but on Juanita it's an adorable and distinctive beauty mark? Love may be triggered by physical attraction and material behavior, but what *is* love? What is this overpowering feeling that captures our hearts? It is argued that love could not exist without physical bodies (brains, chemical reactions, etc.) but is that true? How do we know that love does not exist *outside* our physical bodies? Perhaps our bodies are the "computer" but love is the "software." True, the information on a software program cannot operate without being inside a computer, but to conclude that the computer *is* the information would be a mistake.[6]

Love may not be directly measurable, but its effects are palpable and observable. It is the force that causes people to behave in ways both heroic and tragic. It is responsible for the commonly heroic and

---

[6] We make a similar mistake in our thinking about DNA. The physical component of the DNA, amazing as it is, is not the *information*—it is only the *carrier* of the information. What the information is, how and if it evolved, and who or what created the information with which the DNA was "programmed" are all fascinating questions. These questions led the head of the U.S. Human Genome Project, former atheist and world-renowned geneticist Francis Collins, to conclude that God exists. *See,* Francis S. Collins, *The Language of God* (New York: Simon & Schuster, 2006).

for the terribly wicked. Parents engage in daily acts of selfless care of their children as is evidenced by everything from changing a diaper to exhausting a lifetime of savings on a college education. People will make great sacrifices for love—including their own lives—but will also kill under its influence. Reputations have been ruined, businesses destroyed, and wars waged for love. It is impossible to imagine life without it. Our art, music, and literature exist almost exclusively as attempts to express it. Whatever love is, its existence is made powerfully and unavoidably known. It is, as one wag wrote, "what makes the world go 'round."

The point is that something that one cannot directly touch, feel, see, hear, taste, smell, or measure may nonetheless evidence signs of its existence *indirectly*. If a man kills his wife's lover, the scientific method can tell us that the cause of death of the paramour was due to a massive loss of blood and coronary failure caused by being shot in the chest. The scientific method cannot tell us why the husband shot the paramour. It cannot show us the forces the husband felt about his wife, her lover, or himself that drove him to murder. The scientific method cannot even prove (or disprove) that such forces exist. The scientific method only measures material things—it is neutral regarding things supernatural or metaphysical. Yet only a fool would conclude that passion played no role in this crime.

A Brief Review of the Supernatural in the Gospels

It is tempting to have a "sensible" and "reasonable" Jesus. One who speaks more of love than of hell, of rejoicing more than of repentance, and of tolerance more than of judgment. It would be comforting to the modern mind to have Jesus without angels, demons, and exorcisms. The problem is twofold: first, it is simply historically inaccurate—or more specifically—it is untrue. The Jesus of the Gospels is a miracle worker. He heals the sick, raises the dead, exorcises demons, and is tempted by Satan. To rewrite the story of Jesus without including these supernatural elements would be like writing a history of the United States without mentioning that embarrassing episode of slavery. It would be a lie.

Second, if one removed the supernatural from Christianity, we would no longer have Christianity. The supernatural is absolutely essential to the Christian faith. Not only is it essential to tell a *historically* accurate rendition of the faith, it is *soteriologically* necessary to the faith. The supernatural is necessary to the *salvation* offered by Christianity. If we remove the supernatural from Christianity, we remove *salvation* from Christianity—and if we remove salvation from Christianity, we have removed the very essence of what Christianity is.

Just how prevalent is the supernatural in the Gospels? Could we surgically remove a few stories here and there, cut a miracle or two, reinterpret two or three parables and still save the essential story? No. The Gospels are replete with accounts of supernatural occurrences. To remove the supernatural from the Bible would be to completely obliterate the central messages of the Scriptures. Consider the following episodes found in the Gospel of Matthew:

	Supernatural occurrence	Scripture Reference (Gospel of Matthew)
1.	Mary's pregnancy was caused by the Holy Spirit.	1:18
2.	An angel appears to Joseph in a dream.	1:20
3.	A star supernaturally appears over the birthplace of Jesus.	2:1-2
4.	Wise men are warned about Herod in a dream.	2:12
5.	Angel tells Joseph to flee to Egypt.	2:13
6.	Angel tells Joseph to return to Israel.	2:19
7.	In a dream, God warns Joseph to go to Galilee.	2:22
8.	A voice from heaven is heard at the baptism of Jesus.	3:16-17
9.	The Devil Tempts Jesus.	4:1-11
10.	Jesus heals sickness and other torments.	4:24
11.	Jesus refers to the "evil one."	5:37
12.	Jesus tells us to pray to be delivered from the "evil one."	6:13
13.	Jesus cures a leper.	8:1-3

14.	Jesus heals a centurion's servant.	8:5-13
15.	Jesus heals Peter's mother-in-law.	8:14-15
16.	Jesus calms the sea.	8:26-27
17.	Jesus casts demons into a herd of pigs.	8:28-32
18.	Jesus heals a paralytic.	9:1-7
19.	Jesus heals hemorrhaging woman.	9:20-22
20.	Jesus revives a dead girl.	9:18-25
21.	Jesus heals a blind man.	9:27-31
22.	Jesus restores a man's speech.	9:32
23.	Jesus heals disease and sickness.	9:35
24.	Jesus raises the dead and heals the sick.	10:7
25.	Jesus raises the dead and heals the sick.	11:4-6
26.	Jesus refers to unclean spirits.	11:18
27.	Jesus heals a withered hand.	12:9-13
28.	Jesus heals multitudes.	12:15
29.	Jesus heals the blind and mute.	12:22-23
30.	Jesus refers to demons and Satan.	12:24
31.	Jesus warns against sinning against the Holy Spirit.	12:31-33
32.	Jesus refers to unclean spirits.	12:43-45
33.	Jesus refers to the coming of the "wicked one."	13:18-19
34.	Jesus refers to angels and demons.	13:37-43
35.	Jesus refers to sons of the "wicked one."	13:38-50
36.	Jesus refers to angels and demons.	13:47-50
37.	Jesus heals the sick.	14:14
38.	Jesus feeds 5,000 people.	14:18-21
39.	Jesus walks on water.	14:25-27
40.	Jesus heals many.	14:36
41.	Jesus heals the demon-possessed.	15:21-28
42.	Jesus heals many.	15:29-36
43.	Jesus feeds 4,000 people.	15:32-39
44.	Jesus refers to Satan.	16:23
45.	Jesus claims He will return with his angels.	16:27

46.	Jesus appears with Moses and Elijah at the Transfiguration.	17:1-8
47.	Jesus removes a demon from an epileptic.	17:14-21
48.	Jesus retrieves a coin from the mouth of a fish.	17:27
49.	Jesus refers to angels in heaven.	18:10
50.	Jesus refers to His sitting on a heavenly throne.	19:28
51.	Jesus predicts His death and Resurrection.	20:18
52.	Jesus heals the blind.	20:33
53.	Jesus curses a fig tree and it withers.	21:19
54.	Jesus says He will order angels down from heaven.	24:31
55.	Jesus will judge the eternal destiny of humankind.	25:31
56.	Jesus refers to the Devil and the Devil's angels.	25:41
57.	Jesus says He could summon 12 legions of angels.	26:53
58.	Jesus says He will sit at the right hand of God in heaven.	26:64
59.	An earthquake occurs and some dead rise from their graves.	27:51-53
60.	An earthquake rolls the stone away from tomb and angel appears.	28:1-4
61.	Jesus is Resurrected.	28:16-20

It is evident that the Gospel of Matthew is filled with supernatural acts, beings, and occurrences. Matthew is not alone in this version of events. The other Synoptic Gospels (Mark and Luke) record many of the exact same events. The Gospel of John does not record as many miracles, but its presentation of Jesus is—if anything—more supernatural. Consider, for example, the opening two paragraphs in the Gospel of John:

> In the beginning was the Word, and the Word was with God, and the Word was God. He was in the beginning with God.
>
> All things were made through Him, and without Him nothing was made that was made. In Him was life, and the life was the light of men. And the light shines in

the darkness, but the darkness did not comprehend it (John 1:1-5).

John is referring to Jesus as the "Word." He makes the claim that Jesus existed in the beginning with God prior to the creation of the world. He further claims that everything that was made was made through Jesus. Finally, he claims that Jesus contains life within in Him and this life is the light of men. In the first two paragraphs of the Gospel of John, we see Jesus presented as the supernatural, eternal, creator of the universe and the light of humankind.

Even if one were to dismiss the above miracle stories as exaggerations or metaphorical examples of the healing strength of Jesus (e.g., bringing a person to the recognition of the truth is explained metaphorically by saying He "made the blind see"), it is impossible to logically reconstruct such passages as the first two paragraphs in the Gospel of John—and dozens of others like it. The Gospel of John, for example, has Jesus claim He is "the light of the world" (John 8:12), "the resurrection and the life" (11:25), and "the way, the truth, and the life" (14:6). And how does one possibly dismiss the numerous times Jesus refers to Himself as a supernatural being who will sit at the right hand of God, rise from the dead, and one day return with His angels to judge the nations?

Christianity as a Transcendent Faith

Christianity is based on entirely supernatural foundations. In this I am in complete agreement with atheists. The difference between us, of course, is that atheists point out that Christianity is replete with supernatural claims as if it were some kind of condemnation. The thinking of many atheists goes something like this: "The Gospels claim that Jesus performed many miraculous works. We know that miracles are not real, therefore the Gospels are not to be trusted as historical sources." Under any normal circumstances one would tend to agree with the atheists. What atheists fail to see is that the Gospels are not the recording of *normal* circumstances! They are the record of the *extraordinary* life of the *Son of God*.

The Christian story is that God Himself became man. That this

God-man Jesus died for our sins, was resurrected, and ascended into heaven. The story from beginning to end is extraordinary—and the Gospel writers knew it was extraordinary. The writers of the Gospels were not simpletons who believed it was a "normal" event for a person to rise from the dead. Quite the contrary, they were amazed by it! Thomas, it is recalled, proclaimed he would never believe until he saw the mark of the nails and placed his hand into the pierced side of Jesus.[7] They, like us, did not live in a world where miraculous events were normal, expected, or believable. Jesus' contemporaries were utterly astonished by his miracles. That is why they believed Jesus was the Son of God. That is why they left their normal lives and preached the Gospel to the world. That is why they willingly died for their beliefs. The atheists are right—the Gospels *are* extraordinary. But they are not stories told by naïve nincompoops. They are the story of the incredible life of Jesus as told by rational, sober, intelligent men who saw these miracles with their own eyes.

There are at least three positions one can take on these supernatural stories: the Christian view, the atheist view, and the Secular Materialist view. The Christian view and the atheist view are both logical possibilities—the Secular Materialist view is not. The Christian could be right: God exists; God is a supernatural, eternal, omnipotent being who can do whatever He wants. Walking on water, after all, is child's play compared with creating the universe. The atheist could be right: Nothing supernatural exists; God is supernatural; therefore, God does not exist.

The view that is logically incomprehensible is the currently popular view held by Christians who are also Secular Materialists. That view goes something like this: "Yes, I believe an almighty God created the entire universe out of nothing, but I really can't buy these stories about walking on water and healing the blind." What? Let me get this straight: modern man can believe that a supernatural creator of the universe is real, but they can't swallow the idea that this supernatural, eternal creator is capable of performing miracles? Isn't the creation of the universe a miracle? Isn't an eternal, supernatural being a miracle? Why is it so easy to accept the existence of God but so difficult to accept the idea that Jesus performed miracles? For that matter, why is it socially acceptable

---

[7] John 20:24-29.

to believe in a supernatural being called God, but ridiculous to believe in lesser supernatural beings such as angels, demons, and the Devil?

I think the answer is that Secular Materialism is slowly chipping away at our belief in God, but hasn't quite yet accomplished its mission. After 2,000 years of belief, Secular Materialism arrives on the scene very recently. Our culture was strongly steeped in the Christian faith and it takes a long time to reject the faith of our fathers—but the trajectory of disbelief is frightening. What is happening is that Secular Materialism is slowly disintegrating our faith in everything supernatural. We are reluctant to give up the supreme example of the supernatural—God—but we are quickly abandoning our belief in angels, demons, the Devil, and hell.

There is no *scientific* reason for this rejection—we have simply been indoctrinated with the belief that these things do not exist. Science cannot tell us whether they exist. It is simply part of the Secular Materialist worldview that they do not. The Bible tells us these things are real—and not just the Old Testament. Jesus speaks of hell and the Devil more than He speaks about heaven. The problem for Christians is that if we abandon belief in the Devil and hell because they are supernatural, how can we then continue to believe in a supernatural God? Sadly, for millions of Christians, it is only a matter of time before their indoctrination in Secular Materialism will lead them to the "logical" conclusion that God does not exist either. Belief in God will be the final casualty in Secular Materialism's war on the supernatural. In fact, we see it happening already. People are moving from Christianity, to "Nones," to atheists—in that order.

The Supernatural Message of Jesus

In an attempt to reconcile Christianity with scientific materialism, millions of Christians believe in a faith that is demonstrably *not* Christianity. The "Christianity" they believe in holds that Jesus was a great ethical teacher who gave us a moral code showing how to live better lives. This misguided view of the faith holds, in essence, that Jesus showed us how to live good lives. The essential message of Jesus, according to this popular, but historically inaccurate, view was to be a good person, get along well with your fellow man, and strive to make the world a better place. It is Jesus as Miss America rather than Jesus as the divine Son of God—and it is demonstrably refuted by even a cursory review of the Gospels.[8]

A reading of the Gospels reveals that the message of Jesus is not—in spite of popular belief—to be a good person and make the world a better place. The message of Jesus, according to the Gospels, may be briefly summarized as follows: 1) the kingdom of God in near; 2) nothing but the kingdom of God matters; and 3) Follow Me! I am the way to the kingdom.

Jesus spoke of almost nothing but the "kingdom of God." The phrases "kingdom of God" or "kingdom of heaven" are used over 100 times in the New Testament. Jesus employs ten parables to tell us who will enter the kingdom of heaven, five to describe the kingdom of heaven, and six more to discuss when the kingdom is coming.[9] Of all the parables told by Christ, all but one, are about the kingdom of God. Jesus devoted His ministry, and indeed His life, to the kingdom of God. What is this kingdom? A review of the Gospels reveals that the kingdom is not a secular fellowship of man, where men will—through self-actualization and enlightenment—live in peace and work for the common good. It is not Aristotle's "Golden Mean," Buddha's "Nirvana," or Marx's "dictatorship of the proletariat"—and it is most certainly not John Lennon's place of imagination where there is no heaven or hell.

When Jesus speaks of the kingdom of God, He is referring to the reign of God in heaven, on earth, and in the hearts of men. This reign of God will result in a metamorphosis of our hearts and minds, a transformation of our lives, and the eternal brotherhood of man—but such physical and metaphysical changes are *not themselves* the kingdom of God. These altered states are the *result* of the kingdom of God. The kingdom of God is just that—the *reign of God* in the lives of men. The kingdom is God's will being done on earth as it is in heaven.

It is critically important to remember that Jesus was speaking about God's actual physical and metaphysical reign. A reading of the Gospels

---

[8] For a critique of this secularized view of the message of Jesus, *see* Mark A. Stelter, *The Gospel According to Christ: The Message of Jesus and How We Missed It* (Wipf & Stock, 2011).

[9] Stelter, 55.

makes it abundantly clear that Jesus was not speaking of some vague feeling of goodwill, Nirvana, or glorious state when humankind will, of its own enlightenment, live in peace and harmony. Yes, humankind will live in peace and harmony, but because of the Lordship of God. Almost all scholars of the message of Jesus agree: when Jesus refers to the kingdom of God, He is referring to an eschatological event—an actual time in history when God will reign over the lives of men.[10] It is a real, physical and metaphysical time in history when the will of a real and living God will be done. It is most assuredly a *supernatural* event.

How does man enter into the kingdom of God? Again, it is a thoroughly supernatural event. Man enters the kingdom by repenting of his sin and giving his life to Christ. Jesus, through His atoning death on the Cross redeems our souls, and our acceptance of this freely given redemption results in our eternal life in heaven with God. How this all happens and whether it makes sense to us are interesting questions—but the fact remains this is orthodox Christianity. It is what the New Testament proclaims. Gospel means "good news"—and the good news of the Gospel is that we have eternal salvation through the death and resurrection of Jesus Christ.

Some believe this and some do not, but this is what Christianity is. It is an inescapably supernatural event—the climax of a supernatural story. A story filled with angels and demons, a cosmic battle over good and evil between God and the Devil, and a person who was both fully-man and fully-God. This God-Man through some mysterious, supernatural means provides eternal salvation in heaven for our souls. If one does not believe these things, one is simply not a follower of Christ. There is no other Jesus Christ depicted in the New Testament.[11]

---

[10] Scholars as diverse in their views as Rudolf Bultmann, Bruce Chilton, Rudolf Otto, Albert Schweitzer, and Johannes Weiss all agree that when Jesus spoke of the kingdom of God, he was speaking about a real, event that would occur at the end of times. This is agreed upon by almost all scholars of every political, social, and philosophical stripe. When popular theologians and "new age" spiritualists, and secular humanists refer to "the kingdom of heaven" as anything other than the reign of God they are taking an unorthodox position not supported by the Scriptures. There is nothing wrong with this, but there is something very wrong with presenting this view as the view of Jesus.

[11] See Stelter, *The Gospel According to Christ* for a thorough analysis of the words of Jesus as recorded in the New Testament.

Has Science Disproven the Existence of the Supernatural?

To some proponents of scientific materialism, anything outside of the scientific method is not only incompatible with reason, but is *non-existent*. The supernatural, for example, is considered *a priori* non-existent not because there is conclusive evidence of its non-existence, but merely because it is not subject to the scientific method. To scientific materialists, if something cannot be measured, it does not exist.

Of course, taking such a position is unreasonable, unscientific, and dogmatic. Ironically, those who unreasonably, unscientifically, and dogmatically reject the supernatural mistakenly believe they are acting out of reason and the scientific method. In reality, they are rejecting the supernatural not based on the dictates of reason and science, but based on their own dogmatic worldview. The supernatural has not been rejected because it has been proven false—it is considered false because it has been rejected.

The Apostle John tells us that God is love.[12] Like love, God is immeasurable. He does not subject Himself to a scientist's laboratory to prove his existence. Theologically, this is not merely a matter of God's will (i.e., God does not *feel* like offering Himself for experimentation), but of God's nature. The Creator of all nature must logically stand *outside* of that which He created. God pre-existed the natural world. He existed prior to the existence of time, space, and matter. He is eternal. The attribute of being "eternal," it is important to note, does not mean that God will exist forever (although that is true), it means that *he always has existed*. Being eternal means there was never a time when God did not exist.

So, God, by definition, is immeasurable. He stands outside of the natural world as the eternal being who created that world. He existed *prior to* the existence of time, space, and matter. In other words, God is *super*natural. The scientific method, by definition, cannot measure the supernatural. Because it cannot measure the supernatural, the scientific method stands moot on questions about the existence of God. It must remain agnostic as to such matters. We are simply factually mistaken if we believe that science has disproven the existence of God. It has not and it cannot. To expect the scientific method to answer whether God

---

[12] "The one who does not love does not know God, because God is love" (1 John 4:8).

exists is like conducting a Google search on whether you love your wife. This is not a question your computer can answer. If a person says, "I see no scientific, empirical evidence of God," he is talking nonsense. Of course there is no empirical evidence of the non-empirical. Of course there is no physical evidence of the metaphysical. It is rather like someone saying, "I am not aware of any of my subconscious thoughts."

An important point to make at this juncture: I am *not* saying that God is, by definition, undiscoverable. I am saying that the scientific method may not be the best way to discover God. There is enormous evidence for the existence of God—just not the kind of evidence limited by the scientific method. Furthermore, I am *not* saying that reason, logic, and critical analysis are unhelpful in discovering God. In fact, I believe the opposite to be true. I believe God (and Christianity, as well) can be defended using reason, logic, and critical analysis—among other evidentiary tools. The scientific method, *so long as it excludes any possibility of the supernatural*, will be unable to measure the supernatural. Similarly, scientific materialism—insofar as it insists that only material, physical things are real—has not disproven the existence of God. All it has done is made the *a priori* conclusion that God does not exist. That is not proof—it is dogma.

To less radical proponents of the scientific method, they are in the understandable position of standing mute on the subject. Because science is the measure of material, natural, empirical things, they have nothing to say about the supernatural. Whether the supernatural exists or not is not within the realm of scientific adjudication. This is fair enough, so far as it goes, but in our classrooms this silence on the topic of God walks hand-in-hand with our separation of church and state policy to serve, perhaps inadvertently, as a strong voice for the atheistic worldview. If a student asks a science teacher about the existence of God, for example, the teacher will most likely respond with words to the effect that "As a teacher at a public institution I cannot discuss the existence of God; and, as a scientist I have nothing to say on the existence of a being outside the realm of science." This is all true and appropriate, but it is sadly an answer in such alignment with the answer an atheist would give that it is almost indistinguishable from atheism. While the teacher may simply mean that God is not a topic he or she is allowed or qualified to speak on, the student may well hear, "Look, as a scientist I discuss 'real' facts, not matters of faith or superstition."

It is, by definition, impossible to prove or disprove a metaphysical being using methods that only measure the physical. When the scientific materialist asserts that "science has disproven the supernatural," he is merely expressing a subjective opinion masquerading as science. But what about other, non-scientific methods of inquiry? Have these other methods of evidence disproven the supernatural?

If we look to a purely experiential methodology, we find that many millions of people claim to have had some experience with the supernatural. Millions more acknowledge at least some vague awareness, feeling, or recognition of the supernatural. If we look to history as our guide, we learn that up until very recently the existence of the supernatural was accepted by the vast majority of humankind— and not just the "ignorant masses," but the intellectual elite as well. The majority of the great ancient philosophers from every culture have written approvingly of the reasonableness of belief in the supernatural. The Renaissance rejected much of medieval thought, but belief in the supernatural remained. Likewise, the greatest minds of the Enlightenment did not reject the supernatural. Unfortunately, our educational institutions have promoted the belief that the great thinkers of the Enlightenment were Secular Materialists who rejected the supernatural. Even a cursory reading of their works shows this is patently untrue. Immanuel Kant, one of the leading thinkers of the Enlightenment believed in a supernatural God and he defended this view in his book, *Metaphysics of Pure Reason*. Blaise Pascal, a brilliant philosopher, physicist, and mathematician was a devout Christian. [13] Similarly, John Locke showed his support for a supernatural deity in *Defense of the Christian Institutions*, as did Rene Descartes in *Apologies*. Among the giants of the Enlightenment only Voltaire was a

---

[13] The famous "Pascal's Wager," formulated by Blaise Pascal makes this proposition: It is logical to choose Christianity over atheism because in choosing Christianity you gain eternal life if you are right and lose nothing if you are wrong, whereas in choosing atheism you gain nothing if you are right but risk eternal damnation if you are wrong. Pascal composed a written recollection of his two-hour conversion experience and sewed this note into his coat, so he would never be without a reminder of this illumination by the Holy Spirit.

thorough-going materialist.[14] The great thinkers of the Age of Science, like the best minds of the Renaissance and the Enlightenment, took the study of the supernatural very seriously. The intellectual elite of Victorian England were fascinated with science and the supernatural and saw little tension between the two.

In spite of the historical fact that the world's greatest thinkers thought there was nothing incredible about the possibility of the supernatural, we live in a time where many hold that belief in the supernatural is somehow incredulous: naïve at best and irrational at worst. Today, the idea of the supernatural is so misunderstood, so ridiculed that many dismiss the possibility of the existence of God with the flippant question, "So you believe in the *supernatural*?" Christians often recoil in horror at such questions, not wanting to be thought of as pre-Enlightened thinkers who believe in supernatural things. This is a mistake. Let me make myself clear: *One cannot be a Christian without believing in the supernatural.* To surrender this battle is to lose the war. Christianity is a thoroughly supernatural faith and if one removes the supernatural from Christianity one is not left with a weakened, enlightened, or more rational Christianity—one is left with secular humanism.

Atheists and Secular Materialists are quite correct about one thing: Christians believe in the supernatural. Where atheists and Secular Materialists are quite incorrect is that science has disproven the existence of the supernatural.

What is truly astonishing, however, is that science is coming very close to proving the *existence* of the supernatural. To be sure, most scientists have not yet embraced the existence of the supernatural, but the evidence for its existence is far greater than the evidence against it. Atheists and Secular Materialists, who proclaim to be on the "side of science," are now confronted with the very uncomfortable fact that the evidence seems to be pointing to some supernatural laws or design.

We will now turn to a brief examination of this incredible new evidence that points *to a Creator.*

---

[14] Voltaire once said, "A hundred years from my death the Bible will be a museum piece." Ironically, a hundred years after his death the Geneva Bible Society set up its headquarters in Voltaire's former home.

CHAPTER 11

HAS SCIENCE PROVEN THE EXISTENCE OF THE SUPERNATURAL?

The study of the origin of our universe is fascinating and mind-boggling. The sheer number of stars, the incomprehensible distances between these stars, and the seemingly impossible fact that life exists at all, has led more than one scientist to find faith in God through the study of God's creation. Our sun is one of over 200 billion stars in our galaxy. Each of these 200 billion stars may have their own solar systems; we just don't know. The next nearest star to us is 25 trillion miles away. That is so far that it takes the light from that star four years to reach us. The farthest known star in our galaxy is 300,000 trillion miles away and it takes its light 75,000 years to reach Earth.[1]

The average distance between the stars in our galaxy is 30 trillion miles. Traveling in a space shuttle at 17,000 miles an hour (5 miles a *second*), it would take you over 200,000 years to go 30 trillion miles.[2] And that is in our galaxy—the Milky Way—alone. There are over 2 *trillion* galaxies in the observable universe.[3] The sheer enormity of the universe does not, of course, prove that God exists, but when one

---

[1] Giberson, p. 41-42.
[2] Norman L. Geisler and Frank Turek, *I Don't Have Faith Enough to Be an Atheist* (Crossway, Wheaton, IL 2004), pp. 108-109.
[3] Conselice, Christopher J.; et al. *"The Evolution of Galaxy Number Density at z < 8 and Its Implications"*. The Astrophysical Journal. 830 (2): 83. arXiv:1607.03909v2. Bibcode:2016ApJ...830...83C. doi:10.3847/0004-637X/830/2/83, *2016*.

ponders the universe, he can appreciate why the Psalmist wrote, "The heavens declare the glory of God, and the sky proclaims His hands."[4]

Perhaps the greatest stumbling block for atheists is the fact that the universe exists. How did we get here? One of the greatest mysteries of our universe is that it exists at all. Why is there something instead of nothing? The natural state of the universe, if the word "natural state" even makes sense in this context, would be nothingness. The simplest (and most likely) condition is not creation, but non-creation. It is not life, but the void. Yet, we find ourselves living in an unfathomably complex universe with trillions of galaxies, on a planet perfectly designed for the existence of life. This is not what one would expect if there was no design, intelligence, or purpose. If there is no creator, where did creation come from?

The answer for Christians and other believers is the universe exists because God created it. For years the atheist response was the universe exists simply as a brute fact: it is there because it has always been there. This theory is called the "Steady State" theory and was held by many scientists as the most probable explanation.

The Steady State theory, although popular among atheists, was never a very convincing theory. It left unanswered numerous important questions, such as why would anything simply exist? Wouldn't the default position be that nothing exists rather than something? And of course, the universe isn't just "something," like a large void or black hole. It is very much something more—it contains countless stars and planets and such rather complex things as gravity, electromagnetic forces, light, radiation, and on at least one planet—life. The laws of physics, chemistry, and mathematics exist with no explanation. This is hardly what one would expect to "simply exist" as a brute fact.

There were other problems with the Steady State theory, such as the fact that our sun had not burned out yet. The sun, which is a physical object that is slowly burning itself up, could not have existed "eternally." If the sun had always existed it would have burned out by now.

In any event the Steady State theory has largely been relegated to the dust bin of science. By the late 1960's most scientists had replaced the Steady State theory with what we call, the Big Bang. Interestingly, the

---
[4] Psalm 19.

father of the Big Bang theory, Belgian physicist George Lamaitre, was also a Catholic priest. His theory was widely rejected, in part based on prejudice: Father Lamaitre's theory seemed curiously consistent with the story of creation in Genesis. In fact, the name "Big Bang" was given to Lamaitre's theory in a derisive dismissal of it by Fred Hoyle, the father of the Steady State theory.

Unfortunately for Hoyle, the Big Bang was confirmed by Arno Penzias and Robert Wilson who discovered that the universe was, as predicted by Lamaitre, filled with highly specific radiation patterns that were released at the time of the Big Bang.[5] Eventually, scientists were even able to date the age of the radiation. This, combined with other discoveries, such as Hubble's discovery that the universe was expanding, has convinced nearly all scientists that, lo and behold, Father Lamaitre was correct.

Science tells us that the universe is not eternal, but in fact was created 13.7 billion years ago. What has this to do with the supernatural? To understand this, we must first understand what is meant when we say the "universe was created" 13.7 billion years ago. When we discuss the creation that occurred at the moment of the Big Bang, we are referring to the creation of *everything*. Before the Big Bang, *nothing* existed. It is hard to comprehend, but when scientists refer to nothing existing prior to the Big Bang—they mean *absolutely nothing*. Before the Big Bang there was not merely empty space—there wasn't even space! There was no gravity. There was no material thing. In fact, there was no *time, space, or matter*. There was literally *no thing*.

It is almost impossible to comprehend because we do not have words to explain this event. For example, it is not really correct to say that in a millisecond the universe was created because prior to the creation of the universe, there was no such thing as time. So, at the moment (if "moment" is the right word) of the Big Bang—time, space, and matter came into existence. Stop a moment and reflect on that fact. It is beyond human comprehension. What area did the space occupy if there was no space prior to the Big Bang? Well, that is hard to explain. The best we can do is imagine a vast emptiness that the Big Bang exploded

---

[5] Penzias and Wilson were awarded the Nobel Prize in Physics for this discovery. One can only hope they mentioned the Jesuit priest, George Lamaitre.

into, except this imagining is inadequate because there was no vast emptiness. Emptiness, after all, is something that takes up space and there was nothing—absolutely nothing—prior to the Big Bang. If there was anything prior to the Big Bang, it was, by definition, something supernatural—that is, outside of the natural world—because the natural world did not exist yet. In this way, the Big Bang is consistent with the biblical account that a supernatural, uncreated, eternal being outside of time and space (whom the Scriptures refer to as "God") created the entire universe in a flash of light.

It gets even stranger. The Big Bang produced two kinds of particles: electrons and quarks. The quarks quickly combined into protons and neutrons *under the constraints of* **preexisting** *laws that told them what to do.* Such things as gravity, the laws of physics, mathematics, chemistry, electromagnetism, and thermodynamics were already in place or the Big Bang would have amounted to just an explosion. Because these laws, constants, and conditions are omnipresent and have always been with us (well, for the last 14 billion years at least) we take them for granted. But there is absolutely no reason why these laws of nature should exist at all, much less be constant and predictable. After all, an explosion normally creates nothing but a random mess. A carpenter does not build a house by throwing a bomb into a lumberyard. Of course, the creation of our universe was even stranger than that. It was like a non-existent carpenter throwing a non-existent bomb into a non-existent void and the resulting explosion resulted in the construction of the Taj Mahal. Except, of course, the universe is something far, far more complex than the actual Taj Mahal.

There is, for example, no reason that chemicals had to interact the way they do, that gravity had to exist, that light is inevitable, that the laws of physics had to operate in such ways that they could be called "laws," or that any of this could be understood using the language of mathematics. To reply that those things are "brute facts" of nature, that they have simply always existed is not an explanation, and worse, it is not even true. Those things did *not* always exist. They were created, or "popped into existence," if you prefer, about 14 billion years ago. What existed before that? We do not know, but the two current answers seem to be: God or nothing. If you choose nothing as your answer you have some explaining to do. How did time, space, matter, and the laws of physics, gravity, thermodynamics and much, much more appear suddenly out of *nothing*?

What happens following the Big Bang is perhaps as incredible as the Big Bang itself. All of these elements, forces, and laws begin to interact in ways that create stars, planets, orbits, and other patterns that are necessary for the eventual creation of life on the planet Earth.

Why are these almost incomprehensible facts so important? For three reasons:

1. The Big Bang confirms that the universe is not eternal. That means at some point in time it was created. If "created" is too theologically loaded a word, then let's just say at some point in time it just "popped" into existence. Of course, only a scientist who is strongly averse to the idea of God would prefer to imagine that things just "popped" into existence, since the very premise of science is that things *don't* just "pop" into existence.
2. Second, because *nothing at all* existed prior to the Big Bang, that means that approximately 13.7 billion years ago not only was all matter created, but *time and space themselves were created*. This leaves only two options: either the universe, including all matter, time, and space just "popped" into existence out of nothing (which seems less scientific and even more miraculous than belief in a Creator), or something or someone *outside of time, space, and matter* created the universe. By definition something outside of time, space, and matter is *supernatural*—that is outside of the realm of the natural.
3. While these truths do not scientifically prove the existence of God, much less the God of the Bible, but they are consistent with the creation story in Genesis.

The Bible claims that God—a supernatural, immaterial being, not subject to time or space—created the universe with the words, "Let there be light."[6] This is a rather odd way for a person writing in the 15th Century B.C. Wouldn't it make more sense, prior to having any

---

[6] Genesis 1:3.

knowledge of the Big Bang, to write that "In the beginning God created man," or "In the beginning God made the oceans, the mountains, and the valleys," or some other such more reasonable (at the time) statement? And yet, there it is: "Let there be light." While the Bible is not and was never meant to be a physics textbook, these words are consistent with what modern science tells us about the creation of the universe.

The Bible tells us that God is timeless, eternal, immaterial, and supernatural. Meaning God is outside of time, space, matter, and the natural world. According to the Big Bang Theory, time, space, and matter came into existence about 14 billion years ago. What existed prior to that point in time was, by definition, supernatural. If something existed prior to the Big Bang it or He would be something outside of time, space, and matter. That happens to perfectly fit the definition of God. God is eternal, immaterial, and supernatural. So, the Christian worldview has an explanation for what non-material, non-spatial, non-time bound entity could have created time, space, and matter: God.

Secular Materialists, on the other hand, have no answer for what existed prior to the Big Bang. They simply are at a loss to explain how created things came into existence, and so they incoherently claim created things came out of nothing. This defies all logic, reason, and experience. Worse, it requires a kind of "magic" to simply believe that the entire universe popped into existence out of nothing. It is very odd that Secular Materialists, those alleged champions of reason and science, offer explanations of the universe that defy reason and science.

Christians, on the other hand, have an answer that, if not precisely scientific, is at least internally coherent: the Creator had to have been uncreated. He had to be the "immovable mover," in Plato's words. This Creator would have to be outside of the natural world. He would have to be supernatural. He would have to be outside of time. He would have to be eternal. Happily, this is precisely how theologians describe God. It is the very description and understanding of the God of Moses. One may reject this explanation based on the presupposition that God does not exist, but this Judeo-Christian description of creation is consistent with what we find as we study the universe. The tables have been turned: the atheists, who tell us to rely on the scientific evidence, now tell us to believe in a sort of magical creation because they do not like where the scientific evidence leads. Unfortunately for atheists, scientists keep making discoveries that point not toward randomness, but toward intelligent design.

The Anthropic Principle: The Fine-Tuning of the Universe

The former presumption that there is no need for a Creator because the universe was always here (the Steady State theory) was demolished only as recently as 1965. Without addressing how the Big Bang could have possibly occurred without a Creator, atheists accepted the "brute fact" of the Big Bang. However, they clung to the idea that once you get past the inexplicable creation of the universe, all else falls nicely into line with random occurrences. Inexplicable as all this might be, they were convinced that these random occurrences would eventually lead to life on Earth—and probably in a lot of other places as well. According to atheists, once we get past that pesky problem of the creation of the universe, a perfectly natural explanation for life could be provided.

Unfortunately for my atheist friends, science keeps handing their theories setback after setback. The atheist conception of life being a lucky, random happenstance, much like the Steady State theory, no longer seems plausible. This is so because the more we learn about the universe, the more unlikely it is that we should be here at all. The conditions that are needed for life to exist are so exacting that physicists John Barrow and Frank Tipler refer to the set of conditions necessary as the "Anthropic Principle," coming from the Greek word, *anthropos,* which means "man," or "human." Barrow and Tipler coined that phrase because a review of all of the necessary conditions to make life possible revealed that the likelihood of all such conditions happening by random chance was essentially impossible. It appeared to Barrow and Tipler that the universe was set on a design or course to produce human life.

Of course, such an appearance may be incorrect, but the evidence for some sort of design or preexisting pattern, whether from God or otherwise, is overwhelming. Barrow and Tipler explain this in their book, *The Anthropic Cosmological Principle.* Their book, which is over 700 pages long and includes more than 1,500 scientific references, is highly regarded by physicists and astrobiologists. Renowned physicist Karl Giberson says of the book, "It is the most ambitious and scholarly work I have ever read."[7] Others have written more accessible books on the same topic, such as Alister McGrath's *A Fine-Tuned Universe*, Paul Davies' *The Mind of God*, and Hugh Ross', *Improbable Planet*. The evidence presented by these, and other books, is that the conditions necessary for life on any planet in our universe are improbable beyond imagination.

A very simplified understanding of the fine-tuning phenomenon is this: in order for life to exist there need to be over 100 factors, such as the appropriate electromagnetic forces, position and mass of other planets relative to Earth, atmospheric pressure, distance from the sun, etc. If any of the required forces, distances, temperatures, and other factors, are not precisely—within very small ranges of error—set, then life could not occur. Just one such example: If the gravitational force were altered by just 0.0000000000000000000000000000000000001% our sun would not exist, and thus no life on Earth.[8] Further, all of these variables not only had to exist in the exact amounts necessary, but they had to exist at exactly the right time in exactly the right place in exactly the right sequence. This "fine-tuning" of the universe is compelling evidence that life on Earth is not just a fortunate random happenstance. How compelling is the evidence? Well, when astrophysicists (both theists and atheists, incidentally) calculate the odds that life on earth could "pop into" existence by random chance, they have determined that the chance is less than 1 in 10 to the power of 138. That means that the chance of life occurring anywhere in the universe is less than 1 in 10 thousand trillion trillion trillion trillion trillion trillion trillion trillion trillion trillion trillion.[9] That is 1 chance in 1 with 138 zeros behind it. For a relative comparison that number is about *twice as large as the number of all the atoms in the universe!* Don't worry—I can't comprehend

---

[7] Giberson, p. 159.
[8] Jeffrey A. Zweerink, UCLA Research Physicist, quoted by Norman L. Geisler and Frank Turek, *I Don't Have Enough Faith to Be an Atheist* (Crossway, Wheaton, IL 2004), 102.
[9] Hugh Ross, "Why I Believe in the Miracle of Divine Creation," in *Why I Am A Christian*, ed. Norman L. Geisler & Paul K. Hoffman, (Baker, Grand Rapids, MI, 2006), p. 155.

that number either. However, I know it is large enough that the chances of life randomly appearing on our planet is what we would normally describe as "impossible."

Again, just as with the universe, the more we learn about our planet the more astounded we are. Not only is the existence of our universe inexplicable, but science now tells us that the fact that life exists on Earth is very nearly an impossibility. The chances of it happening at random, with no intelligent guidance or design, are almost zero. It seems, that in some ways, Galileo was wrong and the Catholic Church was right: our planet is in the "center" of the universe—or more accurately, it appears that the entire universe exists so that life on Earth is possible.

It is important to note that this quite recently discovered truth of the universe is almost universally agreed upon, both by believers and non-believers. A sampling of the thoughts of a few of the most distinguished physicists in the nation reveals that scientists are taking a much greater interest in the fine-tuning of the universe than is the average person. Perhaps because they are physicists and understand how truly incredible these recent findings are:

- Robert Jastrow, founder of NASA's Goddard Institute of Space Studies, and an agnostic, writes:

  Now we see how the astronomical evidence leads to a biblical view of the origin of the world. The details differ, but the elements in the astronomical and biblical accounts of Genesis are the same.[10]

- Nobel Laureate, Arno Penzias, the co-discoverer of the radiation that confirmed the Big Bang, said:

  Astronomy leads us to a unique event, a universe that was created out of nothing and delicately balanced to provide exactly the conditions required to support life. In the absence of an absurdly-improbable accident,

---

[10] Robert Jastrow, *God and the Astronomers*, (Norton, New York, 1978), p. 15-16.

the observations of modern science seem to suggest an underlying, one might say, supernatural plan.[11]

- Freeman Dyson, a colleague of Albert Einstein at the Princeton Institute For Advanced Study, concluded:

  The more I examine the universe and study the details of its architecture the more evidence I find that the universe must have in some sense known we were coming.[12]

- Astronomer Fred Hoyle, the atheist of the debunked Steady State theory, commented:

  A commonsense interpretation of the facts suggests that a super intellect has monkeyed with physics, as well as chemistry and biology, and that there are no blind forces worth speaking about in nature.[13]

- Stephen Hawking, in *A Brief History of Time* writes:

  It would be very difficult to explain why the universe should have begun in just this way, except as an act of God who intended to create beings like us.[14]

Finally, Richard Dawkins, perhaps the world's most read atheist, has agreed that it is, in his words, a *miracle* that life exists on Earth. Of course, Dawkins quickly announces that it is in no way a religious or supernatural miracle, but he does at least agree that the likelihood of random chance resulting in life on earth is so infinitesimally small as to be regarded as a miracle.[15] He then goes on to explain, using circular

---

[11] Quoted in Walter Bradley, "The 'Just-so' Universe: The Fine-Tuning of Constants and Conditions in the Cosmos," in William Dembski and James Kushiner, eds., *Signs of Intelligence* (Baker, Grand Rapids, MI, 2001), 168.
[12] Freeman Dyson, *Disturbing the Universe* (Basic Books, New York, 2001), p. 250.
[13] Fred Hoyle, "The Universe: Past and Present Reflections," *Engineering and Science* (November 1981): 12.
[14] Stephen Hawking, *A Brief History of Time* (Bantam, New York, 1998), 144.
[15] Richard Dawkins, *The Blind Watchmaker* (Norton, New York, 1987), p. 139.

reasoning, that because there is no God, this miraculous random event *must* have occurred randomly because, if there is no God, then things *must* occur randomly.

To Dawkins's credit, he does not deny the fine-tuning of the universe. To his discredit he simply presumes that God does not exist, and since God does not exist, there *cannot* be a supernatural or divine source of the fine-tuning of the universe. This being the case, the universe simply must have hit the lucky number in the lottery of life, even though Dawkins admits the probability of getting that "lucky" is so astronomically low as to properly be considered impossible. However, since we are here, and since God does not exist, we must have hit that number, even if it took a non-supernatural miracle for it to occur.[16]

The Anthropic Principle has so confounded atheists that they have offered some truly ridiculous theories to explain the fine-tuning of the universe. Francis Crick, the co-founder of DNA, suggests that the fine-tuning of the universe (and the equally improbable evolution of extraordinarily complex information in our DNA) may be explained not by God, but by aliens.[17] Apparently some people's faith in atheism is so strong that they prefer to believe in aliens rather than God! (Of course, this doesn't really help their argument about the origin of life —after all, who created the aliens?)

Another equally "interesting" theory has been offered, called the "Multiverse." Let's take a brief look at the Multiverse theory to see if it provides a rational explanation for the fine-tuning of the universe.

The Empire Strikes Back—and Strikes Out

While Crick's case for aliens creating Earth has not caught on, the theory of the multiverse has. One is being kind to call it a *theory* because a theory implies some sort of evidence, and currently the concept of the multiverse is more science fiction than science. Nevertheless, it is currently the best answer (aside from a supernatural creator) to explain life on Earth, so we will take it into consideration.

16

17 Christian Orlic, "The Origins of Directed Panspermia," in *Scientific American*, January 9, 2013.

Proponents of a multiverse suggest that there is not just one universe, but rather billions and billions of universes popping in and out of existence all the time from the beginning of time. There is absolutely not a single shred of evidence for this (and this is rather odd considering there are billions and billions of them), but that is the theory. While the multiverse may be a *mathematical* possibility, it does not seem to be an actual *physical* possibility.[18] Even as a mathematical theory, it has a long way to go. Martin Gardner, one of the more influential mathematicians of our day, states, "There is not the slightest shred of any evidence that there is any other universe than the one we are in. No multiverse theory has so far provided a prediction that can be tested. As far as we can tell, universes are not even as plentiful as even two blackberries."[19]

Nevertheless, the idea of multiple universes persists. And let's be clear: by multiple universes, its proponents mean millions or billions or trillions of universes. So many universes that *anything* that could happen *does* happen. Why, you might ask, did this radically unscientific concept become so popular among some scientists? Was it because radiation was discovered suggesting other universes? No. Perhaps there was a gravitational pull detected in our universe that suggested another universe? Nope. Maybe the laws of physics or thermodynamics suggests other universes? Not at all. So why are we even thinking about multiverses? What scientific reason is there to suggest their existence?

The fact is there is no *scientific* reason to support the existence of the multiverse—there is a *religious* reason, or rather an anti-religious reason.

---

[18] The fallacy in this appeal is a form of the gambler's fallacy. A gambler might conclude that an ordinary coin could land on heads a hundred thousand consecutive times if he rationalizes that $2^{100,000}$ coins exist (though he cannot see them), each being flipped 100,000 times by $2^{100,000}$ coin flippers. Statistically, one of these coins could come up heads 100,000 times. Such thinking is incorrect, however, because the gambler has no evidence for the existence of the other coins, coin flippers, or distinct results. If the actual sample size is only one, the rational conclusion to draw is that someone "fixed" the coin to land on heads. In the case of the universe, no evidence can be found for the existence of other universes. So, while an *atheist* might imagine that there exist countless universes, a *scientist*, looking at the best evidence, would have to conclude there is one universe. The multiverse theory, then, is not a scientific theory, but a philosophical or religious theory.

[19] Martin Gardner, quoted in Karl W. Giberson's, *The Wonder of the Universe* (Intervarsity Press, Downers Grove, IL, 2012), p. 182.

The multiverse is not an independent, unbiased theory of science. It is a theory primarily used to refute the possibility that the facts of fine-tuning point to a creator. The multiverse is not so much a scientific theory as it is an anti-theist theory. The entire concept of the multiverse is necessary in order to reject the implications of the fine-tuning of the universe.

How does the multiverse do this? Well, the idea goes like this: The scientific evidence of the fine-tuning of the universe makes it evident that life did not simply appear on Earth by chance. The odds of that are too remote to be considered possible even by such devout atheists as Richard Dawkins. This left atheists with a problem: If science has all but proven that life did not spontaneously appear by chance, what are our choices? Either some supernatural (outside of and before the creation of time) creator designed the universe or…there are so many possible universes that the fact that our universe supports life is not surprising!

While the fine-tuning of the universe makes it clear that life on Earth is not an accident, chance, or series of fortunate events, the existence of a multiverse provides an out from this atheist dilemma. While the random chance that life on our universe is 1 in 1 followed by 138 zeros (in other words not possible), *if* there were billions upon billions of universes popping into existence all the time then the odds would be greatly increased that a planet supporting life would also pop into existence.

This is a nice sleight of hand, a way to stack the deck so the odds of drawing a royal flush increases if you permit billions of attempts. It's a cheap way to increase your odds, but there is still one enormous problem in using the multiverse to eliminate the possibility of a creator. Even if there was evidence for the multiverse (and there is not), we are still left with the irresolvable problem: who created the multiverse? True, if there are billions upon billions of universes the fact that one of those universes supports life is less remarkable. However, atheists are now left with the problem that something or someone still needs to exist to create the multiverse to begin with. If the creation of one universe causes scientists and poets to wonder in amazement at this mystery, how does the fact that there is not one, but perhaps *trillions* of universes, make the mystery of creation any less mysterious?

The more science learns about our universe, the more confidence we can have in the Scriptures. This, admittedly, is odd. One would think that a book written 3,500 years ago would be disproven as science progresses and the knowledge of our universe expands. Instead, the opposite has been true. This in itself is an incredible testament to the Testaments. The Genesis account, while not a scientific textbook and not pretending to be, gets many things right that no other religious (or scientific) account written during that time does. It presumes the Creator would have to be supernatural, eternal, metaphysical, ageless, and pre-existing outside of time and space. This description of the God of Genesis and fits perfectly with what modern philosophers and scientists say a "god" would have to be. Only the God of the Bible fits these descriptions. Genesis describes the universe being created in a moment of light, just as the Big Bang describes the moment of creation. Even the order of the creation of life in Genesis is consistent with science: First Light, followed by the creation of the universe, followed by the creation of the Earth, then living things, then life in the oceans, then life on land, and finally the creation of human beings. Considering this was written over 3,000 years ago, it is remarkably consistent with modern biology. One would expect that the writer of Genesis would have imagined man as God's first creation, but he does not. Instead, he describes the creation in the same order as do modern biologists.

While Christians certainly do not need to rely on science to have faith in God, it is nonetheless comforting to know that the more we learn about our world, the more reasonable our faith becomes. It is important to note, however, that a Christian need not rely on science to have faith in God. Faith requires only faith. I have intentionally been relying on evidence outside of faith to show that *even without relying on faith* one may accept Christianity as true. I have done that intentionally so that my more secular minded readers may be convinced using their own best evidence—namely, science, logic, and reason—and not relying on personal illumination or biblical authority. I should, however, point out that a Christian would be perfectly content relying on faith alone, even if their faith was contradicted by science. In fact, a Christian worldview would confirm *science* because it is consistent with the Scriptures, not confirm the *Scriptures* because they are consistent with science. In other words, there is no reason to presume that Christians need science to confirm their faith. Nonetheless, the Scriptures and science do largely confirm each other.

Amazing new discoveries, not only in astrophysics, but in biology, point to the almost undeniable fact of purpose and design. Recently, the theory that life is the result of random chance has been seriously challenged by the scientific evidence. While priests, ministers, and theologians have argued for centuries that life is ordered, directed, and designed, they now have science on their side. It is one of the failures of our secular culture and educational system that these astounding new discoveries are not widely known among the general public. Most of us learned the "old" science: creation is random. This is no longer the preferred position for many scientists. Even scientists who are atheists recognize that recent scientific discoveries reveal, at a minimum, what appears to be an intentionally designed universe. This is why these atheists are scrambling for some other explanation than a supernatural creator, even if those explanations fly in the face of science.

The renowned astrophysicist Robert Jastrow, after spending a lifetime studying the cosmos for NASA, concluded:

> For the scientist who has lived by his faith in the power of reason, the story ends like a bad dream. He has scaled the mountains of ignorance; he is about to conquer the highest peak; as he pulls himself over the final rock, he is greeted by a band of theologians who have been sitting there for centuries.[20]

Christians have no reason to fear good science. As we believe that God is the God of all things, He is the God of science, too. There is no conflict between science and God—after all, God created science. There is, sometimes, a conflict between bad science and theology or bad theology and science. But in the final analysis Christians can have every

---

[20] Jastrow, p. 116.

confidence that science and its findings will be just one more reason to believe what we already know in our hearts is true.

A Disastrous Compromise With an Intellectually Bankrupt Philosophy

In spite of the fact that reason, logic, experience—and science—are on the side of the Christian worldview, many Christians seem willing—or eager—to compromise on this matter. They want to keep God, and also keep their Secular Materialist disbelief in the supernatural. This is a mistake. What the Christian ends up with in this compromise is an anemic Jesus as "wise moral teacher." We think we can maintain the moral teachings of Christ while abandoning His claims to be the divine Son of God. We cannot—and even if we could, it is a horrible trade.

If Jesus was simply a wise moral teacher, then why did He claim to be the living Son of God? What wise moral teacher makes this claim? As C. S. Lewis points out, if Jesus was not who He claimed to be, then He was far from a wise moral teacher—He was a lunatic! What wise moral teacher claims to be the Son of God? Further, if Jesus was not the Son of God, then why should we listen to His teachings at all? What claim to moral superiority does He have? Yes, some of His teachings seem to make sense, such as turning the other cheek and forgiving your enemies. But some of His teachings seem far less rational, such as giving away everything one owns and dying in order to live. What are we to do with some of Jesus' less conventional teachings? Should we pick and choose which ones we like and which we reject? After all, if Jesus was just a wise moral teacher, why not selectively choose from His teachings? As a mere man, He couldn't have been right all the time, could He? Finally, if Jesus were simply a wise moral teacher, why follow Jesus at all? Why not follow the teachings of say, Buddha, Plato, or Confucius? These men were all "wise moral teachers." Why should Jesus have any special claim on our allegiance? There is no reason, except that we believe Jesus is the Son of God. Now, billions of people reject Jesus as the Son of God. That's fine, but no Christian can reject Jesus as the Son of God and still pretend they are Christians.

But far more importantly, to reject Jesus as the Son of God and accept Him as a mere teacher is the worst trade in the world. We, as Christians, would be giving up the divine Son of God, the eternal and supernatural being capable of granting us salvation and eternal life, in exchange for yet one more wise philosopher. That is a fool's bargain if ever there was one!

Jesus did not claim to be a wise philosopher. He did not ask us to follow His advice or to devote ourselves to His philosophy. He did not even ask us to establish a religion based on His teachings. Jesus told us to follow Him. Not his teachings—but Himself. He did not come to offer us sage advice, but to save our eternal souls. This is the often overlooked, and astoundingly glorious, claim of Christianity: Jesus Christ was not a mere man who came to teach us how to live—but that Jesus is the eternal, living God who forgives us of our sins and grants us eternal life. He does not ask us to learn some new doctrine—He asks us to believe in *Him*.

No other religious teacher claimed to be God. Moses did not claim to be God. Mohammed did not claim to be God. Buddha did not claim to be God. Only Jesus claimed to be God. This is the beauty and the scandal of Christianity. This is why Jesus was executed and it is the claim that has turned the world upside down for the last 2,000 years. This claim—that Jesus Christ is the Lord—is the glory of the Christian faith. It is precisely this supernatural claim that Secular Materialism denies and it is precisely what Christians must never give up.

CHAPTER 12

MORAL RELATIVISM: A BRIEF DISCUSSION OF SECULAR AND CHRISTIAN VIEWS

Having addressed the claim that science has disproven the supernatural, we now turn to the claim that social science has disproven the existence of moral truths. The belief that there are no moral truths is a major component of Secular Materialism. Moral relativism has become such a popular concept that even high school students will tell you with the confidence of a philosophy professor that "morality is relative." To even suggest that such things as moral truths exist is to reveal that one is naïve, at best, and intolerant at worst.

Like scientific materialism, moral relativism is entirely incompatible with Christian belief. Christianity holds that moral truths exist and that God is the source of these moral truths. Moral relativism holds that there are no absolute moral truths, because morality is a social construct, relative to time and place.

Everyone adheres to some moral code—some way of life they embrace to guide their actions and behaviors as they interact with their fellow man. Most of us don't spend a great deal of time contemplating our moral behavior, but a moment's deliberation reveals that the concept of morality raises many crucial questions: What is right and wrong? How do we know? Why do we care? Why should we behave morally? Does moral truth exist? If so, where does it come from?

We cannot think deeply about these moral questions without confronting our most fundamental beliefs about ourselves, our fellow man, and our God. One's view on moral truth will inevitably reflect and influence one's belief in God. When one speaks of his views on moral truth, one is ultimately speaking about his belief, or disbelief, in God.

Because we live in such a secular culture, we may not realize that moral relativism is in direct conflict with Christian thought. Indeed, many Christians believe that morality is relative.[1] They are apparently unaware of how this contradicts their faith. The contradictions are more profound than might be imagined. The problem is not that moral relativists and Christians disagree on what is right and what is wrong. In fact, the moral code of those who believe morality is relative is often indistinguishable from the moral code of Christians. What moral relativists and Christians differ on is the *source* of morality. Christians believe God is the Author of moral truth and moral relativists believe that man creates moral codes.

In some ways, moral relativists are correct. It is easy to claim that morality is relative based on the fact that different cultures in different times have found different things to be moral or immoral. To this I wholly concede. What was considered immoral in the United States in 1923 is not considered immoral in 2024 and may, for all we know, be considered immoral again in 2050. What is considered immoral in Saudi Arabia in 2024 may not be considered immoral in the United States in 2024. But these observations may reveal much less than we imagine. Man does create moral codes and these moral codes are evolving, relative, and often wrong; but to say that man invents moral codes is not the same as saying that morality *itself* is created by man. To presume that the only morality that exists is the shifting, imperfect, and often morally bankrupt laws of man is to presume there is no higher authority than man. Certainly, man creates laws and makes feeble

---

[1] See: "The End of Absolutes: America's New Moral Code," Research Releases in Culture & Media, May 25, 2016, https://www.barna.com/research/the-end-of-absolutes-americas-new-moral-code. 41% of *practicing Christians* agree with the statement: "The only truth one can know is whatever is right for one's own life." The good news is that this is the inverse of the general population (44% disagree, 57% agree). Among those who claim to have no faith, 67% agree that the only truth one can know is whatever is right for one's own life.

attempts at creating, determining, or interpreting morality. This is not evidence that there is no morality—it is evidence that man is not God. Man's morality is relative and imperfect; God's morality is absolute and perfect. This belief is the difference between secular morality and Christian morality.

The Devolution of Moral Relativism: Truth Exists; There Are Many Truths; There is No Truth

The historical trajectory of morality in America, while filled with nuances and subtleties, could be described in this simplified linear progression (or regression): We began as a relatively homogeneous culture with largely shared moral values, the vast majority of Americans coming from similar religious, ethnic, cultural, and geographic backgrounds. This gave way to the "American melting pot" where immigration brought more diversity in religion, culture, and geography—and with that a concomitant divergence of social conventions. However, until very recently the overwhelming consensus was that moral values existed, right and wrong were real choices, and truth was something discoverable. We may not have always agreed on what was the right thing to do in every given situation, but we agreed that there was such a thing as the "right thing"—that moral values were real, were important, and could be ascertained if men and women of good faith reasoned together.

The classic orthodox position was modified over time by the secular view that morality exists with or without God. Secular humanists hold that murder is wrong not because God prohibits it, but because it is morally wrong to harm another human being without just cause. The source of secular morality is different from the source of theistic morality, but both the Christian view and the secular view agreed that there is such a thing as morality—that, for example, murder is wrong.

What started off as a belief in God-given morality evolved into man-made morality. But, while Christians believed morality sprang from the laws of God and secularists believed that morality was created by the laws of man, both camps believed there was such a thing as "right" and "wrong." That is no longer true. Today there is a large segment of the population that does not believe we can discover the truth—because the truth does not exist. This third view on morality is called nihilism.

We have, then, three general possibilities when it comes to moral truth: 1) the theistic moral view, which is the belief that moral truths exists because God exists. This is the view held by Christians; 2) moral relativism, which is the belief that morality is determined by men and differs from culture to culture and generation to generation; and, 3) nihilism, which is the view that there is no such thing as morality. Nihilism holds that no act is "good" or "evil" because "good" and "evil" and "right" and "wrong" do not exist.

Although moral relativism may be the most popular view among those who consider themselves well-educated, ironically, it is the least intellectually satisfying view. The Christian and the nihilist are in agreement that in order for morality to exist, God must exist. The Christian believes both God and morality exist; the nihilist believes neither exists. The moral relativist, however, takes the view that morality can exist without the existence of God. Although moral relativism is the view held by most atheists, agnostics, and secularists because of the imagined logic of its position, a good case can be made that moral relativism is the least logical of the three possible views.

We will begin by discussing nihilism because it is not a view accepted by many Secular Materialists and it can be dispensed of fairly quickly because, although it is intellectually fascinating, in reality it is a view held by very few people (aside from college freshman who may have had a bit too much to drink).

Nihilism

Nihilism, from the Latin nihil ("nothing") is the belief that nothing exists. Philosophically this view traces back to Gorgias, a Greek philosopher who lived between 483 B.C. and 380 B.C. Gorgias claimed that nothing existed, and if it did it could not be known, and even if it could be known it could not be communicated. Theologically, nihilism is most closely associated with Nietzsche who popularized the idea that God is dead. The idea that nothing exists has some obvious practical problems. Did Gorgias, for example, believe he existed? For these rather obvious difficulties, nihilism has never really had much influence in the world.

There are, of course, modified versions of nihilism that do not reject all existence, but instead reject all meaning. We exist, but there is no purpose or meaning in life. In terms of morality, nihilists reject the very notion of morality. Because God does not exist, there can be no moral absolutes. Nihilists do not believe that murder is wrong, nor do they believe that murder is right. They simply do not believe in the concepts of "right" and "wrong." Nihilism posits that there is no right, no wrong, no good, no bad, no evil, no God.

The great practical problem of nihilism is it is a philosophy that works in theory only. No culture—or person—could really exist in a world where nothing exists. While nihilism may be a romantic philosophy for young radicals to espouse, it is interesting to note that these "nihilists" still very much behave as if things existed. Not only do nihilists live in a real, physical world, but they seem to obey the laws of the allegedly non-existent state as much as the next fellow—not to mention the laws of physics. Nihilism, the belief in the absolute nothing, doesn't seem to stop nihilists from enjoying their "non-existent" iPods and iPhones or from being morally outraged about things they disagree with. It is, as a practical matter, very difficult to journey through life without meaning, purpose, or belief that some things are right and other things are wrong. The most that can be said for it is that if it is correct there is really no reason to ponder life's mysteries for there are no mysteries. We merely exist (or do not exist) and nothing much can be said about our existence (or non-existence). If there are no truths whatsoever then any laws, rules, or moral codes are entirely arbitrary and have no moral authority (if such a thing as moral authority even exists).

In theory, Christian orthodoxy agrees with one aspect of nihilism: If God does not exist, then nothing exists. There can be no existence outside of God. In this sense, the Christian worldview is in agreement with the nihilistic worldview. If there is no God, there is no such thing as right and wrong and good and evil. Without God there is only the void—absolute nothingness.

This view seems so irrational (not to mention abhorrent) to most people that if a choice were forced on us between nihilism and belief in God, I dare say even most atheists would choose God over a meaningless, purposeless, amoral existence. Which is why those who reject God but still want to retain some meaning and purpose in their lives, embrace moral relativism. They presume it provides a rational basis for moral behavior without the pesky necessity of belief in God. As we will see, they are mistaken.

Morality As Part of God's Essence: The Christian View

In the dialogue "Euthyphro," Plato presented the following etiological moral dilemma: "Is the good 'good' because God wills it? Or does God will it because it is good?" The dilemma is this: If the good is good because God wills it, then God could will something horrible, such as the Holocaust, and we would have to call it good. God could, theoretically, engage in acts of evil and call it good. On the other hand, if God wills the good because it is good, then the good stands independent and apart from God. It is self-defining, and in some sense superior to God. If God is judged by what is objectively good, then the objective good is the highest source of morality, not God. This makes the objective good the judge of God's behavior. Many Christians unwittingly believe that God is, in fact, subordinate to the good. This is because they believe God cannot do anything evil or immoral. They are right; God cannot do anything evil or immoral. But *not* because the good is superior to God—something that exists outside of God that God Himself must obey. Rather, it is because God's very essence is all good.

Christianity resolved this dilemma (and answered Plato's theretofore unanswerable question) by holding that the good is not something God arbitrarily creates without regard for justice and righteousness, nor is it something independent of God that God Himself must be obedient to. Rather, the good is part of the essence of God. It is an outflow of God's nature.

The Christian worldview holds that morality emanates from God as part of God's character. God can only act morally and cannot act immorally. Goodness, or morality, is simply part of who God is. God is self-existent, eternal, omniscient, omnipotent, and omnibenevolent. Omnibenevolent meaning all-loving, just, merciful, compassionate, and good. Because this is the essence of who God is, God cannot, by definition, enact evil. Since God is all-knowing and all-good, what He commands is necessarily moral. Plato's clever dilemma is not applicable to God. According to Christian theology, there are no self-existing moral laws. God is the source and creator of morality. God does not obey self-existing moral laws nor does he arbitrarily call evil good. Nor can God ever do anything that is immoral because that is opposed to his very nature.

The concept that something is a part of one's unchangeable essence may be difficult to understand. Let's use the color yellow as an example. Part of the essence of the color yellow is that it is yellow. If the color yellow was red, it would no longer be the color yellow. Indeed, it is impossible for the color yellow to be red. Part of the essence, or very being, of the color yellow, is that it is yellow. If it was red, or any other color, it would no longer be yellow.

Non-believers, and even some Christians, may reject the idea that God is all-good. This rejection, however, does not make the Christian definition of God irrational. It is entirely rational to suppose that a god, by definition, could be entirely and exclusively good. In fact, it would make sense that a god worthy of worship would be entirely and exclusively good. There is nothing impossible or irrational about such a theoretical god and indeed one would suppose that a perfect being would be all-good. This theory of god is exactly how the Bible describes God. Now, if God is omniscient (all-knowing) and omnibenevolent (all-good) then it is completely rational to obey the moral imperatives established by God.

Because God is omniscient and omnibenevolent His moral standards are perfect and obedience to them is in our best interest. Not because God will punish us if we are immoral, but because immorality hurts us. Our Creator is loving and acts in our best interest and gives us the moral law for our benefit.

There are other reasons Christians strive to act morally. We know, as moral beings made in the image of God, that acting morally is the right thing to do—whether it benefits us or not. We believe moral truths exist and we believe these moral truths emanate from God Almighty. Therefore, we are called to adhere to these moral truths whether we agree with them or whether we can recognize their benefit. Finally, Christians endeavor to act morally as an act of obedience. Christian philosophy holds that our God is not only the Lord and Master of the universe, but also the Lord and Master of each individual human being. Obedience to our Lord is central to the life of a practicing Christian.

Of course, it goes without saying that Christians do not always obey God. In fact, Christians regularly disobey God. Christians refer to this disobedience as sin. Christian theology holds that not only do all people sin, but that all people are sinners. That is to say, it is in our Fallen nature to sin. Often, we are quite aware of our sins. We recognize we have behaved immorally, feel remorse, and hopefully repent and endeavor to do better next time. Sometimes, however, we commit the greater sin of not simply disobeying God, but of rejecting God's moral standard. We know God prohibits something, but we disagree with God's moral law and commit sin without remorse or repentance. We, like Adam and Eve, want to judge what is good and what is evil for ourselves.

But the fact that we sin in no way refutes that there are absolute moral laws. In fact, it confirms them. We would not refer to something as a "sin" or even as "wrong" if we did not believe there were moral truths.

For the Christian the ontological question is easily resolved: Does morality exist? Yes. The Scriptures make it clear that belief in the concept of moral truth exists as the concepts of good and evil and of right and wrong are inextricably interwoven throughout almost every chapter of both the Old and New Testaments. Indeed, Jesus refers to Himself as the truth. For some Christians (and for many unbelievers) the Bible and the Christian religion in its entirety is primarily about living a moral life. This, as it turns out, is not the primary teaching of the Bible or of Christianity. The primary teaching of Christianity is that Jesus Christ is our Lord and Savior and one is to love God with all his heart, mind, and soul. The second most important article of the Christian faith, is, however, to love one's neighbor as oneself. So, while adhering to the moral teachings of the Scriptures is not the primary teaching of Christianity, it is of tremendous importance. Christians believe that morality exists because the Scriptures tell them morality exists.

Morality emanates from God. Man may and does determine what is legal, but only God determines what is moral. Sometimes man's laws are consistent with God's morality; sometimes they are not. When they are not it is the duty of the Christian to obey God, not man.

The epistemological question (i.e., how can we know what is moral?) causes the most practical problems for the Christian view of morality. Assuming morality exists and that it emanates from God, how can we know what is the moral thing to do? For Christians the answer is found in reviewing the laws, commandments, prohibitions, and moral exhortations found in the Scriptures. The Ten Commandments and the Sermon on the Mount are good examples of moral truths being revealed. It is true that there are situations that are not specifically covered in the Scriptures and that such situations provide a challenge to Christians struggling to find guidance. For example, is it morally right to kill in self-defense or during times of war? While a simple reading of the Sixth Commandment may suggest that thou shall not kill is absolute, a more complete reading in context of the entire Bible reveals that the best Hebrew translation is "thou shall not murder," and that killing in self-defense and in times of just wars was not prohibited.

Finally, Christians believe the moral law is written in their hearts. At Romans 2:14-15 Paul writes, "So, when Gentiles, who do not have the law, instinctively do what the law demands, they are a law to themselves even though they do not have the law. They show that the work of the law is written on their hearts. Their consciences testify in support of this, and their competing thoughts either accuse or excuse them on the day when God judges what people have kept secret, according to my Gospel through Jesus Christ."

Where Scripture may be silent or confusing, God has provided us a conscience to guide us and the Holy Spirit to speak to us through our conscience. So, while the Christian reference to the Bible for moral guidance may not always provide easy or simple answers to all of life's moral quandaries, it mostly certainly provides an excellent source of moral truth—indeed, it has been the source Western culture has relied on for two millennia.

Moral Relativism: Man As The Measure of Morality

Moral relativism is the view that man creates his own morality. There are no absolute moral truths handed down by God—only rules invented by man. Because morality is not the creation of God but the invention of man, morality is not absolute but changes from culture to culture and generation to generation. There is no such thing as "right" and "wrong," but only rules and codes invented by man that are constantly changing as society deems proper. Moral relativism often results in the following beliefs:

- Not everyone agrees on the truth, therefore there is no absolute truth—there is only "your" truth and "my" truth.
- Morality is created by man to benefit the progress of man—it is relative, evolving, and subjective.
- No moral claims are superior to any other moral claims; therefore no one has the right to impose his moral views on anyone else.

A cursory review of the history of humankind would seem to confirm this view. Certainly, man creates laws, revises laws, and discards laws at his pleasure. Not only does man create his own laws, but even what man considers to be moral or immoral changes over time. What was considered moral in 1820 was not considered moral in 1920 and what is considered moral in Thailand may not be considered moral in France.

Does morality exist? Unlike the nihilist, the moral relativist would agree with the Christian that morality exists, however, they would argue that it is relative. What is moral is what the culture in any given place at any given time determines is moral. Morality exists, but it is dynamic, changing with the culture. It is not the creation of God, but the creation of man.

If morality is relative to the culture and the culture is the source of morality, this presents a bit of a thorny dilemma for the moral relativist.

On the one hand moral relativists argue that a culture determines what is moral. Obeying the law is moral and breaking the law is immoral. The problem arises when the law conflicts with one's *personal* sense of what is morally right. Can such a problem theoretically even exist for a moral relativist? If there are no absolute moral truths and morality is relative to the culture, what if one disagrees with the moral pronouncements of his or her culture? Imagine the German who disagreed with the laws regarding Jews in Nazi Germany. If morality is relative, determined by the culture, were the laws in Nazi Germany regarding Jews "moral"? If not, why not? If there is some "greater" morality that transcends the state, then morality is not relative, but absolute. We now turn to this question and will compare the Christian view of morality with the Secular Materialist concept of moral relativism.

CHAPTER 13

MORAL TRUTH V. MORAL RELATIVISM: JUDGING GOD AND FINDING HIM WANTING

Let's concede at the outset that there are problems with all human concepts of morality, be those Christian concepts or Secular Materialist concepts. That is not to say that there is a problem with *God's* concept of morality. After all, by definition God is a perfectly moral being. The problem arises with mere mortals attempting to discern and apply God's morality.

In this chapter we will look at the problems inherent in the Christian understanding of morality and the problems inherent in the Secular Materialist understanding of morality. While not all Secular Materialists adhere to the doctrine of moral relativism, for our purposes the Secular Materialist position will be that of moral relativism, as that is the dominant theory competing with the Christian understanding of morality. Indeed, moral relativism is a position held by many Christians, even though it is logically inconsistent with orthodox Christian belief.

The problem inherent in both the Christian moral worldview and moral relativism are essentially the same: What does a person do when he or she finds that their own personal moral beliefs conflict with the objective moral standard they claim to believe? More specifically, if one is a Christian, what does he or she do when their own moral beliefs conflict with the Bible? If one is a moral relativist, what does he or she do when their own moral beliefs conflict with the laws of the state?

Judging God

If you are a fellow Christian, let's admit it: We often judge God and find Him wanting. We question the commandments we do not like. We do not understand how it could hurt anyone to violate our least favorite commandment—whatever commandment that may be. I knew a man who was a good and decent man in most every respect—but he was in love with a woman who was not his wife. He made an excellent argument that the pesky commandment about not committing adultery did not really apply to him in his particular situation. Adultery, he claimed, meant having sexual relations with a woman whom you did not love. If you love the woman you are sleeping with—even if you are married and she is not your wife—that is not really what God meant by adultery. Because this man was so eager to be with his lover his "reasons" (or excuses) were boundless. "In fact," he "reasoned," if you sleep with someone you do not love, even if she is your wife—that is the real adultery. Sleeping with the person you love is beautiful and must be ordained by God." Sure.

Of course, like most of us, this man came to see the error of his ways; but, all of us at one time or another have questioned God's moral code when it did not align with whatever it was we wanted to do. This behavior should not be surprising; it is described in the Scriptures. In Romans 1:28, Paul writes: "And because they did not think it worthwhile to have God in their knowledge, God delivered them over to a worthless mind to do what is morally wrong."

In fact, the Scriptures tell us that it is impossible for man to know what is morally right without the assistance of God. Christian theology tells us that because of the Fall, sin entered the world and every human is affected by sin. Part of the effect of sin is our inability without the grace of God to be able to reason correctly. The Scripture tells us that man's inability to reason without the assistance of God is the result of the Fall, which was caused by man wanting to be like God, determining what is good and what is evil. The story of Adam and Eve, which we will discuss is greater detail in Chapter 16, is not about eating an apple or discovering sex. It is about man wanting to determine for himself what is good and what is evil. In the story, the serpent says to Eve: "No! You will not die. In fact, God knows that when you eat it your eyes will be opened and you will be like God, knowing good and evil" (Genesis 3:4-5).

Christian theology on the Fall, Original Sin, and the nature of morality may be rejected by those who choose not to believe and it may even be questioned by Christians, but it is not illogical or inconsistent. It provides an entirely logical and consistent theory of morality that has not been refuted by science or logic. In fact, the biblical story of the nature of sin, as incredible as it seems, has been entirely consistent with the experience of humankind. One may reject the idea that all men are inherently sinful but one cannot deny the fact that all men have sinned. Even a cursory review of humankind reveals that the biblical description of man is right on the mark. As G.K. Chesterton commented, "Certain new theologians dispute original sin, which is the only part of Christian theology which can really be proved."

We may reject God's moral code and choose our own, but in the very act of doing so we are confirming and replaying the story of Adam and Eve. We may reject the worship of God and choose instead to worship man or nature or evolution or science, but in doing so we are confirming Paul's words in Romans 1:21-23:

> For although they knew God, they did not glorify Him as God or show gratitude. Instead, their thinking became nonsense, and their senseless minds were darkened. Claiming to be wise, they became fools and exchanged the glory of the immortal God for images resembling mortal man, birds, four-footed animals, and reptiles.

The more one studies the Bible the more obvious it becomes that the history of humankind has been perfectly described therein. Those who believe the Bible has been disproven by science or philosophy or reason, are simply not serious students of the Bible. Before I was a believer, I, too, considered the Bible a book consisting of many fanciful "just so" stories; but once I took off my secular glasses, I began to read the Bible without the presuppositions of a secular worldview. As with all things, our assumptions will shape our conclusions. When I re-read the Bible without secular bias or prejudice, I recognized how remarkably the Bible describes human desires, thinking, and behavior—and our irrationality.

The stories in the Bible, whether they are literal recordings of real events or metaphorical or allegorical stories (and there are some of both) point to the fact that to disobey God can only be the result of sin. Notice I wrote that to disobey God is the result of sin, not is a sin. It is both, but for our purposes it is disobedience as a result or product of sin that is pertinent when we imagine that God behaves immorally. Sin has its consequences and one of its consequences is that humans are not always able to reason due to what theologians refer to as the noetic effect of sin. That is, one of the effects of sin is to cloud our reasoning. An example of the noetic effect of sin is our belief that God has behaved immorally. There are many instances of us questioning God's morality. Examples of God behaving badly might include the flood, God asking Abraham to sacrifice Isaac, the slaughter of the Canaanite children, the existence of hell, or even the Crucifixion itself! This is not a book on theodicy (the justification of the behavior of God) and many excellent books have been written that do just that.[1] But whatever doubts one may have as to God's moral character, these questions, while fascinating explorations into morality, may be dispensed of by using simple logic: If God is omnibenevolent (all good) and is incapable of sin, then it is an impossibility that God ever behaves immorally. We may not understand God's behavior (indeed, as Fallen humans we *cannot* understand God's behavior), but as believers we can securely rest assured that God does not sin.

Let's reason through this. If one does not believe in God, then

---

[1] See: Bruce A. Little, *God, Why This Evil* (Hamilton Books, Lanham, MD, 2010); Alvin Plantinga, *God, Freedom, and Evil* (Eerdmans, Grand Rapids, MI, 1977); Kenneth Surin, *Theology and the Problem of Evil* (Wipf & Stock, Eugene, OR, 1986); and N.T. Wright, *Evil and the Justice of God* (InterVarsity, Downers Grove, IL, 2006). For a less scholarly and more personal exploration of the problem of evil, See: C.S. Lewis, *A Grief Observed* (HarperCollins, New York, 1961).

it is irrational for him to believe God acts immorally. If there is no God, He cannot act immorally, or any other way, because He does not exist. So, atheists cannot logically claim that they do not believe in God because He acts immorally. They are certainly free not to believe, but they cannot rationally blame it on God's allegedly bad behavior. I suspect what atheists really mean is they cannot believe in God because if God existed, He would not act immorally, and atheists have judged the behavior of the Judeo-Christian God and concluded that He has acted immorally. Even then, atheists face a bit of a dilemma because they can hardly judge God based on moral standards, as many atheists do not believe in objective moral truths. Perhaps what they are really saying is that God does not act rationally, and therefore He cannot be God. This, of course, begs the question of why atheists presume their definition of rational behavior is correct or of whether a god would have to behave rationally.

The Christian who believes that God has acted immorally has an even harder time than the atheist. If one is a Christian, he cannot reasonably claim that God acts immorally because, by definition, a Christian is someone who believes in the God of the Scriptures. The Scriptures tell us that God is perfectly good, all-moral, omnibenevolent. If so, and we must believe so in order to call ourselves Christians, it is completely irrational for an omnibenevolent God to act immorally. It is simply a logical impossibility.

Yet we struggle with the morality of God. We question, we doubt, we judge a perfect God by the imperfect morality of Fallen man. This is the picture of irrationality.

Irrational though it may be, it is entirely consistent with what the Bible says men will do. This gives us another reason to believe in the reliability of Scripture. Consider: We believe God exists. We believe this God is perfectly moral. We believe that man is Fallen, sinful, and behaves immorally. We believe that man, due to the noetic effects of the Fall, is sometimes incapable of rational thought. We believe that our sinful nature encourages us to find fault in God. We believe that we desire to be like God—determining for ourselves what is moral and what is immoral—in fact, we believe this was the Original Sin of Adam and Eve. And yet, believing these things, we often conclude that God behaves in ways that are inconsistent with our understanding of morality and, therefore, God behaves immorally!

Think about this. It may take a while to truly comprehend the irrationality of the above description of human nature. Yet, here we are, knowing we are Fallen and God is perfect and still judging Him using our imperfect reason and our imperfect understanding of morality! And what's more, the Scriptures predict all of this:

> To the pure, everything is pure, but to those who are defiled and unbelieving, nothing is pure; in fact, both their mind and conscience are defiled. They profess to know God, but they deny Him by their works. They are detestable, disobedient, and disqualified for any good work.
> –Titus 1:15

> For the mind-set of the flesh is hostile to God because it does not submit itself to God's law, for it is *unable* to do so. Those whose lives are in the flesh are *unable* to please God.
> –Romans 8:7-8 (emphasis added).

In the above passages, Paul explains that those who do not believe have minds and consciences that are defiled—incapable of belief, incapable of reasoned analysis. Paul does not say that men sometimes choose not to submit to God, but that men *cannot* submit to God. To make sure no one misses this crucial point Paul repeats it immediately in the passage. He goes on to explain that while men are unable to submit to God's law, all is not lost. With faith in Christ and through the prevenient grace of God men can and do submit to God—although not always and not perfectly in this life. This is true of believers and non-believers alike, according to Christian theology—and as is evident by observing the world around us.

While it is irrational for a Christian to conclude that God has behaved immorally, it is not wrong to have questions about God's behavior. Having such questions should not be surprising to Christians—and it is certainly not surprising to God! Christians (and others) should not be afraid to have questions or even doubts about their faith. God knows you have questions and He is not afraid of your questions. God wants you to openly and honestly reveal your heart to Him and to come to Him with your questions and doubts. This is true for believers, unbelievers, and believing skeptics. Mark's Gospel tells the story of a father whose son was possessed with a demon that caused the boy to have convulsions. Jesus asked the man, "How long has this been happening to him?" The father answered, "From childhood. And many times it has thrown him into fire or water to destroy him. But if You can do anything, have compassion on us and help us." Jesus replied, "If You can? Everything is possible to the one who believes." To which the father of the boy replies to Jesus: "I do believe! Help me with my unbelief."[2]

What a beautiful passage. How honest. How like us. Did Jesus rebuke this doubting but desperate father? No. Jesus did what Jesus does: He healed the father's son.

While Christians often do not understand God and often find his ways mysterious, perplexing, or even shocking, we should remember that the Scriptures tell us that this will happen and if we keep our faith in the perfection of God's love and morality that in time—whether in this life or the next—God will be revealed to us more fully and we will better understand his perfection. In my own life, I have questioned God on one topic or another and either through research or experience, time after time, I have learned that God was right. This should not come as a surprise! Yet, as a sinful and Fallen human being, it always surprises me that—guess what?!—the Lord of the Universe was right and I was wrong! As my pastor, Aaron Dorman, once remarked, "I disagree with God all the time; but I usually know who is right."

Christians will doubt. Christians will question. This is not a sign that the Scriptures are wrong—it is a confirmation of the Scriptures. We know, as Christians, that we are Fallen and that our best reasoning is often flawed; but, when we doubt, we can know, through faith, through experience, and through the Holy Spirit moving inside our hearts that our God is all-loving and perfectly moral. This, for believers, is not an illogical conclusion but the only logical conclusion. We believe

---

[2] The story is told at Mark 9:17-29.

in absolute moral truths because the Bible tells us there are absolute moral truths. This is how Christians determine what is moral, and, assuming God exists, an entirely logical and rational way to define morality. It may not be entirely satisfying, but it is not illogical. And I believe we will see that it is more satisfying than the secular belief in moral relativism.

Moral Relativism: Fighting With Our Relatives

The Christian has a moral code that is logically sound and internally consistent: God is perfectly good. God has established a moral code that is consistent with his moral perfection. We may not like this code, we may disagree with it, and we most certainly will not always follow it—but none of these things detract from its logic.

Moral relativism does not fare as well. To begin with, the premise of moral relativism is fatally flawed. Moral relativists assert that humans create their own moral codes. This is an assertion that is self-evident and agreed upon by all. However, it proves nothing. Of course humans create their own moral codes…but that does not mean that there is no moral code outside of and surpassing our feeble man-made codes. Just because we get morality wrong, does not mean there are no moral truths—it simply means we are often mistaken in determining what those moral truths are. For example, if an entire culture believed the Earth was flat and later determined the Earth was round, this is no evidence that the shape of the Earth is relative—it is simply evidence that we were mistaken about its shape. Because some people believe 2 + 2 is 4 and some believe 2 + 2 is 5, we do not come to the rather irrational conclusion that math is relative!

Blinded by our self-centeredness, we presume because we have made poor moral choices that there is no such thing as morality. We imagine we are the authors of morality, the center of the universe, the Alpha and Omega. In believing we are the creators of morality we necessarily presume that God is not. In this worldview, we determine what is right and wrong—not God.

Moral relativism is often accompanied by the pretense that moral relativism leads to greater tolerance of opposing views, thus making the world a more peaceful place. Even this claim, which is not a claim based on the *truth* of moral relativism, but merely on the expediency that it leads to greater tolerance, is terribly flawed. First, even if there are no absolute truths, this does not mean all truths are equal. Some truths may be better than other truths in terms of logic, reason, application, consistency, etc. For example, even if we did not know how fast light traveled, an answer of 150,000 miles a second is better than 8 miles an hour, and 8 miles an hour is a better answer than "yellow." So, accepting the idea that there are no moral truths does not logically lead to the conclusion that we must then accept all moral claims as if they were moral truths.

Second, a person may believe there are absolute moral truths and still be tolerant—indeed, may even be more tolerant than a moral relativist. After all, prior to postmodernism "tolerance" meant not that all views are equal, but that even if you believe your position is superior you should be tolerant of opposing views. Tolerance does not mean giving up one's beliefs, it means treating other beliefs with the respect they deserve. Whether one believes in moral truth or in moral relativism has very little to do with whether one is a tolerant person or not. A person can believe in absolute moral truths and still be very tolerant of moral relativists; and one can be a moral relativist who is very intolerant of those who believe in moral truths.

In the real world, I have yet to meet a true moral relativist. No matter how wedded to moral relativism we may be intellectually, we seem incapable of abandoning our instinct for justice. For example, an animal lover who happens to also be a prostitute may be a firm believer in moral relativism when it comes to legislating sexual behavior, but is completely convinced that clubbing baby seals is an act of wanton immorality. A pro-choice woman who insists that we should keep "our laws off her body" might entirely support laws prohibiting prostitution. The reality is that most supporters of moral relativism support it when they find it convenient to disregard conventional morality, but are quite happy to invoke morality when it suits their needs. Moral relativism is used when one disagrees with another's morality. Few regard their own morality as relative. When we encounter a position that we find immoral it would be more helpful, and do less harm to truth, if instead of pretending that morality was non-existent, we simply disagreed with the morality of our opponents' position.

But for our purposes, let's look at moral relativism in its purest theoretical form. Moral relativism may be true even if its adherents are hypocrites. After all, one would not want the truth of Christianity to be judged based on the behavior of some Christians. But moral relativism, even in its purest form, contains an internal contradiction that destroys its premise.

The contradiction within moral relativism is that most moral relativists claim there is a morality that transcends mere human laws or cultural norms. There is a very good reason for moral relativists to hold to a morality that transcends the morality of human beings. After all, none can deny that societies often create moral codes that are, well, *immoral*. Few would argue that slavery was moral even though it was perfectly legal in the antebellum South. Few would argue that the Holocaust was moral even though it was carried out in perfect accordance with the law in Nazi Germany.

Moral relativists have, we know, disobeyed laws they found immoral. The question is, can a moral relativist logically appeal to a "higher law" or his "conscience" when disobeying the law? If morality is relative and entirely dependent on one's culture, how can one claim there is a "higher law"? Where does this higher law come from? How can there be a higher law if morality is the creation of men? To what higher authority do we appeal if there is no higher authority?

When confronted with an immoral law, moral relativists often defend disobeying that law by saying such things as, "Well, we all know that certain behaviors are wrong." I was once debating an atheist about the immorality of murder. He readily conceded that his position was there were no moral absolutes because there was no God. I asked, "If there is no God and there are no moral absolutes, why is murder wrong?" He attempted to justify his position by alluding to secular ideas, but was unable to arrive at one that really made sense. For example, perhaps none of us wants to be murdered, but so what? None of us wants to pay taxes, either. He suggested that if murder went unpunished, that would lead to a rather unstable society. I countered, "Murder can be punished, we just can't say it is 'wrong.' It simply leads to instability so we discourage such instability by punishing it, but that does not mean it is morally wrong." Becoming frustrated, he threw up his hands in despair and blurted out, "It's just wrong, because... you know...Thou shall not kill!" Of course, one cannot rest on a biblical commandment to claim that morality is a social construct, created by man. My friend was relying on the vestiges of a Christian culture to defend the post-Christian world of moral relativism. This is common in our current culture. We have largely abandoned our Christian worldview but we retain its benefits. How long such borrowed benefits will last in a post-Christian culture remains to be seen.

Most moral relativists, when confronted with a law they find immoral will rely on remnants of our Judeo-Christian heritage or such metaphysical concepts as the "conscience" to guide us. Some things, as my friend said, we all know are just wrong. But if that is true (and I think it is) then one has admitted that moral relativism is false. Man does not create morality; he only creates laws.

Herein is the fatal flaw with moral relativism. While it is obviously true that man creates laws it is not obvious that man creates morality. In fact, for one to claim that a law is immoral he or she is implicitly saying that there is something or someone greater than the law. He or she is making the claim that the law is subject to a higher authority. But if one is a moral relativist, one believes that morality is created by man. If morality is created by man to what or whom does one claim is the higher authority? If the moral relativist answers, "God," then he or she is not a moral relativist but a believer in moral absolutes. Indeed, if one were to reply that morality exists apart from God and apart from man as some kind of free-floating Platonic form, existing in nature like gravity, one has still admitted that there are moral absolutes.[3] Either way he or she has rejected the belief in moral relativism.

---

[3] I find it interesting that many moral relativists are quite content to hold that there actually are absolute moral truths, so long as they are not truths created by God. For example, some moral relativists believe that there are certain moral truths floating about in the universe like gravity, simply truths that are a part of the natural order. Why they prefer an absolute truth found in nature rather than one found in God can only be explained by their animosity toward the concept of a god—or perhaps worse, their animosity to the Judeo-Christian God. When pressed as to how some force of

If moral relativism is true then it is a logical impossibility for man to enact an immoral law. Morality, by definition under moral relativism, is created by man. What is moral is what man determines is moral and what is immoral is what man determines is immoral. So how can a moral relativist ever claim a law created by man is immoral?

The moral relativist has no such authority as God as the font of ultimate moral good. The moral relativist holds that morality is not absolute but is created by man. How, then, can the moral relativist logically claim that any moral behavior by the creator of morality is immoral? There is no way to check the bad behavior of the government under the theory of moral relativism. Perhaps this is why public schools, the handmaidens of the State, are so fond of teaching the "truth" of moral relativism. As a personal anecdote I recall learning the "truth" of what is called Legal Realism in law school. The students were taught, basically, that there are no natural laws or higher laws or unalienable rights. Rather, the law is whatever the lawyers and judges say it is. Any rights individuals have been given to them by the State. No rights exist outside those graciously bestowed upon us by a benevolent government. As repugnant as this is, this teaching was generally well-accepted among my fellow law students. And why not? We were being told we were the princes who would determine what rights people had. It is easy to believe man is the Master of the Universe if are told you are in the inner circle of the ruling class.

If Moral Relativism Is True, Does It Have Any Moral Authority?

A brief synopsis of a rather troubling philosophical dilemma is that if there is no God then there is no higher authority than man. If man is the ultimate authority, why should any man obey the moral dictates of another man? The answer is that he should not. The result is moral nihilism. While nihilism has the advantage of being logically consistent,

---

nature could create morality they have no scientific explanation, of course. What seems paramount to these people is that whatever there is, whatever caused creation, whatever created moral truth—*it is not God!*

it has the rather unpalatable conclusion that if there is no God then there is no truth means which means there is no morality, which leads to the conclusion that there is no reason or purpose for anything. He who dies with the most toys wins.

The logical conclusion of moral relativism is not quite as bleak as nihilism. Moral relativists are not anarchists. They believe laws have their practical benefits—they keep us all from killing each other, for example. However, they see the prohibition against murder not as a moral statement, but simply as a useful rule to have so that men and women can enjoy their lives as much as possible while interacting with one another. To the moral relativist, it is not wrong to murder our neighbor—it is just not a good idea in a well-ordered society. Murder is not evil; it is just very inconvenient.

In short, the problem for a Godless morality is this: How does secular morality arrive at its moral imperatives? If there is no God, how can there be absolute moral truths? For example, secular morality holds, as does Christian morality, that murder is wrong. When asked why murder is wrong, the ultimate Christian reason is because it is prohibited by God. God says it is wrong. God is all-knowing and perfectly righteous. Therefore, murder is wrong. This is an authoritarian answer to be sure, but not an irrational one.

How does the secular humanist answer this question? If she replies, because it is wrong to hurt other people, this begs the question, "Why is it wrong to hurt other people?" Why indeed? If the secular humanist says, "It just is," they are probably relying on the shadows of a Judeo-Christian morality that they claim to reject. To "feel" murder is wrong, secular humanism borrows from the Judeo-Christian capital our culture was built upon while at the same time denying the source of that capital. It is not reasonable for an atheist to say that murder is wrong "just because it is." They must give a reason why murder is wrong. Christians, too, must give a reason, but their reason is readily available: God prohibits murder; therefore, it is wrong.

I challenge moral relativists to construct a logical secular reason why we should not kill one another that would withstand the scrutiny of critical examination. True, a murderous society would be enormously destructive to the species, but being enormously destructive and being "immoral" are two different things. Further, we are not attempting to determine why a society should prohibit murder, we are attempting to give a reason why it is morally wrong for an individual to commit murder. For example, if it is in my best interest as an individual to kill my business partner provided 1) I don't get caught, and 2) everyone else doesn't behave the same way as I do. If I don't get caught, I won't personally suffer and I will gain a great deal by getting my partner's share of the business. As long as others in my society don't engage in my murderous behavior, the culture I live in will be relatively safe for me to enjoy my ill-gotten gains. Yet most people would agree that it is morally wrong for one to murder his or her business partner. But why? Is it only because you might get caught and go to prison? This might be a very good reason for not committing murder but I would hardly call it a "moral" reason.

Moral relativism means when contemplating whether I should commit murder I should not ask, "Is it right to commit murder?" but rather, "Will I get caught?" Our greatest moral questions are reduced to a simple cost-benefit analysis. If I can get away with murder, I should do it. After all, if there is no God there are no moral truths; therefore, my only consideration should be my personal costs and benefits of engaging in any particular act.

The historical trajectory of moral relativism, then, goes something like this: The belief that our Creator imputed into man's heart certain moral truths gives way to the idea that morality is a social construct, created not by God but by man. This in turn leads to the logical proposition that if man creates morality, what is right and wrong is relative—it changes over time and varies among cultures. If so, then what we call morality is simply a set of rules created by some men to regulate the behavior of other men. This leads to the inevitable question, "Why, then, should I follow these rules?" The logical conclusion is that there is no reason!

Let's revisit slavery in America as a brief example. If slavery was not immoral until the moment Lincoln signed the Emancipation Proclamation, why did the Emancipation Proclamation all the sudden make slavery immoral? It made it illegal, yes, but immoral...why? Further, should Lincoln's signature carry any moral (or legal?) weight in the Confederacy? If not, then with the signing of the Emancipation Proclamation slavery was suddenly immoral in the North but was still moral in the South. Finally, why should any individual care what a Northern president signs or what a Southern president signs? Imagine you are a Southern slave holder. Lincoln's signature carries no moral authority for you. But why, pray tell, does the signature of Jefferson Davis? Imagine that not only Lincoln but Davis as well enacted legislation outlawing slavery. Does this legislation make slavery immoral? If so, then slavery was moral prior to the legislation. But this is to confuse law with morality.

Moral relativism and scientific materialism share in common the belief that nothing exists but the material, the physical, and the natural. If moral truth exists, they would transcend the laws of man. They would be something more than mere legislation. They would be metaphysical, immaterial things that are nonetheless as real and consequential as a freight train. This is something moral relativists seem to fear.

Notice how moral relativism and scientific materialism walk hand-in-hand here. If the only things that are real are those things that can be proven by the scientific method (objectively measured, with empirical data emerging from repeated experimentation) then such things as right and wrong and good and evil are not real. They do not exist. They are ephemeral metaphysical thoughts that exist only in the minds of men, but they are not part of reality. Good and evil, right and wrong are simply objective sounding labels that we place on subjective feelings. They are meaningless words that do not correspond to any real thing that exists in the material world. When one says it is wrong to microwave kittens, she is really saying, "I don't like it when people microwave kittens." To say it is wrong to microwave a kitten is saying nothing more and nothing less than to say, "I prefer vanilla ice cream to chocolate." Moral relativists argue that if we lived in a society that regularly microwaved kittens (or human babies), we would not look at such behavior as morally wrong because it was acceptable behavior in our society—hence the term "moral relativism." And, indeed, if we lived in a society that regularly microwaved kittens, it is no doubt true that we would not consider such behavior as morally wrong. The question, however, is not would *we* consider it wrong, but would it *be* morally wrong regardless of how we regarded it?

The Consequences of Moral Relativism: The Authoritarian State

A tragic consequence of moral relativism is that it inevitably leads to authoritarian government. As we have seen, because moral relativists deny the existence of absolute moral truths created by God and instead claim that morality is invented by man, there is no good reason for people to be obedient to this man-made morality. The only reason to follow morally relative, man-made rules is the fear of being punished by the state. Raw power is the only real source of authority in a society that embraces moral relativism. This is why in nations that have abandoned belief in God (i.e., the former Soviet Union and Maoist China) we see totalitarian governments emerge that attempt to control every aspect of their citizen's lives—even their thoughts. This is also why disobedience to the totalitarian government results in draconian penalties—because the only means to enforce morality is the raw power of the state.

If moral relativism is correct, does an individual ever have a moral right to disobey the laws, customs, and mores of his culture? To what higher authority would this imaginary conscientious objector appeal? If there are no moral truths then a dissenter has no basis to claim that the culture is violating the laws of nature, God, or any other "higher" authority. It is no wonder that authoritarian regimes the world over reject the idea of unalienable rights given to us by our Creator. What is less understandable is why a liberal Western democracy, such as the United States, would want to embrace the concept of moral relativism.

Historically, free people have held fast to the idea that their government is not the highest authority but is itself subject to a Higher Law. It is sad to see people embracing moral relativism thinking that it is tolerant when in reality moral relativism has been used by the most intolerant governments as a way to suppress dissent. A truly tolerant philosophy is a philosophy that holds there are certain moral truths and civil rights that even the government cannot outlaw. This is why the Declaration of Independence is rightly celebrated for declaring that people have been endowed by their Creator with certain unalienable rights. This concept of limited government is essential to a free people. But what or who could be so powerful that even the rulers must obey certain rules? It would have to be a source of moral authority greater than men and their governments. In the American tradition this greater authority is God. If there is no God there is no higher authority than the government. It is not a coincidence that some of the most totalitarian and brutal governments in the world were also officially atheist.

Sadly, this also explains the proliferation of laws in our own nation. If there are moral absolutes given to us by God, there are certain things even the government cannot do. This is the underlying philosophy of limited government. The Founding Fathers, whether Christian or Deist, were all informed by the common belief in natural law. It is from this shared agreement that there are natural laws that Jefferson was able to speak of "unalienable rights." This commonly held view was the foundation upon which limited government rests. All men have certain natural rights, given to them by their Creator. These rights are moral absolutes and are not granted by, nor can they be taken away by, the government. The Framers thought of law as being bifurcated into two kinds: Ordinary law and natural law. Ordinary law could be granted or taken away through legislative due process. But natural law was something given to man by his Creator, and as such, was "unalienable." These things included the right to life, liberty, and the pursuit of happiness. No government had the right to take away anything granted to man by his Creator.

Moral relativism holds that there are no such things as natural laws or unalienable rights. According to moral relativists, all laws are mere creations of men, and as such can be granted or taken away at the whim of the government. As a commonly agreed morality disappears, the state is left to fill in the vacuum. The less moral a nation is, the more it has to legislate morality. Ironically, in an effort to escape the loving authority of God, we end up with the oppressive authority of a godless government. As Bob Dylan sings, "You gotta serve somebody."

The United States has avoided the totalitarianism that has plagued other nations for three principal reasons: we have a proud history of being fiercely independent and hold a healthy suspicion of government; we have a near-reverence for our Constitution and the concept of limited government; and, in spite of concerted efforts otherwise, most Americans still adhere to Judeo-Christian principles, especially on matters of morality. Sadly, every one of these three bulwarks of a free people is being rapidly eroded. Signs are everywhere evident of a culture that embraces government and its imagined benefits, that is willing to ignore or judicially amend the plain meaning of the Constitution, and that is ready to abandon Judeo-Christian principles of morality. Already we see this happening under the guise of "tolerance" and the totalitarian demand that those who are not "tolerant" will be punished.

The Christian view of morality has many enormous advantages over secular moral relativism. First, it permits Christians to logically engage in civil disobedience when man's laws violate the higher laws of God. Second, it keeps the State in check so that Christian cultures may logically hold that individuals have certain unalienable rights given to them by their Creator that even the government may not abrogate. Third, it allows Christians to logically defer to their consciences when opposing a law, action, or behavior they find morally repugnant.

Is Moral Relativism Compatible With Christianity?

Many people believe that moral relativism and Christianity are, if not entirely compatible, at least not incompatible. They reason that whether moral values are absolute or relative to the changing needs and mores of the community, they are still guidelines to help people live virtuous lives. And, so they imagine, any decent moral values—relative or otherwise—are compatible with Christianity.

The truth is that moral relativism is diametrically opposed to Christian orthodoxy for at least three reasons:

First, Christianity holds that there are objective moral truths. Christian morality posits a number of morally unacceptable behaviors throughout the Bible from the Ten Commandments of the Old Testament to the Sermon on the Mount in the New Testament. Moral relativism holds that morality is subjective, based on the whim of man.

Christians hold that God is the ultimate Author and Arbiter of morality whereas moral relativists hold that man is the ultimate author and arbiter of morality.

Second, and perhaps more abstractly, the worldview throughout the Bible is that there is an ongoing battle between good and evil. The Bible is not merely a book of moral rules, but it is in its entirety a sort of morality play. It boldly proclaims there is right and wrong, good and evil, justice and injustice. To deny good and evil is to deny the fundamental teaching of the Bible.

Third, moral relativism is inconsistent with Christianity because it provides, or attempts to provide, an atheistic—or godless—source of morality. Let's imagine that a secular humanist could come up with a convincing argument for living a moral life. Perhaps the logic that moral relativism ultimately leads to nihilism is not sound. Perhaps there is some good reason, aside from the existence of God, that we should be loving, kind, and law-abiding in matters concerning our fellow man. Imagine further, that in such a world everyone is loving, kind, and law-abiding. That no one murders his neighbor, or covets his neighbor's wife, or steals his neighbor's car. In fact, let's imagine this world was peaceful, prosperous, and an all-around wonderful place to live. Would such a world necessarily be consistent with Christianity? Of course not. Such a world could be atheistic, Islamic, Jewish, Buddhist, Hindu, or something else altogether. After all, in this imaginary world, there is no reason to believe that only Christians would behave in morally exemplary ways. Indeed, in the real world we all know Jews, Muslims, Buddhists, atheists, and others who live exemplary lives.

So, if Christians are not the only people capable of living morally sound lives, then what separates Christians from non-Christians? The answer, of course, is Jesus Christ. Christians believe that Jesus Christ is the supernatural Son of God whose atoning death on the Cross brought our salvation. Christians believe that Jesus Christ is their Lord and Savior. If our imaginary world was filled with wonderful, law-abiding people who do not accept Jesus Christ as their Lord and Savior, then obviously such an imaginary world would be inconsistent with a Christian worldview. The Christian worldview is not just about loving our neighbors, it is also (indeed, primarily) about loving the Lord our

God with all our heart and mind and soul. Any world, no matter how morally upright that does not place Jesus Christ as its Lord and Savior is incompatible with Christianity.

Any society—even a moral one—that bases its morality on anything outside of God is inconsistent with Christianity. Here's why: The Christian worldview is that God—not man—is supremely worthy. Man is worthy only because he is created in the image of God.

In a secular world, man does not kill his fellow man because humans are, for some inexplicable reason, given special consideration. Why humans are special is not explained—and perhaps cannot be explained—in a secular world. From a Christian worldview, humans are given special consideration because God granted humans special consideration when He created them in His own image—when He endowed them with an eternal soul. Moral relativists hold that man should behave morally toward his fellow man because of the dignity of man. Christians hold that man should behave morally toward his fellow man because of the dignity of God. The secular view is that man is so important, so great, so wonderful, so aggrandized that all moral behavior is for the benefit of this elevated creature—Man. Christians hold that only God is worthy of our worship—not man. We behave morally because God is the embodiment of morality, the Author of morality—and that as our Lord, He knows what is in our best interest and that it is not only in our best interest to obey His commands, but that it is our duty to do so. This is the reason a Christian should disobey the law of man if it conflicts with the law of God.

Christians believe there is a greater cause and higher law than man-made law. For any man-made law to be a just law, it must not violate the higher law—the law of God. God's laws keep man's laws in check. Men can, indeed should, disobey any man-made law that conflicts with God's law. Nations that adhere to the belief that there are higher laws than the laws of men are nations of limited government. Nations under the spell of moral relativism have no higher authority than the State. There was no appealing to a "higher law" in the former Soviet Union or Communist China. The world is painfully aware of the result.

The reason there is a greater cause and higher law than man-made law is because there is a greater cause and higher purpose than man.

Man, according to Christians, is not the most elevated being and his progress is not the ultimate end. For Christians, the greatest being is God, our greatest purpose is to know Him and love Him, and our ultimate end is to worship and enjoy God for all eternity with Him in heaven. This is why for Christians there can be no true morality outside of God. Moral relativism—a morality based on the whims of man—is not moral at all. God is the Creator and Sustainer of morality and without God there can be no morality. Morality springs forth from the being of God. It is the essence of God.

The City of Man or the City of God?

Which worldview is more reasonable? The secular worldview or the Christian worldview? Again, I do not ask you to have faith or believe in God because the Bible tells you God exists. Faith and Scripture are excellent reasons to believe, indeed, they are ultimately the best reasons to believe, but I am willing to engage in combat with the secular worldview on its own battlefield using the weapons of its choice: logic and reason. Which view of morality is the more logical and reasonable view: secular moral relativism or Christian moral truth?

The secular worldview holds that there are no moral truths. But if there are no moral truths, why do humans feel that some acts are inherently wrong? Why do we feel in our innermost being that some things are right and some things are wrong? Why do great thinkers such as Socrates, Plato, Paul, Augustine, Aquinas, Descartes, Kant, and King—to name a few—conclude that there are moral truths that transcend human laws?

Further, if there are no moral truths, does moral relativism make sense? If there is no absolute moral truth, can a "relative" moral truth exist? What is this relative moral truth relative *to*? Need there not be an absolute for something to be relative to it?

Finally, if there are no moral truths and only man-made laws, why should we obey these laws? If we should obey them merely because they are laws, then doesn't it reason we should always and everywhere obey them regardless of how unjust or immoral we may think they are? After all, if there are no moral truths, then there is nothing we can point to—no higher law to appeal to—whenever we find our culture behaving unjustly. Moral relativists cannot protest an unjust law, because there is no higher authority than the law itself. We are bound to do whatever the government orders us to do because there is no higher authority than the collective will of man as expressed through the government.

This secular view was very popular among the intellectual elite and those who wished to imagine they were in that group. Today, secular thought has spread so deeply throughout our culture that many of my freshmen students eagerly explained to me that "all serious thinkers know that morality is a social construct." These same freshmen are not really sure what a "social construct" is, but they know there are no moral absolutes. In fact, the only thing they are absolutely sure of is that there are no moral absolutes. Of course, most freshmen have not spent many hours reading philosophy and contemplating the nature of morality. Their beliefs are not conclusions they have developed—they are dogmas with which they have been indoctrinated.[4]

Most students (and many of their teachers) are blissfully unaware that many of the intellectual elite have largely abandoned moral relativism—and with good reason. While the average American may think he is on the "cutting edge" by embracing moral relativism, many philosophers have come to the realization that the choice is not between theistic (God given) morality or secular morality, but between theistic morality or nihilism. It is either God or nothing. As Dostoyevsky wrote in *The Brothers Karamazov*, "If there is no God then everything is permitted."

This is because serious moral relativists, those who have given a good deal of thought to their philosophy, realize that if morality is an illusion, a mere social construct, then what is right or wrong is nothing more than the subjective opinion of the group in power forced upon everyone else through social indoctrination and criminal sanctions. The law, under this view, is not a reflection of what is right, moral, or true—it is the creation of what we label right, moral, or true. But this invention of what we label "moral" has no

---

[4] See: Bloom, *Closing of The American Mind*, (New York: Simon & Schuster, 1987), 25.

basis in reality. There is no absolute principle upon which to build a foundation for why something is moral or immoral in the world of moral relativism.

It turns out the choice is not between a God-based morality and a human-based morality, but between morality and amorality. There are either moral absolutes or there are simply laws created by man at the discretion of man, determined by whatever group is in power at any particular time. And if the latter is true, it is hard to call such arbitrary rules "moral" in any sense. Man-made rules may be useful for social order, they may even reflect God-given morality, but because they are created by men, not God, they cannot really be considered moral imperatives. They are only rules that may—or may not—be a good idea to follow. And because they have no real moral authority outside of man himself, they will inevitably be enforced through the barrel of a gun. The only authority they have is raw power and the individual has not even a theoretical right to point to some "higher authority," because no higher authority exists.

The Christian worldview, on the other hand, provides some rational explanations to the world as we find it. We feel a deep abiding sense of justice and injustice because we are made in the image of God and God has created us with this internal sense of right and wrong. We feel justified in protesting or even violating man-made laws that do not comport with God's higher law. We place limits upon governments because governments are made up of fallible men and we subject these fallible rulers to the infallible laws of God. We recognize that man might misinterpret, misunderstand, our maliciously disobey God's moral laws, but that does not mean moral absolutes do not exist, it simply means we have been mistaken or disobedient in our application of them. The fact that men behave immorally is no evidence that morality does not exist. It is, ironically, evidence that morality does exist—or how would we say that men are behaving "immorally"? Similarly, the fact that men do not obey the Bible is no evidence that the Bible is mistaken. On the contrary, it is evidence of the veracity of the Bible, which fully acknowledges and anticipates that men will disobey the commandments of the Bible.

The secular worldview imagines a world that is foreign to our consciences—a world that denies truth, justice, right and wrong, good and evil. While this thinking may make for scintillating pseudo-intellectual conversation, we know moral truth exists. We know this because we feel it in our hearts and because it is the logical outcome of serious thought.

What we must recognize is that the denial of moral truth is not only illogical, but it is a covert attack on Christianity. Like scientific materialism, moral relativism is not so much a conclusion based on facts as it is part of an atheistic belief system. Moral relativism, again like scientific materialism, masquerades as a theory that is the result of unbiased and objective observation about the world. The truth is that both scientific materialism and moral relativism *begin* with the presumption that there is no God and then build their conclusions upon that premise. If there is no God there cannot be moral truths. Since there is no God there must not be moral truths. Starting from that atheistic belief the moral relativist works backward from his beliefs into his theory.

The unrecognized agenda of those who espouse moral relativism is to promote atheism. After all, moral relativists behave exactly as if moral truth existed. Those who deny moral truth act in ways that indicate they believe in moral truth: they become enraged at injustice, they believe some things are right and some things are wrong, they praise virtue and shame vice. What they are really trying to accomplish is to eliminate God. They want to keep their morality while abandoning God. Of course, that is not possible. Christians recognize that morality springs forth from God and we cannot have morality without God any more than one can bask in the afternoon heat and deny the existence of the sun.

Christians believe in moral truth because we believe in truth and we believe in truth because we believe in The Truth. Jesus Christ said, "I am the way, and the truth, and the life."[5]

Which brings us to another false foundation of Secular Materialism: that there is no truth.

---

[5] John 14:6. The full quotation is "I am the way, the truth, and the life. No one comes to the Father except through me."

CHAPTER 14

THE TRUTH ABOUT TRUTH

Christians seem fixated on the truth. This obsession with and insistence on knowing the truth is one of the major grievances non-Christians have with Christians. Why, they wonder, do Christians have to insist not only that their faith is true, but that it is *exclusively* true? Why, they lament, can't Christians just be happy to have "their" truth and let atheists have "their" truth? Why are Christians so insistent on knowing the truth? Can't they be happy just enjoying the search for the truth? Why are Christians so concerned with being on the right road? Isn't the journey all that really matters?

No matter how tolerant, compromising, and politically correct such admonitions to Christians are, for some reason Christians insist on having the truth. Being on a journey will not do. Having *a* truth will not satisfy them. Christians, maddeningly to many, not only believe in such a thing as truth, they believe they know the truth, and they believe Jesus is The Truth. If ever one claimed a monopoly on truth—surely this is what it would look like!

Why can't Christians be happy with their faith and not always be evangelizing, handing out silly pamphlets, debating with non-Christians, looking for archeological evidence, and writing books like the one you are reading? Why is it so important to Christians that what they believe is actually true?

Truth is central to the Christian faith. We see this vehement defense of truth among Christians revealed in many ways. Christians do not

simply regard their faith as a religion they adhere to, or as a set of doctrines that they accept. Rather, Christians believe their faith is *true*. They do not regard Christianity as a set of "just so" stories, created to explain mysteries of the universe, but as true, historical recordings of real events. Serious Christians do not regard Jesus as a person who was one with God symbolically or as the metaphorical savior of the world, but rather as God Himself and as the literal Savior of the world. Whatever else may be said of the beliefs of devout Christians, they believe that their beliefs are true and that the events described in the Gospels are real—that they actually happened.

This may seem a self-evident truth about any and all faiths, but it is not. Many Hindus, for example, do not feel that their faith is hindered in any way by the fact it may not be the literal truth. Buddhist stories, as well, need not be taken literally for them to express some transcendent truth. This is not so of Christianity. To be sure, some passages in the Bible are *meant* to be metaphorical. They are written as similes, metaphors, allegories, or poetry. But much of the Bible, particularly the New Testament, is meant to be a literal history of real events that took place in history. They refer to actual historical people living in actual places at a very specific point in time. The Christian faith includes some metaphor, such as Jesus saying He is the Lamb of God, but when Jesus speaks this metaphorical language, Christians believe that He actually existed and actually spoke those words.

In fact, the *truth* of Christianity—or its purported truth—is at once its most audacious, scandalous, and greatest claim. However unlikely that God Himself would physically come to earth as a human child, born of a human woman, be crucified, die, and be resurrected from death—these are things Christians actually believe to be true. However inadequately a Christian may explain such events, he believes them to be true. To the true believer no other truth is as certain as the truth that Jesus Christ is her Lord and Savior. This they believe.

This insistence on knowing the truth may seem, at a very minimum, annoying to non-Christians. We will address this soon enough. But first, we should take a moment to consider the implications of the fact that devout Christians are absolutely, adamantly, even radically fixated on the truth. What does this tell us about the claims that Christianity is a fantasy, a wish-fulfillment, or some escapist desire to *avoid* the truth? Let's set aside whether what Christians believe is true actually *is* true for the moment. The undisputable fact is that Christians are extraordinarily concerned about the truth. They believe there is such a thing as truth and they want to know the truth. These would be strange attributes of people interested in wish-fulfillment or truth avoidance. If Christians were naïve optimists looking for a religion that brought them easy comfort and unquestioned bliss, wouldn't it be more likely that they would not insist on knowing the truth? Wouldn't it be more likely that they would be content with metaphorical "truths" or "true myths" or transcendent "truths" that need not necessarily be historically true?

One may claim that Christians are wrong, or deluded, or intolerant, or even psychotic—but one cannot say that Christianity is a faith for those looking for comfort and fantasies and wish fulfillment. Christians are seriously, studiously looking for the truth. Theirs is a religion based on truth claims. This does not prove that Christianity *is* true, but it proves that Christians are making claims they *hold to be* true. They are not interested in "feel good" stories designed to bring comfort and alleviate fear.[1]

Why are Christians so focused on truth? This can be answered in one word: Jesus. While such virtues as faith and forgiveness are often associated with Christianity, and rightly so, Jesus actually spoke more about truth than either of those virtues. In fact, the New Testament has Jesus using the word "truth" over 100 times. And this does not even include all of the times he says, "Amen," at the end of a passage, which means "verily," or "truth." Jesus, standing before Pilate, says, "I was born for this, and I have come into the world for this: to testify to the truth. Everyone who is for the truth listens to My voice."[2] And, of

---

[1] How Freud and others could imagine that a religion that believes in a place called hell is a religion designed for comfort and "wish-fulfillment" has always puzzled me. What kind of man-made religion, designed to bring comfort, would create a place of eternal suffering and torment? Wouldn't the more secular New Age religions fill this role better? After all, they offer the very comforting ideas that all roads lead to the right path, that love is all there is, that there is no punishment, no judgment, no hell. If I were looking for a religion that gave me easy comfort, I would most certainly not choose Christianity.

[2] John 18:37. It is interesting to note that the oldest writing we have from the New Testament, the John Rylands Papyrus, contains these words of Jesus.

course, famously Jesus refers to Himself *as the truth*: "I am the way, the truth, and the life. No one comes to the Father except through Me."[3]

Christians believe that moral truths exist and that God is the Author of those truths. They believe that morality emanates from God. They believe morality exists because God exists.

It is not a mere coincidence that until very recently Western culture at large and Christianity in particular held the same view of truth. That is, Western culture believed there is such a thing as truth. Unlike many Eastern cultures, the West had an almost child-like literalism. This belief in discoverable truth helps explain the West's dominance in science. We may disagree on what that truth is, but we adhere to the fundamental notion that truth exists. The great fear of Western civilization has been that barbarians just outside the gates of the culture do not follow the same rules. These barbarians do not adhere to the civilized principles of truth, justice, and morality. The rejection of these principles by the barbarians is what will lead to the downfall of Western culture—not the weapons of the barbarians or the different cultures of the barbarians—but the fact that barbarians, by definition, do not respect any norms, morality, ethics, reason, or agreed upon judicial process.

Today, those barbarians have arrived. They are not hordes swinging battle axes, but intellectual elites wearing tweed jackets with arm patches. Nonetheless, they have wreaked havoc on Western thought and civilization at least as effectively as armed marauders. Alisdair MacIntyre writes: "This time the barbarians are not waiting beyond the frontiers. They have already been governing us for some time."[4] They are, in the words of Richard John Neuhaus, "the party of emancipation from the truths civilized people consider self-evident [and] [t]hat the barbarians are composed of the most sophisticated and educated elites in our society makes them no less barbarian."[5]

Christianity is perhaps the last stronghold of the concept that there are non-material truths to be known. Much of the West has succumbed

---

[3] John 14:6.
[4] Alisdair MacIntyre, *After Virtue* (Notre Dame, 1981), 245.
[5] Richard John Neuhaus, *The Naked Public Square: Religion and Democracy in America* (Eerdmans, Grand Rapids, MI, 1984), 87.

to the post-modern barbarians who have convinced us that the only truth is there are no metaphysical truths. Indeed, who have convinced many of us that there may be no metaphysical at all! Christians, by stubbornly clinging to their belief in metaphysical truth may be the last line of defense for such things as beauty, mystery, and humanity. An acceptance that the material world is all there is and that human beings are merely advanced animals, devoid of purpose, meaning, or souls is certainly a bleak worldview. While the purpose of this book is not to assess the success of Christian Europe with post-Christian Europe, it seems self-evident that few cultures have ever surpassed Europe under Christendom in matters of literature, art, architecture, sculpture, philosophy, and music. Post-modern art and architecture do not compare favorably to most any observer with the art and architecture created during the Age of Faith. Christianity, if nothing else, seemed to nurture the disciplines of the soul.[6] Christians stubbornly defend the concept of truth because they believe Jesus is the truth, but a happy by-product of this belief is respect and honor for the human soul.

Secular Materialism and Truth

Secular Materialism's belief in moral relativism is closely related to the Secular Materialist view that there are no absolute truths. Secularist Materialists believe that morality is relative because they believe all truth is relative. Their worldview about truth is that truth, if it exists at all, is relative. What is true for you may not be true for me and what is true for me may not be true for you. This view is popular for at least two reasons:

First, it allows us to avoid the hard work of thinking through often complicated and difficult dilemmas. It is always easier when presented with a problem to opt for the convenient, "There is no right answer" as the solution. Sometimes there is, indeed, no right answer—but often there is a right answer, it just takes some good thinking to arrive at it.

Second, allowing that "my truth is true for me and your truth is

---

[6] Francis Schaeffer, *How Then Should We Then Live: The Rise and Fall of Western Thought and Culture* (Crossway, Wheaton, IL, 1976).

true for you" helps us to avoid confrontation and dissension. It makes us appear tolerant of opposing viewpoints. Again, sometimes this is fair and reasonable. When discussing matters of opinion in which there truly is no right answer, showing respect and tolerance for differing opinions is wise and judicious. However, when discussing something that is a matter of *fact*, not opinion, the claim that "my truth is true for me and your truth is true for you" is nonsense. In matters of fact, there is an answer that is true and an answer that is false, and to claim otherwise is to insult truth while paying false tribute to tolerance. To pretend otherwise is not to show tolerance to our fellow man, it is to show disrespect by patronizing him.

Intellectual humility and tolerance for opposing views are excellent virtues and I applaud our culture's desire to have more of both. But as we will see, pretending there are no truths or that all truths are equal is being neither intellectually humble nor tolerant. It is casting aside real intellectual humility and true tolerance in favor of a sort of intellectual shrugging of the shoulders and replying, "Whatever." That is insulting to both the concept of intellectual humility and tolerance.

Three Types of Questions

The view that my truth is true for me and your truth is true for you in all matters is what logicians refer to as a categorical mistake. For *some* types of questions, one opinion is as good as the next. But for *other* types of questions, one opinion is right and one opinion is wrong. Some further clarification here is necessary: Questions may be broken down into three broad categories:[7]

1) Questions of Opinion
2) Questions of Judgment
3) Questions of Fact

---

[7] My thanks to Drs. Linda Elder and Richard Paul of The Foundation for Critical Thinking for insight on these categorical questions. While occasionally flawed by a politically liberal bias, their work on critical thinking is still highly recommended. An affordable (and easy to carry) pocket guide to critical thinking may be found on their website: www.criticalthinking.org.

It is important to know which category of question one is asking. For questions of opinion, such as, "Which flavor tastes better, chocolate ice cream or vanilla ice cream?" the answer is entirely subjective and depends completely on the view of the person being asked. For such questions your truth is *the* truth and my truth is *the* truth because we are being asked a question which calls for our opinion as an answer. There are no "right" or "wrong" answers for questions of opinion.

For questions of judgment, such as, "What is the cause of poverty?" there may not be one correct answer, but it is not exactly simply a matter of opinion, either. Rather, there are *better* and *worse* answers. If someone said that vanilla ice cream causes poverty, that is a much worse answer than if someone said the cause of poverty is lack of education. While a poor education is certainly not the only cause of poverty, it is a much better answer than vanilla ice cream. Social science can provide empirical data showing that low educational achievement is correlated to poverty, whereas there is no reasonable correlation between vanilla ice cream and poverty. Questions of judgment may not have right or wrong answers, but they are hardly mere matters of opinion, either. The answers to questions requiring judgment can be said to be better or worse, whereas answers to questions of matters of opinion cannot be assessed at all.

Finally, there are some questions of fact, such as what is the sum of 2 + 2? These questions have right and wrong answers. The sum of 2 + 2 is not a mere matter of opinion, nor is it a matter of judgment. There is a right and wrong answer to this question. If Adam believes that the capital of the United States is Washington, D.C. and Bob thinks the capital of the United States is Chicago, Bob is simply incorrect. It is not true for anyone, not even for Bob, that the capital of the United States is Chicago. Bob's opinion on this matter is not "as good" as Adam's opinion, because the question is not one that addresses a matter of opinion or a matter of judgment, but rather a matter of fact.

In a way, even matters of opinion or judgment may be said to be true universally, and not just for the person holding the opinion. For example, if Bill's favorite color is blue, then it is not just true for Bill that his favorite color is blue. It is universally and absolutely true that Bill's favorite color is blue. Todd's favorite color may be red, but that in no way changes the absolute truth that Bill's favorite color is blue. So, it would be incorrect to say that "It is true for Bill that his favorite color is blue, but that is only his truth." That is not so. If Bill's favorite color is blue, then it is true for everyone that Bill's favorite color is blue. However, because it is a question of opinion, it is not universally true that the best color is blue. It is true that blue is the best color for Bill, and it is absolutely true, but it is not true that it is everyone's favorite color.

If, however, it was a question of fact, such as "Which color is the most popular color in the world?" then there would be one universally true and absolutely true answer to that question. A poll could be taken of everyone in the world and each favorite color could be tallied—the color that the most people selected as their favorite color would then be, as a matter of fact, the most popular color in the world. This is not to say that said color has to be *your* favorite color or the *best* color in the world, but it is true that it is the most popular color in the world. And its popularity is a fact whether it is your personal favorite color or not.

Secular Materialists sometimes say that truth is relative or that truth is in the eye of the beholder. But this is demonstrably not so. *Opinions* are in the eye of the beholder, but *truth* is not. An oft used example by those who deny absolute truths is the story of the three blind men and the elephant. Each of the blind men feels a different part of the elephant and when asked to describe what an elephant looks like the blind man who felt only the trunk replies, "An elephant is rather like a large, fat snake." The blind man who felt only the leg replies, "An elephant is like a tree stump." Finally, the blind man who felt only the side of the elephant replies, "The elephant is like a big, flat wall." According to relativists, the story is supposed to illustrate that each of the men has described his truth about the elephant, proving that truth is relative. But this conclusion is ridiculous. An elephant does have an actual shape and look. The reason the three blind men describe the elephant incorrectly is because they are *blind*. It is true that if one only feels the trunk of an elephant, he will describe the elephant as looking something like a large, fat snake. But this does not prove an elephant actually looks like a large, fat snake—it only proves that the part of the elephant felt by the blind person resembles a large, fat snake! That person's truth is not true—even for him. It is only true that he *thinks* the elephant looks like a large, fat snake—but he is *wrong*. The story illustrates not that truth is relative, but that truth is absolute and people sometimes make mistakes in determining what truth is. In more rational times the story was used to illustrate that if you only see part of the whole, you will be misguided as to the truth. In our postmodern culture the story is used to show that truth is relative. The story does no such thing.

Christianity and Truth

The popular worldview that there is no absolute truth, only "your truth" and "my truth," is in direct contradiction to the Christian worldview. A careful reading of the New Testament shows that truth is at the very heart of the Gospel. In fact, the ultimate Christian claim is not that the Bible makes sense or that the Bible shows us the best way to live. Rather, the foundation upon which the Bible rests is simply this: it is the truth. Whether we can understand it, explain it, defend it, or agree with it—it remains the truth. Like all truths, our approval or disapproval of it has absolutely no bearing on its veracity. It is true with us just as it is true without us. If it is true, it would be true even if not one person in the entire world believed it was true.

Truth and Christ are inseparably intertwined. Indeed, they are one. Jesus tells us, "You will know the truth and the truth will set you free" (John 8:32). Christianity is a faith built on the foundation that truth exists. Christians hold that there is such a thing as truth and that Christianity is the truth. Even more, Christians hold that Jesus *is the truth*. What is this truth that will set us free—this truth that Jesus was born for? He tells us: "*I* am the way, the truth, and the life" (John 14:6, emphasis added).[8] Jesus Christ, Himself, *is* the truth. The Christian view, properly understood, is not that Jesus was a wise teacher who revealed great truths, but that He is the divine Son of God who *is the truth*.

---

[8] *The Truth Project*, an extensive group study video set published by Focus on the Family is an outstanding resource in understanding the Christian worldview.

These concepts can be easily forgotten, even by Christians. Many Christians hold a view of Jesus and the Bible not much different from non-Christians. Secular humanists and Christians generally agree that the Bible contains powerful stories that illustrate the truth about the human condition. Christians and non-Christians generally agree that the Bible establishes a sublime moral code. Christians and non-Christians generally agree that Jesus Christ was a great moral teacher who showed us the way to a better life. This is all fine and good as far as it goes. But authentic Christianity is not about a sublime moral code or a profound moral teacher. Jesus proclaimed to not only show us the way, the truth, and the life, but that He *is* the way, the truth, and the life!

Many of us today are uncomfortable with truth claims of any kind. Yet Jesus made extraordinarily bold truth claims—one of which was that He Himself is the truth. That is why the attack on truth in our culture is an attack on Christianity. When truth is attacked, the real object of that attack is the One who proclaimed that He is the truth. After all, do we see attacks on scientific truth or mathematical truth or even on more subjective truth claims, such as the truth claims that everyone is equal or that no beliefs are more valid than any other beliefs? These are all truth claims, yet none are questioned by our culture.

The only truth claims questioned are *religious* truth claims. Our secular culture's attack on truth is in reality a backdoor attack on any truth claims about God. This becomes evident when one engages in an extended conversation with an atheist or secular humanist about truth. When they say that truth is an illusion or that truth is relative, they really mean that morality is an illusion or that morality is relative. And by "morality," they are almost always referring to Judeo-Christian morality. For instance, most postmodern doubters of truth are zealous believers in the truth of the scientific method. They are fervent in their defense of the truth of Darwinist evolution. They are convinced of the truth of a good many other things as well, such as the mathematical proposition that $2 + 2 = 4$; that Michigan is to the geographic north of Alabama; and that the nation of Germany is not in the continent of Africa. They are convinced of many other truths without which they could not function in the real world, such as that they exist; that they are able to communicate with other human beings in spite of language being imperfect; and that reason and logic are reliable methods for determining that propositions correspond with reality. Similarly, they are just as offended as the next guy when someone lies to them or commits a wrong against them—even though they profess that there is no truth nor any right or wrong. They even, when pressed, admit to holding certain positions they regard as morally wrong, such as destroying the rainforest, dumping toxic waste into rivers, or killing innocent people.

Those who deny moral truth often have very strong moral opinions of their own and they most certainly believe in truth—it is incoherent for them to do otherwise. For example, is it *true* that there are no absolute truths? If yes, then there are absolute truths. If no, then they have contradicted their own position. What most proponents of moral relativism mean is that they reject *Christian* morality. What most critics of the existence of truth mean is that they reject *Christian* truth. Denying moral truths is simply a covert way of denying Christianity. It is a clever way to tell a lie about the truth.

What Is The Truth?

Many Christians today blissfully live in two worlds: the secular world and the Christian world. For the most part, this bifurcated existence is a pragmatic solution to the Christian position of being *in* this world but not *of* this world. Most of the great proponents of the Christian faith were not hermits or monks. Peter, Paul, Augustine, Luther, Calvin, and Mother Teresa, were fully-engaged in the world. They were not captured by the world's materialism nor mesmerized by its shiny trinkets; they were not seduced by its sensual pleasures nor fooled by its fleeting fame; but they did not live in isolation satisfied in their own salvation and willing to let the world go its own way. Their example is one we should emulate. Peter and Paul founded the world's largest religion; Augustine was a leading bishop; Luther led a revolution; Calvin ran a city-state; and Mother Teresa served as a living example of self-sacrificial love. Living *in* the world but living *for* Christ, is the path of the Christian.

However, this happy conjunction of things secular and things sacred does not always work. An acceptance of the secular view of truth, for example, is not compatible with Christianity. One cannot logically accept the Christian worldview and believe that truth is relative. Paul tells us, "Do not be conformed to this age, but be transformed by the renewing of your mind, so that you may discern what is the good, pleasing, and perfect will of God" (Romans 12:2). Peter, Paul, Augustine, Luther, Calvin, and Mother Teresa all lived in the world, but they did not conform to the secular world. They were most certainly not moral relativists.

Christians must be uncompromising on the nature of truth because it was so central to the message and mission of Jesus Christ. Contrary to some modern thought, Jesus did not come to show us how to be good. He did not come to establish a high ethical standard or to show us how to live in peace with our fellow man. He came to proclaim the truth—to tell the world that He *is* the truth—but the world rejected Him. Perhaps most relevant to the secular view of truth is the brief but telling conversation Jesus has with Pontius Pilate before Pilate has Jesus crucified:

> Then Pilate went back into the headquarters, summoned Jesus, and said to Him, "Are you the King of the Jews?"
>
> Jesus answered, "Are you asking this on your own, or have others told you about Me?"
>
> "I'm not a Jew, am I?" Pilate replied. "Your own nation and the chief priests handed You over to me. What have You done?"
>
> "My kingdom is not of this world," said Jesus. "If My kingdom were of this world, My servants would fight, so that I wouldn't be handed over to the Jews. As it is, My kingdom does not have its origin here."
>
> "You are a king then?" Pilate asked.
>
> "You say that I'm a king," Jesus replied. "I was born for this, and I have come into the world for this: to testify

to the truth. Everyone who is for the truth listens to My voice."

"What is the truth?" said Pilate.[9]

The context makes it clear that Pilate is not asking a question, but making a statement about truth claims. John's Gospel gives no record of Jesus' response, because it is clear a response is not expected. One can imagine the tone in Pilate's voice, cynical and weary, a man jaded by years of governing in the far outposts of the Roman Empire. When Pilate says, "What is the truth?" he is questioning the very existence of truth. Like so much else in the Bible, we are struck at how modern this passage appears to us. The reality, of course, is that our postmodern cynicism is not new. While college sophomores (and many of their professors, who should know better) strut about filled with intellectual arrogance, questioning all the old ways and imaging they are killing every sacred cow, the truth is that Solomon got it right when he said, "There is nothing new under the sun" (Ecclesiastes 1:9).[10]

This exchange between Jesus and Pilate shows the gravity of the matter. Truth is at the center of the mission of Christ. Jesus tells Pilate, "I was born for this, and I have come into the world for this: to testify to the truth." Those who hold there is no truth are not disputing some minor point of the faith: they are directly refuting the mission of Christ. This is why it is logically inconsistent for one to believe that truth is an illusion—or at best relative—and yet claim to be a Christian. This is also why many atheists and Secular Materialists are also moral relativists: they are not really questioning the existence of truth; they are attacking Christianity.

Truth is what conforms to reality. Truth is at the very center of the Christian faith. Jesus made truth claims unlike any other religious or secular philosopher. He not only claimed to know the truth, He claimed to *be* the truth. Jesus not only showed us the way, He said He *is* the way.

---

[9] John 18:33-38.
[10] The full passage reads: "What has been is what will be, and what has been done is what will be done; there is nothing new under the sun." The Book of Ecclesiastes is a brilliant lament of the futility of life. I recommend it to any college student (or professor) who thinks he is the first to experience existential angst.

He revealed the truth by revealing Himself. The truth and Jesus are one, just as the truth and God are one and Jesus and God are one.[11]

Truth is central to Christianity. Christians hold that our faith is based in the reality of a historic events committed by historic people. Christianity is not meant as a myth or a series of wise metaphorical tales. It is a faith based on real events that happened in real places to real people. Further, Christianity holds that the teachings of Jesus are true. They are not the wishful thoughts of a kind man or the maniacal rantings of a lunatic. We believe in the truth of the actions and words of Jesus Christ.

Jesus came to reveal the truth, but we were too blind to see. We see now dimly, as through a mirror, but in heaven we will see God face to face. Then we will know what reality looks like. Then we will understand how confused we were—and how blind.[12]

Truth is absolutely fundamental to Christianity because Christians hold that Jesus Christ *is the truth*. In the final analysis Christians offer nothing more or less than the truth. Christians, at the end of the day, are Christians not because we hold that Christianity is the most popular faith or the most rational faith or the most rewarding faith—although it may be all of those things. Rather, we believe in Christianity because we think it is the truth. We think it is the truth when it provides great benefits, and we think it is the truth when it causes us great losses. We think it is the truth when it is completely reasonable, and we think it is the truth when we cannot find the reasons. We think it is the truth when God's presence is like the bright light of the day, and we think it is the truth when we suffer the dark night of doubt.

Christians believe not only in the truth, but also in The Truth—The Truth that is more reasonable than our reason, more logical than our logic, and more real than our reality.

---

[11] *See, e.g.,* Matthew 10:40, 11:27; Luke 9:48, 10:16, 10:22; John 1:1, 8:58, 10:30, 14:7, 14:11; 15:23, 16:15, 17:10.
[12] See, e.g.: Isaiah. 53:1; John 3:3; John 3:19; 1 Corinthians 13:12.

CHAPTER 15

THE INTOLERANCE OF TOLERANCE

For many people in our current culture, believing that something is absolutely true is worse than a sin—it is an act of ignorance. The reasoning of the modern secularist is 1) truth, if it exists at all, is relative; 2) because truth is relative, tolerance is the greatest virtue; and 3) because truth is relative and tolerance is essential, any truth claims that are absolute or exclusive of other possible truths are not to be tolerated.

Tolerance, properly understood, means showing patience and consideration for views one *disagrees* with. Unfortunately, tolerance has come to mean *agreeing* with all views. Of course, since it is logically impossible to agree with opposing views, the new tolerance really means *believing in nothing*. If by tolerance we mean offending no one, refusing to take sides, playing the agnostic to all questions—then the only way to accomplish these rather pusillanimous goals is to believe in nothing. For example, if Ashley says that Muhammad is a prophet and Brenda says that Jesus is the Son of God—and assume nothing more about Muhammad or Jesus—it is possible for each of them to agree with each other. But if Ashley claims that Jesus is not the Son of God and Brenda claims that Jesus is the Son of God, it is not possible for them to agree with each other. At this juncture they can show classic tolerance, holding to their respective positions while agreeing to disagree with mutual civility and respect; or they can embrace the new tolerance and hold that truth is relative, there is no absolute truth,

Jesus is not the Son of God in Ashley's world but Jesus is the Son of God in Brenda's world.

This, of course, is ludicrous. Either Jesus is the Son of God or He is not the Son of God. He can be one or the other, but He cannot possibly be both. Ashley may be wrong or Brenda may be wrong, but they both cannot be right. It is logically impossible.

As a college professor, I extolled the virtues of classic tolerance to my students. Students were not expected to leave their beliefs at the door—in fact—they were encouraged to vigorously defend them. They were, however, encouraged to have an open mind and to be tolerant of other views so that by listening respectfully to each other we could defend, modify, or change our positions as reason dictated. The purpose of classic tolerance *is to determine the truth*. Unfortunately, what I have found is that many students believed that we should be tolerant not in order to determine the truth, but because *there is no truth*. In this popular worldview tolerance is not a position we adopt while we continue to search for the truth—tolerance is an excuse to stop searching for the truth. Classic tolerance is the position we temporarily hold while searching for the truth. But today, many people see tolerance not as a temporary position to hold while on a journey in search of the truth, but rather as the destination itself.

When tolerance is used as a means to help us discover the truth, then tolerance is indeed a virtue. But when tolerance becomes the end in itself—when we settle for tolerance because we reject the very idea of truth—then tolerance ceases to be a virtue and becomes an insurmountable obstacle in the path that leads to truth.

One of the major purposes of education is to develop students' critical thinking skills so they can make better assessments of the information they receive. However, much of what happens in schools today is simply indoctrination of tolerance. Students are forced to be tolerant at the penalty of ridicule, failure, or expulsion.[1] Controversial

---

[1] Lest one think I am being alarmist in the disturbing level of intolerance on college campuses, a simple internet search will reveal many stories on students being expelled or re-educated for holding views that are not currently in vogue. Such discrimination has been decried by those on the left and the right. See: "Liberal Intolerance is on the Rise on America's College Campuses," https://www.washingtonpost.com › opinions › 2016/02/11; "College Bias Leads to Grade A Intolerance," by Tony

issues that once called for reasoned analysis ("Is democracy preferable to dictatorship?" "Is the death penalty just?" "Does capitalism or communism more efficiently distribute economic goods?") may now be entirely avoided with the trite and dogmatic answer, "It is up to each individual's opinion. There are no 'right' or 'wrong' answers."

This would all be tragic enough if the only result of the new tolerance was to make reasoned analysis a lost art. Unfortunately, the new tolerance, like the doctrine that there are no moral truths, is not quite as tolerant as it pretends. Certain ideas are "less tolerated" than others. Christianity, it seems, comes under special attack for being "exclusivist" and "intolerant."

But Aren't Christians Exclusive and Intolerant of Other Faiths?

One of the most common complaints about Christians is that they are exclusivist and intolerant. These charges are not entirely untrue. But what, precisely, is meant by these allegations? If by "exclusive" people mean that Christians believe that their faith is true and that any statement that is contradictory to that truth is false, then I agree: Christians are exclusive. Of course, they are no more exclusive in their faith than are believing Muslims, Jews, or atheists. Christians, for example, believe that Jesus Christ is the divine Son of God. They think anyone who disagrees with this is wrong. Muslims, Jews, and atheists believe that Jesus Christ is not the divine Son of God and they think anyone who disagrees with this is wrong.

This commitment to one's religion is criticized by such popular writers as Sam Harris (*The End of Faith*), Richard Dawkins (*The God Delusion*) and others. They bemoan the fact that religious truth claims are exclusive and intolerant. But that is the nature of *all* truth claims. If

---

Perkins, September 12, 2019, https://www.dailysignal.com/2019/09/12/college-bias-leads-to-grade-a-intolerance/; "A New Campus Survey Reveals Just How Students Are 'Unlearning Liberty'," by David French, National Review, March 13, 2018; and "Fmr NYC Mayor Michael Bloomberg calls out college campus 'intolerance' in blistering op-ed", by Jon Street, Campus Reform, September 17, 2019, https://www.campusreform.org/?ID=13723.

something is true, then its counter cannot be true. This is not the *vice* of truth claims—it is their *virtue*. It may be uncomfortable or inconvenient that 2 + 2 = 4, but it is a brute fact. And if it is true that 2 + 2 = 4, then it is an *exclusive* truth—as are all truths. In other words, if 2 + 2 = 4, the possibility that 2 + 2 also does not equal 4 is *excluded*. As a matter of logic, something cannot equal X and *not* equal X at the same time. Whether we are comfortable with it or not, either Jesus Christ is the Son of God or He is not. One cannot be both the Son of God and not the Son of God.

Christians do make exclusive truth claims—or at least they *should*. Any Christian who claims that Jesus is not the Son of God cannot really be said to be a Christian any more than a Muslim who claims that Mohammed is not God's prophet can really be said to be a Muslim. Do Christians believe that statements that contradict their beliefs are wrong? Of course they do. Do atheists make exclusive truth claims? Of course they do. They believe that God does not exist and they adhere to this belief exclusively. They do not believe that God exists and they hold that anyone who believes that God exists is wrong. Atheists believe that truth is exclusive just as Christians believe that truth is exclusive: It is exclusive in that anything that contradicts the truth has to logically be excluded from being the truth.

Now, this exclusivity in no way means that Christians (and atheists) need be intolerant. A Christian (or an atheist) may disagree with your belief about God, but still respect your opinion. Holding that something is true does not necessarily lead to intolerance.

There is another kind of exclusivity that Christians are wrongly accused of. Some people believe that Christians exclude certain people from becoming Christians—that there are *some* people who aren't allowed in the "Christian club." Perhaps these people include prostitutes or homosexuals or liberals or evangelicals. While it is true that some Christians may be biased, prejudiced, and exclusive in this sense, this is *not* Christian behavior. In fact, Christians, beginning with Jesus, have been criticized, persecuted, and even killed because of their extraordinary *inclusiveness*. Indeed, many of the early martyrs of Christianity were killed for promoting the radically inclusive belief that God had opened his arms to not only the Jewish people, but to the Gentiles.

A reading of Paul's letters, for example, reveals that he spent much time trying to convince his fellow Jews that one could enter the kingdom of heaven without circumcision, without the temple, and without adherence to Jewish dietary restrictions. Indeed, Paul spends so much time on these matters that modern readers might form the mistaken impression that Paul was obsessed with circumcision and kosher food! The truth is that Paul was writing about these issues not because *he* was obsessed with them, but because he was trying to remove their obsession from a *culture* that was obsessed with them. Paul was introducing an unprecedented liberal freedom to a very intolerant culture.

The early Christians were not only inclusive, they were *radically* inclusive. Not only were all people capable of eternal life in God's kingdom, whether Jew or Gentile, but Paul also wrote that God equally loves slave and master, Greek and Jew, Roman soldiers and Palestinian peasants, men and women. In fact, a close reading of Paul's epistles shows that he was a radical egalitarian—and that he suffered for his egalitarianism. In his letter to the Colossians Paul writes, "Here there is not Greek and Jew, circumcision and uncircumcision, barbarian, Scythian, slave and free; but Christ is all and in all."[2] Again, in his letter to the Galatians Paul writes: "There is no Jew or Greek, slave or free, male or female; for you are all one in Christ Jesus."[3] In the First Century, it was unthinkable that Jew and Gentile, men and women, slave and master, Roman citizen and conquered subjects of Rome were all equal in the eyes of God. This was a major—and majorly controversial—part of the Christian message. It is ironic and sad that some Christians today are as intolerant and exclusive as the enemies of Christianity were when Christians were the minority group.

While some individual Christians are exclusive and intolerant, Christianity as a worldview is diverse, inclusive, open, and tolerant. Nowhere in the world are Christians persecuting non-Christians. Every nation in the world that is majority Christian is open and welcoming to other faith groups. This is not an accident. Christian orthodoxy

---

[2] Colossians 3:11.
[3] Galatians 3:28.

teaches that people cannot be forced to accept God. That belief must be heart-felt and unforced. No other human can violate another human's free will in matters of faith. This is a Christian principle. Christians believe that if one comes to God against his will, that person is not truly a believer. A believer must come to God of his or her own free and voluntary act. Any Christian who attempts to exclude believers from becoming Christians or force unbelievers into becoming Christians is no Christian.

Christians are certainly capable of being intolerant. After all, Christians are humans and they share with their fellow humans all of the same follies and vices. Christians can be petty, vindictive, jealous, envious, greedy, bigoted, and intolerant—just like every other human being. But Christianity, in principle, is among the most tolerant of any religion, philosophy, or belief system the world has ever seen. Unlike some faiths, Christianity is open to all. Anyone, anywhere, at any time can become a Christian. Unlike some faiths, Christianity holds that believers must come to God freely and voluntarily. No one can be forced into real Christianity. Christianity, unlike some faiths, does not discriminate based on gender, race, ethnicity, nationality, —or *any other human trait, condition, or circumstance.* Those with even the most limited understanding of the Gospels know that Jesus entertained tax collectors, touched lepers, broke bread with criminals, and forgave prostitutes. One of his last acts in life was to forgive a thief dying on a cross next to Him and welcome this man into paradise.[4] Among His last words, spoken directly to the Roman soldiers and the crowd mocking Him as He hung dying, but indirectly spoken to all of us, were, "Father, forgive them, because they do not know what they are doing."[5]

Do Christians believe that the message of Jesus Christ is the truth? Absolutely. In fact, if believers in the truth make you nervous, Christians can be a very unnerving bunch. Not only do they believe that the message of Jesus is the truth—they believe that Jesus *Himself is the truth!*

But while Christians believe in the truth and in The Truth, they are extraordinarily tolerant (or should be!) of those who disagree. Nowhere in the world do Christians persecute people of other faiths. Nowhere

---

[4] *See* Luke 23:39-43.
[5] Luke 23:34.

in the world do Christians force anyone to join their faith. Nowhere in the world are people forced to attend a Christian church.

This is not so with many other faiths. We are only too aware of certain radical Muslim nations that discourage or prohibit other faiths from being practiced in those nations. We are aware of radical secular nations, too, that persecute or even kill believers. It would be an enormous misunderstanding of world religions to believe that it is only the Christian faith that makes truth claims. In many Muslim nations, those who are not Muslims are killed, converted, or treated as second-class citizens with rights vastly inferior to those of Muslims. Even Buddhists, it turns out, believe Buddhism is true. When the Dalai Lama was asked whether only the Buddha can provide man's ultimate destiny or salvation, he replied:

> Here, you see, it is necessary to examine what is meant by liberation or salvation. Liberation in which "a mind that understands the sphere of reality annihilates all defilements in the sphere of reality" is a state that only Buddhists can accomplish. This kind of *moksha* or *nirvana* is only explained in the Buddhist scriptures, and is achieved only through Buddhist practice.[6]

The purpose of this book is not to engage in a thorough, or even cursory, study of religions of the world. It is safe to say, however, that all religious beliefs (and *all other truth claims*, whether about religion, math, chemistry, or history) are exclusive. It is also within reason to claim that Christianity—at least in theory—is the most inclusive, diverse, and open religion in the world. None is barred from the Christian faith based on birth, race, nationality, ethnicity, or social class as is the case in many other religions. But what of non-traditional faith systems, such as atheism, secular humanism, or Secular Materialism? Are they tolerant?

---

[6] His Holiness the XIV the Dalai Lama, "'Religious Harmony' and the Bodhgaya Interviews," in *Christianity through Non-Christian Eyes*, ed. Paul J. Griffiths, as quoted in D. A. Carson, *The Intolerance of Tolerance*, 117.

Is The Secular Worldview Tolerant?

The historical record of nations that were or are officially atheist is one of outright discrimination, terrible intolerance, and totalitarian enforcement of the official state religion. The former Soviet Union, Maoist China, and modern-day North Korea are stark examples of secular exclusivity and intolerance. Secular Materialists complain of the past horrors of the Christian Crusades—and indeed there are embarrassing and shameful moments in the history of Christendom. However, what often goes unnoticed is that far more people have been killed by atheist regimes than were ever killed in the Christian Crusades.[7] It is estimated that approximately 1.7 million people perished in the Crusades whereas World War II took an astonishing 70 million lives. Indeed, the common myth that religion is the cause of most bloodshed is completely unfounded. The atheist regimes of Stalin and Mao alone were responsible for over 60 million deaths. Not that anyone is counting, but the fact is that atheism has caused far more deaths than Christianity.[8]

These atrocities do not in any way excuse Christian intolerance or violence but they do point out the truth that intolerance is not an exclusively Christian vice. Indeed, if one were to make an unbiased assessment of the facts, he or she would have to conclude that atheist states are far more intolerant than Christian states. If one were to choose a belief based solely on which belief system was less violent and more tolerant, one would have to logically reject atheism and accept Christianity. It is true that religion has sometimes led to wars, persecutions, and unjustifiable killing—but atheism has far surpassed Christianity in terms of the sheer number of people who have died on its altar. This is especially remarkable considering the enormous number of people in the world who are theists and the relatively tiny number of

---

[7] Further, the Crusades were not launched to force people into becoming Christians. They were an attempt to regain the Christian Holy Land from Muslim occupation. The Crusades were not evangelical campaigns to convert people, they were military campaigns to regain territory. For a good review of the Crusades, I recommend Rodney Stark's, *God's Battalions: The Case For The Crusades* (HarperCollins, 2009).

[8] See: *The Devil's Delusion: Atheism and Its Scientific Pretensions*, David Berlinski, Crown Forum, 2008 (New York).

people who are atheists. Christian nations have dominated the world for the past 2,000 years, while officially atheist nations have arisen only in the last half of the 20th Century. And yet these few nations in such a brief period of time unleased unimaginable horrors on humankind. That is not conclusive evidence that all atheist nations will resort to violence nor does it say anything about the behavior of any individual atheist. It does, however, refute the claim that if we rid ourselves of religion, the world would be a peaceful place.

Few people would defend militant atheism. But what of Secular Materialists? Are Secular Materialists more tolerant than Christians? Just as secular deniers of morality are true believers in a *secular* morality, it turns out that many secular champions of tolerance are actually radically intolerant. They reject, rather intolerantly, any view that makes universal truth claims, unless, of course, they are universal truth claims consistent with Secular Materialism. As the Christian apologist Ravi Zacharias puts it, "Philosophically, you can believe anything, so long as you do not claim it to be true. Morally, you can practice anything, so long as you do not claim that it is a 'better' way. Religiously, you can hold to anything, so long as you do not bring Jesus Christ into it."[9]

The reason the new tolerance is utterly intolerant is that it does not tolerate any worldviews that claim to be true. This seemingly neutral position is, in fact, biased toward secular agnosticism and prejudiced against any view that makes truth claims. It is skewed unfairly toward relativism and rejects any meta-narratives. For one to deny that there are any truths is not to be neutral—it is to be extremely intolerant of anyone who claims anything is true. While it sounds tolerant to hold that there are no truths, the truth is that this eliminates every and all versions of truth. It is extraordinarily exclusive and intolerant. The only views allowed are those views that conform to the belief that there are no truths and *any* truth claim outside of this belief is not tolerated.

Of course, in reality, the truth is even worse. If Secular Materialists denied *all* truth claims they would, at least, not be discriminating against any particular truth claims. Alas, much of the time Secular Materialists do not really deny *all* truth claims, they only deny those truth claims with which they disagree. Those who claim to believe that there are no

---

[9] Ravi Zacharias, *Jesus Among Other Gods*, vii.

absolute truths seem perfectly willing to accept truth claims made in the fields of astronomy, biology, botany, chemistry, cosmology, engineering, geography, geology, mathematics, oceanography, physics, quantum mechanics, statistics, and zoology—to name a few. The secular claim that there are "no absolute truths" seems to be reserved principally for Christianity. Similarly, the Secular Materialist worldview often shows great tolerance for all worldviews *so long as it is not a Christian worldview.*

Either out of ignorance or intention, the intolerance of any claims of truth in reality often means an intolerance of any *Christian* claims of truth. For example, the *Los Angeles Times* pulled Johnny Hart's cartoon strip, "B.C." because on Easter Hart showed his caveman character penning a poem that included the words, "Never to mourn the Prince who was downed, For He is not lost! It is you who are found." The *Times* declared that this was "insensitive and exclusionary."[10]

Some worldviews hold that there are no universal truths; some hold there are universal truths. Each of these views is making a *universal truth claim.* Christians (as well as Jews, Muslims, atheists, and others) are making the universal truth claim that there are certain truths. Moral relativists are making the universal truth claim that there are no universal truths. The position that there are no universal truths is not a neutral or objective stance. It is a position that fervently holds to the subjective opinion that there are no universal truths. To allow this viewpoint to be taught in our classrooms while prohibiting any viewpoint that differs with it is showing extreme bias, prejudice, and intolerance.

This is particularly unfair to Christianity because, as we have seen, Christianity is an evangelical faith whose adherents are called upon by God to share the Good News. As the great Christian thinker John R. W. Stott puts it:

> We seem in our generation to have moved a long way from this vehement zeal for the truth which Christ and his apostles displayed. But if we loved the glory of God more, and if we cared more for the eternal good of the souls of men, we would not refuse to engage in

---
[10] *Slouching Towards Gomorrah,* 291.

necessary controversy, when the truth of the gospel is at stake. The apostolic command is clear. We are "to maintain the truth in love," being neither truthless in our love, nor loveless in our truth, but holding the two in balance.[11]

As Christians, and for that matter as rational thinkers, we must reject the current social climate that redefines words to fit the social constructs of the politically correct. Tolerance, which once meant permitting views with which we disagreed, now means eliminating any views with which we disagree. Diversity once meant a community of many peoples with many views, now means a community of many people with the same views. Pluralism once meant divergent groups retaining their views and letting the marketplace of ideas choose which views made the most sense, now means eliminating the differences of groups. We are told at "diversity" conferences that we show tolerance by denying that our beliefs are true; we show diversity by acting like everyone else; and we embrace pluralism by eliminating any views that do not conform to these new definitions of tolerance and diversity. Professors teach students that right and wrong are judgments that reveal ignorance; that truth is relative, if it exits at all; and that all religious beliefs are equally invalid. Black is white, up is down, yes is no. Welcome to our Brave New World.

A Modest Proposal to Return to Sanity

To intelligently discuss Christian exclusivity and truth claims, we must first have an understanding of truth and tolerance. All people make truth claims, including those who claim there are no absolute truths. It seems impossible to make any propositional statement without making a truth claim. Whether we can prove what we believe is true or not is a different issue. For example, either God exists or He does not. This side of heaven no one may be able to prove the truth of this claim, but that does not mean it is not true. Not knowing whether something is

---

[11] John R. W. Stott, *Christ the Conversationalist*, 22.

true in no way detracts from the actual truth of something. Christians make truth claims, but so does everyone else. Christians make certain claims that may not be provable in this life. But so does everyone else. Christians, as well as Muslims, Jews, Buddhists, atheists, and Secular Materialists, should be able to make truth claims. Their opponents have every right to reject those claims, but they have no right to forbid Christians from making such claims. Christians should be able to express what they believe is true as firmly and unapologetically as anyone else.

Because most rational thinkers will come to the conclusion that conversation, thought, and reasoned discussion are impossible without truth claims, the opponents of Christianity attempt to demonize the faith by claiming it is "intolerant." D. A. Carson exposes this tactic in his excellent book, *The Intolerance of Tolerance*, where he writes: "The grounds for [prejudice against Christians] are not, formally speaking, that the Christian is a Christian, but that the Christian is intolerant, which cannot be tolerated."[12]

Indeed, calling Christians intolerant is a very effective way to shut down the conversation before it begins. I sympathize with the Christian who attempts to explain her views only to be met with the inaccurate rebuttal, "Well, believing Christ is the only way is not very tolerant." A person who believes that Christ is the only way may or may not be tolerant, but one thing is certain: She is not automatically intolerant by holding this belief.

Tolerance, properly understood, does not mean having no convictions. It means allowing others to hold convictions that may be counter to yours. Intolerance, properly understood, does not mean thinking your opponent is wrong. It means not allowing your opponent to express her beliefs. Ironically, one who holds that a Christian is intolerant because he believes that Jesus Christ is Lord is himself being intolerant.

Before Christians can defend their worldviews, they must understand that having a worldview that includes truth claims is not irrational, intolerant, or uncommon. Indeed, *all* worldviews make truth claims. Making a truth claim is not, in itself, a sign of intolerance. Being prohibited from making truth claims, on the other hand, is. Christians should defend the rights of others to hold differing viewpoints and they should demand

---

[12] D. A. Carson, *The Intolerance of Tolerance*, 33.

that others allow them that same privilege. As Voltaire, that secular son of the Enlightenment is credited with saying, "I disapprove of what you say, but I will defend to the death your right to say it."

Christians, it seems, have the right to believe in Christianity. An unbiased review of the facts reveals that Christianity holds its truth claims to be exclusive, but so do every and all truth claims. History shows us that Christianity is a most welcoming, open, and tolerant religion. Christianity is open to all, tolerant of all, forgiving of all, loving of all. In light of these facts, why does Christianity generate so much controversy? Could the discomfort be caused not by the fact that Christians make truth claims, but rather by the *specific* truth claims they make?

Know The Truth and The Truth Will Make You Uncomfortable

Christians believe that Jesus Christ is the Son of God, the second person of the Triune God, and that through Him we receive salvation. These claims are not offensive, in and of themselves. They are simply truth claims about a particular faith. They are offensive not because they are truth claims, but because they conflict with *other truth claims*. To say Jesus is the Son of God is inoffensive, except to the person who believes that Jesus Christ is not the Son of God. To hold that Jesus is the second person of the Triune God is inoffensive, except to those who believe it is blasphemous to think of God as three persons. That we receive salvation through Christ is inoffensive, except to those who make other truth claims about salvation. The point is that Christians are not offensive because they go around making truth claims—they are offensive because they go around making truth claims that conflict with other truth claims. Christianity is especially offensive to those who make truth claims that the supernatural is an illusion and that morality is a man-made social construct. These Secular Materialist truth claims are no less fervently held by their adherents than any religious truth claim is held by people of faith.

If a Christian and a Muslim each hold conflicting truth claims, how is this the Christian's "fault" any more than it is the Muslim's "fault"? If a Christian and a Secular Materialist each hold conflicting truth claims, why is the Christian the one "causing trouble?" It cannot be because Christians claim to know the truth because Muslims and Secular Materialists claim to know the truth, too.

Perhaps it is because Christians evangelize and Muslims and Secular Materialists do not? But, of course, this is not true. One would have to be completely ignorant of world history (not to mention current events) to believe that Muslims do not proselytize. As for Secular Materialists, try saying a prayer in a classroom, posting the Ten Commandments in a courtroom, or supporting legislation based on your religious beliefs. The proselytizing of Secular Materialists has been so incredibly effective because it has been largely covert and duplicitous. Secular Materialists imagine (or pretend) that they are only interested in neutrality and equal treatment of all religions. The fact is that the "neutral" and "equal" treatment they want is that all religious beliefs are removed from every corner of public life. This may be neutral in theory but it is fatal in fact. If we were to treat political discourse in the same way, we would ban all public political discussion under the guise of not wanting to show favoritism or offend any of the many political groups in the nation. We would be treating all political views equally—they would all be equally suppressed. If one's goal is the suppression of political beliefs, equal suppression is not neutral—it is precisely the result the oppressor desired. Similarly, if the goal is no religion, equal suppression of all religious viewpoints is precisely the result atheists desire. When one group (the anti-religious) wins every time, this is not what I would call a "neutral" public policy.

So, we do not find Christianity offensive because it makes truth claims—all people, religious and non-religious—make truth claims. Nor is it because Christians promote their faith—all religions seek converts. (For that matter so do all commercial establishments, sports teams, cities, philosophers, political parties, public interest groups, community associations, television stations, rock bands, newspapers, authors, artists, actors, animal lovers, environmentalists, and automobile dealers).

Christians do believe that their faith is true, but so do all believers (and unbelievers) of every faith in the world. Nonetheless, Christianity is one of the most *inclusive* religions in the world. There are no barriers to Christianity based on nationality, ethnicity, race, gender, or achievement. One does not become a Christian by family bloodline, tribal ancestry, or service to the church. There are no tests, qualifications, or acts to be performed to prove one's worthiness. There are no secret ceremonies, rituals, or rites of passage. Christians come in all shapes, sizes, ages, genders, nationalities, ethnicities, income brackets, and educational levels. There are liberal Christians, conservative Christians, gay Christians, Chinese Christians, communist Christians, and Jewish Christians. Indeed, one of the criticisms of Christianity is that its membership is too inclusive, too easy, open to anyone at any time without any qualification—except that they believe in Jesus Christ.

We have seen that Christianity is the same as other faiths, philosophies, and worldviews in that it makes exclusive truth claims. It is beyond dispute that modern Christianity is among the most inclusive and tolerant religions in the world. Yet, it is undeniable that there is *something* about Christianity that causes many people to react with feelings ranging from acute annoyance to rabid repulsion. Maybe the uneasiness, ridicule, and even hatred derive from what Christians *believe*? Maybe this man, this Jesus, is not a mere moral philosopher—a wise sage preaching peace, love, and understanding? Maybe He is something more. Maybe Jesus was right when He said:

> I came to bring fire on the earth, and how I wish it were already set ablaze! But I have a baptism to be baptized with, and how it consumes Me until it is finished! Do you think that I came here to give peace on earth? No, I tell you, but rather division! From now on, five in one household will be divided: three against two, and two against three. They will be divided, father against son, son against father, mother against daughter, daughter against mother, mother-in-law against her daughter-in-law, and daughter-in-law against her mother-in-law.
> —Luke 12:49-53

Jesus and His followers have *always* been controversial. They have, from the very beginning, created powerful reactions—feelings both of total commitment to the faith and of zealous persecution of the faith.

Jesus told His disciples, "You will be hated by everyone because of My name" (Matthew 10:20), and "If the world hates you, understand that it hated Me before it hated you" (John 15:18). Paul describes his Christian ministry in his second letter to the Corinthian church:

> We give no opportunity for stumbling to anyone, so that the ministry will not be blamed. But in everything, as God's ministers, we commend ourselves: by great endurance, by afflictions, by hardship, by pressures, by beatings, by imprisonments, by riots, by labors, by sleepless nights, by times of hunger, by purity, by knowledge, by patience, by kindness, by the Holy Spirit, by sincere love, by the message of truth, by the power of God; through weapons of righteousness on the right hand and the left, through glory and dishonor, through slander and good report; as deceivers yet true; as unknown yet recognized; as dying and look—we live; as being chastised yet not killed; as grieving yet always rejoicing; as poor yet enriching many; as having nothing yet possessing everything.[13]

Have you suffered for Christ lately? Have you offended anyone by sharing the Gospel? Have you boldly proclaimed your faith? Does anyone at your place of employment even know that you are a Christian? Do you defend Christianity when it is ridiculed and attacked? Or do you prefer the praise of men over the praise of God? We would bode well to remember the words of Jesus, "Therefore, everyone who will acknowledge Me before men, I will also acknowledge him before My Father in heaven. But whoever denies Me before men, I will also deny him before My Father in heaven."[14]

---

[13] 2 Corinthians 6:3-10.
[14] Matthew 10:32-33.

CHAPTER 16

GORGING ON THE TREE OF THE KNOWLEDGE OF GOOD AND EVIL

We are approaching the end of our comparison of the secular worldview with the Christian worldview. In our study we have seen that the major tenets of Secular Materialism are the radical separation of religion from our culture, the conviction that science has disproven the supernatural, and the belief that morality is created by man.

All three of these secular principles share a common belief: man is the master of the universe. The radical separation of religion from our culture is an attempt to keep God away from our lives and it is diametrically opposed to the principles our nation was founded on. The conviction that science has disproven the supernatural is not only in contradiction to science, but offers no particular advantage or insight into the universe save that God does not exist—something any unbiased scientist will admit science has absolutely no way of knowing. The belief that morality is created by man is a self-evident attempt for man to create his own subjective moral rules. These pretentions lead to the belief that man is the ultimate source of authority; an obvious rejection of any power higher than man himself. While all three of these beliefs masquerade as being the logical conclusions of constitutional interpretation, scientific discoveries, or objective sociological insights, we have seen that in reality, they are nothing of the sort. They are, in fact, simply beliefs about the world based on an atheistic worldview. They are, in the final analysis, an attempt to be God.

Man's desire to be God is nothing new. In fact, the desire to be God is the *original* sin—or in Christian theology—*Original Sin*. To understand how we have fallen so far astray, we need to start at the very beginning with man's original sin: our desire to be God.

We would be remiss in our analysis of Secular Materialism if we did not discuss the Bible's primary source of information on the nature of good and evil. No, we do not look to the Ten Commandments for that source, nor even the Sermon on the Mount. The Bible's seminal teaching on good and evil is found in Genesis—the very first chapter of the Bible—in the story of Adam and Eve. For my more secular readers a digression into this ancient story might seem superfluous or even ridiculous. After all, are we *really* going to explore a story about eating a forbidden apple? Yes, we are. And I believe even the most skeptical reader will discover brilliant truths and insights about the human condition in this story, even if one presumes the story is allegorical, metaphorical, or mythical. It is also an excellent place for skeptics to begin a serious study of Scripture because, as we will see, the story of Original Sin is not a simple fairy tale for children. It is a complex, sophisticated source of insight into the human condition. Of further benefit to skeptics is that if the "obviously silly" story of Adam and Eve can be revealed as something with profound philosophical perception, then there is at least the possibility that many of the other seemingly ridiculous stories of the Bible might offer the same—if given half a chance.

The story of Adam and Eve is universally known. Adam and Eve ate the fruit of the forbidden tree, Original Sin was introduced into the world, and we have ever since suffered the consequences. This story is rich with wisdom on a variety of topics and raises many profound questions. While the story reveals many truths, are the characters that convey these truths meant to be taken literally? Were Adam and Eve real human beings? Did God literally walk with them in the Garden? Does the serpent symbolize the Devil or were Adam and Eve tempted by an actual speaking serpent?

These are all fascinating questions filled with important theological implications, but for our present purposes we do not need to address those issues. Whether the story is a myth, an allegory, or an historical event does not change the profound truths revealed about humanity. This is not to say that whether the events that took place in the Garden of Eden were true or metaphorical is unimportant. Far from it. It is simply that for our purposes now, whether the serpent, for example, was real, metaphorical, or symbolic is not dispositive of the particular question we are going to address. And that critical question is this: What is the nature of good and evil?

Back To The Garden

If it has been a while since you read this story, you might want to re-read it. It is not an unsophisticated story about an apple or a snake or sex. It is a profoundly philosophical story about the nature of good and evil.

The tree in the Garden represents the knowledge of good and evil. This is plainly stated in the text. "And the Lord God commanded the man, 'You are free to eat from any tree of the garden, but you must not eat from the tree of the *knowledge of good and evil*, for on the day you eat from it, you will certainly die'"(Genesis 2:16-17, italics added). The forbidden fruit is not sex. It is not power. It is not even evil itself. It is the *knowledge* of good and evil.

But what does this mean? What does it mean to "eat from the tree of the knowledge of good and evil"? Reading the passage in its context provides the answer. When the serpent tempts Eve with the forbidden fruit, Eve tells the serpent that if she eats from the tree she will die. The serpent's reply to Eve holds the key to the entire story:

> "No! You will not die," the serpent said to the woman. "In fact, God knows that when you eat it your eyes will be opened and you will be like God, knowing good and evil" (Genesis 3:4-5, emphasis added).[1]

---

[1] It should be mentioned that the serpent is lying to Eve. However, this is irrelevant to the fact that Eve wants to be like God, "knowing good and evil."

What the serpent offers Eve, and what Eve desires, is to be like God. *Original Sin is man's desire to be God.* Now, certainly most of us do not think we can breathe universes into existence or walk on water. However, there are many ways to "be God" and the specific way that Adam and Eve desired was to "know good and evil." Again, what does this mean?

To "be like God, knowing good and evil," is to *determine* what good and evil is. It is to judge, adjudicate, or decide what is good and what is evil. It is, in short, to accept the Secular Materialist worldview that morality is whatever man says it is. It is, in a greater sense, to declare our independence from God and his decisions and to strike out on our own—autonomous and independent—and become our own judges, our own arbiters of what is good and what is evil, our own gods.

Prior to man's bold attempt to "be like God," as the serpent entices, man was innocent (and ignorant) of the knowledge of good and evil. He lived in complete happiness trusting on the word of God to determine what was right and what was wrong, what was permitted and what was prohibited, what was good and what was evil. Because God is all-knowing (omniscient), He always knows what is good and what is evil, and because God is all-loving (omnibenevolent), He always gives us what is good and prohibits what is evil. But man decided he wanted to "be like God," knowing good and evil, i.e., determining for himself what is right and what is wrong. We disobeyed God and attempted to become gods ourselves. This was the Original Sin committed by Adam and Eve and this is the Original Sin committed by each of us today.

Ironically, it is the very sin committed by those who question God's existence and justice. Atheists mock the Bible as a collection of irrelevant and outmoded stories, then they proceed to commit the very sin warned against by these "irrelevant and outmoded stories." First, they deny the Bible has anything important for modern man to know, and then they commit the exact sin warned about in the story of Adam and Eve by declaring that morality is relative and created by man. If it wasn't so tragic it would be humorous to watch these misguided souls behaving in precisely the way the Bible says they will behave—and then denying the relevance of the Bible to our modern times!

Humans seem to have a penchant to disbelieve and disobey God. This disbelief often leads to us becoming separated from God. And nowhere is this separation more evident than when we declare our independent ability to determine what is right and wrong, without reference to God. We then, rather irrationally, blame God for the evil in the world, and bemoan, "What kind of God would allow this evil?" The answer, of course, is the kind of "god" man is. Men, not God, create evil when they disobey God's commandments, determine what is good and evil on their own—and then, when confronted with the awful mess they've made—turn around and shake their fists at God for the evil that they themselves have done.

As also foretold in the Bible, the evil committed by humans leads humans, in their Fallen nature, to irrationally conclude that either God does not exist, or that He is not a god worthy of their worship. What could be more diabolical (and I use the word intentionally) than for me to conclude that the God of the Universe is unworthy of my worship? Yet I have heard intelligent, well-educated people—some of them theologians—say this exact thing: "If God allows evil to exist then He is not worthy of my worship." How twisted. How sad. How evil. Yet this is precisely the nature of the Fall and its consequences upon the human mind and soul. We have eaten from the tree of the knowledge of good and evil and have gained only the great hubris and flawed insight to determine that God—the Creator and Sustainer of heaven and earth—is unworthy of our worship.

God gave us free will. It is obvious man could choose to disobey God—we did. It is obvious we could choose to eat from the forbidden tree—we did. And the consequences are equally obvious. Whether one believes Adam's sin was passed on to us or whether one believes we each are free to make our own choices in spite of Adam—or, for that matter, whether one rejects the story altogether—none can deny that we live in a world filled with pain, suffering, and evil and that each and every single human being is, and always has been, capable of committing great evils upon their fellow man. In this much, at least, the story of Adam and Eve is readily convincing.

One could argue that God should not have given us free will, but then we would not be truly free creatures, capable of making real choices and meaningful decisions. We would be mere robots, programmed by

God to do whatever God desired. Such a person would not be human, would not be "real," and would not be able to freely and authentically decide to love God. We are God's children, and so an apt analogy is to our own children. What parent has not wished that their children did not have free will? How much better life would be, we sometimes imagine, if our children would just do what we say! They would suffer so much less because we know what is best for them. Yet, upon further reflection, parents realize that their children must be allowed to make their own decisions. That, at some point in their development, children must be totally and completely free of their parents' control. They must be allowed to fly from the nest and make their own decisions—even if those decisions result in tragedy. And as all parents know, the free will of children sometimes does end in tragedy—in readily foreseeable divorces, drug abuse, prison, and sometimes even death. But what loving parent would want to so control her child's life that the child was not a free, independent human being? What lover would want to control his beloved so that she had no choice but to love him in return? Controlling another human in this way would not be an act of love, but of profound disrespect—and the love they returned would not be love, but merely a programmed response dictated by a puppet-master.

God gave us free will because He loves us. He warned us not to eat from the tree of knowledge of good and evil, but we did not listen. We disobeyed. We rejected God as God. Yes, Adam and Eve still believed in God as a real entity. They knew He existed. But they did not believe in Him as their Lord and Master. They accepted Him as a force in the universe but rejected Him as their God.

How many of us do that today? How many of us believe in God, but reject His commandments—at least the ones we find disagreeable, irrational, or outdated? I know I am guilty of this grievous sin. I know that I, like Adam before me, want desperately to be my own god—to determine for myself the nature of good and evil. And whether one takes the story of Adam and Eve to be literal or figurative, the truths it conveys are profound. This magnificent story of the human condition is yet another example of this "irrelevant and outmoded" book describing the human condition better than any philosopher, psychologist, or sociologist ever has.

The story of Adam and Eve, ridiculed and rejected by Secular Materialists, describes the cause of man's problems with frightening accuracy: man is lost because he has rejected God and chosen to rely on his own judgment to determine what is right and what is wrong. He has rejected God as his Lord and Savior and has either denied His existence altogether or has safely placed Him in a very small box that he calls upon on those few occasions when he thinks he needs help.

In the final analysis we can either submit to God's determination of what is good and evil or we can reject God and decide on our own what is good and evil. Of course, that is a bit like the lunatics running the asylum, but this is precisely what humans often do. Secularist Materialists have determined that they are the final arbiters of what is good and evil, what is right and wrong, and whether God lives up to their "high" standards. Secularist Materialists have judged God and found Him wanting. And this insane behavior masquerades as "reason."

How can a rational human being reach such an irrational conclusion? This, too, is explained by Christianity. Like Adam and Eve, when we alienate ourselves from God, in that great fall, we also alienate ourselves from reason and morality. This is so because God is not just some other being, similar to us but with greater powers. No, God is life, love, reason, morality. Reason, morality, love and even life itself do not exist outside of God. They are by-products of God and they emanate from His being. God not only creates life, He sustains life. Without God, the world would not simply be a dark place—the world would not exist at all.

We are like lost children, groping around in the dark, who have rejected our Father's flashlight, but curse Him for the darkness. What sounds reasonable to us is often unreasonable. What seems rational to us is often irrational. This is the result of the Fall—the result of our declaration of independence from God—both through Adam and Eve in the Garden and through our personal daily decisions here and now. As Paul writes in Romans, "...their thinking became nonsense, and their senseless minds were darkened. Claiming to be wise, they became fools and...[t]hey exchanged the truth of God for a lie..."[2]

Paul precisely describes the secular worldview. Secularist Materialists, claiming to rely on reason, have rejected God and worshipped Man.

---

[2] Romans 1:21-25.

They have, claiming to be wise, become fools, and exchanged the truth of God for a lie.

Although these words were written in the First Century, they perfectly describe our world today. This, too, is not a surprise. At least not for Christians. Christians understand the Bible to be the word of God. It is no surprise to believers that this ancient book so perfectly describes the human condition and so marvelously answers our most troubling questions. It should, however, cause non-believers some serious pause and reflection. Sadly, in perfect consistency with what the Bible predicts, most non-believers simply reject the Bible offhand, without even bothering to seriously consider its message. They have, as the Bible says, become fools, exchanging the truth of God for a lie.

And because of this Fallen condition that we find ourselves in, we cannot always rely on our own reason to reveal the truth. Our reason is fallible—indeed, it is Fallen! Relying on our own independent reason and logic will not lead us to the truth. This is why independence, so highly valued and prized among humans, is disastrous when applied to our relationship with God. We cannot know the truth living independently from God. It is only by submitting to God that we can know the truth. As Augustine wrote, "Therefore, do not seek to understand in order to believe, but believe in order to understand."

Modern, secular man wants to see before he will believe. Augustine tells us we must first believe, and then we will see. This, of course, is impossible to do without faith. And faith only comes by laying down our independence at the feet of God and submitting ourselves to Him. Then, and only then, will our reason be restored and we will be able to see clearly. This is why independence and autonomy, while excellent virtues in a wide-variety of situations in life, are considered the Original Sin when applied to our relationship with God. Humans may act wisely in declaring their independence from their parents, their government, or their employers, but they act foolishly in declaring their independence from God. Humans were created to be in relationship with God. That is their purpose. To reject this relationship is to reject the very purpose of our being.

Jesus said He was the supernatural Son of God. He spoke of heaven and hell as real places. He referred to Satan as a very real being. And yet in spite of this, and based only on our extraordinarily limited knowledge of the world and its mysteries, we have determined there is no such thing as the supernatural. The Bible tells us God is the author of morality, the very essence of Good. We are told in the story of Adam and Eve that man's Original Sin is to reject God's definition of good and evil and to determine for himself what is good and what is evil. And yet in spite of this, and in disregard of man's long history of wars, violence, death, and destruction, we have determined that man—not God—is the author of morality.

Then, armed with this "knowledge," we reject both the supernatural and morality, in effect rejecting the existence of God. With this rejection of God comes the elimination of His influence on our culture. And this is nowhere better illustrated than in the radical separation of God from our public lives. A culture built on the foundation of the combined wisdom of over 2,000 years of Christian thought does not merely dismiss God overnight. The process is slow and incremental. We are at the rather late stage in this process of eliminating all vestiges of God and religion from the public square. We are not quite ready to eliminate God from our culture entirely. He is, after all, still allowed to exist in our churches and in our hearts. But His influence is largely limited to those confines. We now live in a post-Christian society where God is forbidden, either by law or by custom, from playing any meaningful role in our businesses, our schools, or are government. It is all fine and good to confess Christ as one's Lord and Savior—as long as we keep Him out of our government. And our schools. And our television programs. And our movies. And our books. And our shopping centers. In fact, talk all you want about the omnipotent, omniscient, omnipresent God of the Universe—just don't let Him influence anything in the "real world."

This relegation of our faith to the confines of our churches and homes is justified by the secular worldview that the Constitution requires it; that science has disproven the supernatural; the morality is relative; and that the individual is the ultimate arbiter of good and evil. How well have these presumptions held up under the scrutiny of reason and experience? How well have they served our culture? Perhaps it is time to forge a new path forward.

Chapter 17

What Now Shall We Do?

Secular Materialism is the default worldview in our current culture. It is the majority view held by what passes as our modern "intelligentsia"—journalists, comedians, novelists, academics, and entertainers. That this ragtag bunch of miscreants represents our modern intelligentsia says much about our culture. Would we have a more enlightened culture if its shapers were, say, doctors, engineers, and businesspeople? Or, God forbid, members of the clergy? After all, the clergy and statesmen were the primary shapers of our culture until the 20th Century. Nonetheless, it is the view that one must hold if he or she wants to be considered enlightened by "serious thinkers" and, more importantly, cool at parties. We have examined the central tenets of Secular Materialism. Those three "truths" are:

1. **Religious Irrelevance**
   Religious belief is based on faith, tradition, and ritual. Since the Enlightenment humankind has endeavored to throw off these chains and use the tools of reason, logic, and science rather than relying on the authority of the church. This is why the United States was founded as a secular nation with an impenetrable wall of separation between church and state. One's religious beliefs should have no influence on public policy and should, preferably, be banned from the public square and restricted to the confines of church, home, and individual conscience.

2. **Scientific Materialism**

   The material, natural world is all we can know and the scientific method is the only legitimate way of discerning facts about this world. Anything outside of the material world (the supernatural) is at best unknowable, and at worst, illusory.

3. **Moral Relativism**

   Morality is a social construct, relative to time, place, and culture. One person's "truth" may not be another person's "truth." Because this is so, making universal truth claims is exclusionary and intolerant.

In what I hope was a fairly objective review of these three principles, it was shown that not one of them performs well under the tests of reason, logic, or experience. The Secular Materialist belief that the United States was founded as a secular nation is entirely refuted by the facts. The truth is our federal government was prohibited from establishing a national religion. Aside from that, the states were free to engage in whatever religious activity they desired, including the establishment of religions. More importantly, there were (and are) no prohibitions on the practice of religion by *individuals*. Indeed, the First Amendment to the Constitution explicitly protects religious freedom. The idea that religion should be kept private and have no influence in the public square would be unimaginable to the Framers, and indeed, to most Americans from the founding well into the 1960s. Nothing, of course, prohibits people from choosing to keep their religious lives private, but we should not be under the illusion that this is required by the separation doctrine. History reveals that it clearly is not. The Constitution simply declares that the government shall not establish a national religion as was the practice in Europe. That is a long way from proclaiming that we should keep God out of our public lives.

Has science disproven the supernatural? Not even close. In fact, while science may not be suited to prove or disprove the supernatural, the evidence we have thus far seems to favor the possibility of the supernatural. Unless the entire universe, including time, space, matter, and even the laws that control the behavior of matter, were all created out of absolutely nothing by absolutely nothing—a concept itself that is utterly irrational, illogical, and against all scientific knowledge—then something or someone existed prior to the creation of anything. Such a thing or being would be, by definition, supernatural. Whether the supernatural exists or not may never be answered this side of heaven. But it is certain that science has not *disproven* the supernatural.

Is morality relative? Certainly *man's* laws are created by humans and change over time. But to presume that the only moral truth is that created by humans is an example of the biased and circular reasoning of Secular Materialists. Of course laws created by man are relative, changing, and often wrong. But for us to even know that they are sometimes wrong suggests a higher law. How can we even claim that a law is wrong unless there is some higher moral law than the law of man? The truth is, if God exists, higher moral laws exist. If God does not exist, then morality is relative at best, but more logically it does not exist at all. But to presume that morality is relative is to presume there is no God. This is begging the question. Secular Materialists presume morality is relative because they presume there is no God. Neither of these presumptions is based on the slightest shred of objective evidence.

Secular Materialism fails critical scrutiny. That, in itself, would not be especially meaningful. After all, many beliefs might fail the tests of reason, logic, and experience. What makes the failure of Secular Materialism so important is that Secular Materialism holds an elevated place in our culture—one might even say a dominant place in our culture. In fact, it is not too bold to claim that Secular Materialism is the prevailing worldview in modern Western culture. It is what we are taught and it is what we are expected to believe.

We have seen, I trust, that the foundational beliefs of Secular Materialism are on shaky ground, at best. They amount to little more than the conclusions one might reach if one began with the presumption that there is no God—which, incidentally, is precisely what secular reasoning assumes. That presumption, in itself, is not problematic—so long as one understands that it is the *presumption* upon which the conclusions are based. Because religious presumptions are forbidden from public schools, the only teaching permitted is that based on atheistic presumptions. By "atheistic," I do not mean professors are teaching that there is no God.

I mean that the secular presumption is, by definition, (a)theistic—that is, relying on the presumption that there is no God, because God-based theories and worldviews are prohibited from the classroom.

As a result, the secular presumption has taken on the imprimatur of what passes for "scientific truth," when in reality is it simply a secular worldview. The beliefs that religion should play no role in public life; that science has disproven the supernatural; and that morality is relative is the ultimate source of authority are just that: beliefs. None of it is based on empirical evidence, scientific fact, or logic. It is simply a set of beliefs held by the secular world, just as belief in the Resurrection of Jesus is a belief held by the Christian world. The major difference is that one of these worldviews is taught in our nation's schools and the other is prohibited from even being mentioned.

What Now Can We Do?

It seems clear that the foundation of our post-Christian culture is based more on bias against religious faith than it is on reason, logic, or experience. What do we do with this knowledge? That may depend upon whether the reader is an unbeliever, a nominal Christian, or a committed Christian.

For the unbeliever: I hope (and pray) that the evidence presented in this book will help you to open your mind to the possibility of faith. We have not set out an argument for the existence of God in these pages, but we have established that many of the reasons not to believe are weak—at best. If the possibility of God was rejected because Secular Materialism seemed to provide a better explanation of the world, that reason for rejection should no longer remain logically plausible. We have shown that Secular Materialism is itself a faith-based worldview, and one that simply does not stand the test of reason, logic, and experience. This fact certainly does not prove that God exists, but it does show that Secular Materialism is intellectually bankrupt. With the false narrative of Secular Materialism removed, one who wishes to pursue the possibility of God has many sources in which to turn to further that amazing journey. For the scientific minded I recommend *I Don't Have*

Enough Faith to Be an Atheist, by Norman Geisler and Frank Turek and *The Case For Christ*, by Lee Strobel. For those of a philosophical bent, I suggest *Death on a Friday Afternoon*, by Richard John Neuhaus and *Why I Am A Christian*, an excellent compilation of leading thinkers who explain why they believe. For the more poetic and mystical among you, try *Blue Like Jazz*, by Donald Miller, *The Return of the Prodigal Son*, by Henri J.M. Nouwen, and *Your Life in Christ*, by George MacDonald. And thousands upon thousands of good thinkers have been brought to Christianity by the works of C.S. Lewis. I have also included a more complete list of books categorized by specific topic in Appendix A. I wish you Godspeed on your journey!

To those who are doubting Christians, know that there is no shame in having difficulty believing. In fact, the Scriptures tell anticipate that we will have trouble believing. It is part of our Christian struggle in this life. If part of that unbelief was the result of learning the "truths" of Secular Materialism, I hope this book has provided you with some evidence against the lies of Secular Materialism. Know that your faith is reasonable. Go forward with renewed confidence that Christianity will outlast Secular Materialism as it has survived innumerable other heresies and false doctrines over the last 2,000 years.

For those readers who are committed Christians: We know in our hearts that God is real. We know in our minds that Secular Materialism is based on lies, misinformation, half-truths, and an atheist view of the world. Nevertheless, this is the culture we find ourselves living in at the opening of the 21st Century. What can we do to turn the tide of atheism and agnosticism in America? Many things, but none of them will be accomplished by continuing on the current path of Christian passivity. They will all require positive action on the part of believers. Here is a blueprint for a revival of not only faith, but of reason and tolerance, in our nation:

1. **Understand What It Means To Be a Christian**

One of the reasons that Christians are not more confident of their beliefs is because they don't know what their beliefs are. Many are uncertain of the history and theology of their own faith. It can be embarrassing to engage in a discussion with an atheist who knows more about Christianity than you do! There are two ways to resolve this problem and they were both addressed by the Apostle Peter:

> ...[A]lways be ready to give a defense to anyone who asks you for a reason for the hope that is in you. However, do this with gentleness and respect, keeping your conscience clear, so that when you are accused, those who denounce your Christian life will be put to shame.[1]

As is evident by the above passage, the necessity of defending the faith is nothing new. Peter wrote these words almost 2,000 years ago. An important part of the Christian life has always been promoting and defending the faith. It is part of our Christian duty.[2]

Peter provides a two-part approach to what theologians refer to as "apologetics." Apologetics does not mean apologizing for the faith, as we commonly use the word, but rather means a defense of the faith. Peter tells us to be informed and prepared ("be ready") but also to defend our faith with gentleness and respect. It is impossible to defend our faith if we ourselves do not know what it is. This does not mean we need to be theologians, understanding everything from the dating of the Gospels to the varied interpretations of the Second Coming. In fact, that kind of knowledge is often detrimental in convincing the non-believer if we do not present it with humility and love. After all, there is disagreement even among theologians as to the "right" answer in many of these areas, just as there is in the fields of medicine, law, and philosophy.

What we need to do is understand some basic principles of our faith. Ironically, it is these basic principles that are often most misunderstood, even among Christians. It may be helpful to continually remind ourselves what Christianity is *not*. It is not, like most other religions, a system of punishment and rewards. Many unbelievers (and sadly, many believers) think that Christianity is about rules set down by God, and if we follow

---

[1] 1 Peter 3:15-16.
[2] See Matthew 28:19-20: "Go, therefore, and make disciples of all nations, baptizing them in the name of the Father and of the Son and of the Holy Spirit, teaching them to observe everything I have commanded you."

those rules, then we go to heaven. If we break those rules, then we go to hell. This is *not* Christianity. Christianity, at its heart, is about a loving God, who though His grace, gives us the unearned blessing of eternal life. Christianity is about an unfathomable gift from God, not because we earned it or deserve it, but purely out of the incomprehensible love of our Creator. This is the message that unbelievers need to hear. Whether they should join the Baptist church, the Methodist church, or the Catholic church pales in significance compared to the incredible gift of love we have in Christ. Whether one should tithe, smoke, dance, swear, or use wine or grape juice during communion is utterly irrelevant in light of the unspeakable gift of eternal life given to us by God. This is why Paul was so dismissive of questions asked by early Christians about whether they should refrain from certain foods or be circumcised or not. Paul essentially told them, "Who cares?" We, just as Paul advised the first Christians, should not dwell on these trivial earthly concerns, but should keep our eyes fixed on the glorious salvation given to us through Christ Jesus.[3]

The basic principles of Christianity should be etched on our hearts: We believe that Jesus Christ is the Son of God. That He died for our sins. That though Him we will have eternal life with God in heaven. These beliefs may be best appreciated when simply expressed with heartfelt and sincere conviction, rather than when explained logically. If you look an unbeliever in the eyes, and tell him with confidence that you actually believe these things, it almost never fails to have an impact. You may not be aware of that impact immediately, and the unbeliever may not reveal the impact to you, but it will register. It will register because God has made us with a God-shaped hole in our hearts, and we are restless until that hole is filled. After all, there is a reason that unbelievers are so interested in Christianity…even if they express that interest with cynicism and doubt.

It is also helpful to show humility. It is impossible for a human to fully understand the ways of God, and that is alright. If we mere mortals were able to completely comprehend the ways of the Creator of the Universe, He wouldn't be much of a God, would He? There is

---

[3] This is not to be diminish the importance of religious rituals, rules, and traditions. It is only to say that the salvation offered by Jesus Christ far surpasses these things.

no shame in admitting that we simply don't know everything about how God works. Admitting this reveals our humanity and makes our message more inviting to unbelievers who often complain that Christians are smug and arrogant. We can disarm unbelievers by being comfortable in our belief that God loves us, even as we admit that we do not fully comprehend the brokenness of this world. For example, if you are asked, "Why does God permit little children to suffer and die?" instead of lecturing on the concepts of Original Sin, the Fall, and free will, it may be best to simply reply, "I do not know. I can't explain it. I know our world was broken by man, not by God, but I don't pretend to understand all the suffering in the world. I just know in my heart that God loves us and suffers with us, and that in the end He will remove all death and suffering." Similarly, if someone asks why God's Son had to die so we could be forgiven of our sins, it may be better to simply reply that you don't completely understand all of God's ways, but that you completely trust in His love, rather than to give a seminar on the theories of the Atonement. On the other hand, if you are prepared to do so and if the questioner is interested in theories of the Atonement, by all means be willing to engage in the conversation.

It is also important to understand that being a Christian is not about knowing a set of theological doctrines or engaging in religious rituals. It is an entire worldview. It provides believers with a whole new way of seeing everything. We must be careful not to make Christianity just another religion, or even the "best" or most "reasonable" religion. We should not compartmentalize Christianity the way secularists want us to. It is not a part of our lives, or even the most important part of our lives. It is not a part—it is a whole. It is the way we see and do everything that we see and do. It is not merely our religion; it is our life. If Christian theology can be explained, and it usually can, through the use of reason, logic, and science—that's fine. But if not, we must remember that what it means to be a Christian is that we do not judge Christianity against man's standards of reason, logic, and science; rather, we judge man's understanding of reason, logic, and science against the higher truth of Christianity. In other words, having a Christian worldview means that if science and Christianity appear to conflict, we believe our understanding of science is mistaken, not our belief in Christianity.

Peter tells us to always be ready to defend the faith, but he also cautions us to do so with gentleness and respect. We fail if we are not willing or able to defend our faith, but we fail also if we do not maintain our Christian love and composure when doing so. Each part of this formula is difficult, but when applied in unison our duty becomes much easier. When we fail in our knowledge, we can recover by simply showing Christian patience and love. This is often not easy. It has been my experience that many unbelievers are not really interested in listening or understanding, or even engaging in a discussion in good faith. A typical conversation with an unbeliever often sounds something like this:

Unbeliever: "So you actually believe in all that stuff?"

Believer: "I do. A lot of it is well-documented…"

Unbeliever: "The Gospels were written hundreds of years after the death of Jesus, if Jesus even ever existed! How can you believe those books?"

Believer: "Well, actually most scholars believe they were written somewhere between 20 years and…"

Unbeliever: "Oh, right. So Christian scholars, which is an oxymoron, believe something no one else does! Who cares what Christian scholars think? They are biased!"

Believer: "Actually, those are the beliefs of Christian and non-Christian scholars…"

Unbeliever: "Besides, the church destroyed all the gospels they didn't like and anything that spoke out against the church. The Gospels are just propaganda written by the church hundreds of years after Jesus died."

Believer: "Uh, actually, that's just not true. The church…"

Unbeliever: "So you believe in miracles and angels and ghosts and fairies and unicorns?"

Believer: "Well, I don't think ghosts and fairies and unicorns…"

Unbeliever: "And in dead people rising from the grave and a person living inside a whale for three days?"

Believer: "Yes, I believe Jesus was resurrected. There are actually many good reasons to believe that He was. For example…"

Unbeliever: "The early Christians did not even believe in the deity of Jesus. That was decided at the Council of Chalcedon, 300 years after his death!"

Believer: "Well, I think you are referring to the Council of Nicaea, which was not the first time the deity of Christ was proclaimed. The deity of Christ was proclaimed from the time of His resurrection. The Council of Nicaea was held to determine…"

Unbeliever: "From the time of his alleged resurrection, you mean. Have you seen the Da Vinci Code? What do you think about that? Was Jesus married to Mary Magdalene? You know, they found the bones of Jesus. How could He be resurrected if they found His bones?"

Believer: "OK, first of all, they have not found his bones. Second…"

Unbeliever: "So you think all Muslims are going to hell? What kind of God would send people to hell?"

You get the idea. It can be extremely frustrating even for someone who is knowledgeable enough to answer all of the questions tossed about in a machine-gun style manner, seeking only to badger and not to understand. This is where Peter's second piece of advice comes into play. Try to be loving and kind, patient and gentle with our accusers.

After all, they are, according to Christian theology, under the influence of a force that has blinded them to the truth:

> To the pure, everything is pure, but to those who are defiled and unbelieving, nothing is pure; in fact, both their mind and conscience are defiled. They profess to know God, but they deny Him by their works. They are detestable, disobedient, and disqualified for any good work. Titus 1:15

> For the mind-set of the flesh is hostile to God because it does not submit itself to God's law, for it is unable to do so. Those whose lives are in the flesh are unable to please God. Romans 8:7-8

> They are darkened in their understanding, excluded from the life of God, because of the ignorance that is in them and because of the hardness of their hearts. Ephesians 4:18

When we are confronted by such people, we probably cannot win them over using reason and logic. They will claim to be reasonable and logical, imagining their fallacious arguments are based on facts, but in reality, they are blinded to even the possibility of the truth. It is best not to tell them this, but to show them the Christian love and patience that resides in you. This may influence them more than any argument you could present.

So, Peter, one of the world's greatest defenders of the faith, tells us we must do two things: be informed, and be loving. Oftentimes a discussion with an unbeliever can quickly become heated and angry. When you see this beginning to happen it is best to simply smile and sincerely offer him or her the opportunity to discuss Jesus with you any time they feel comfortable. By disengaging and not becoming frustrated, the unbeliever will see both your complete confidence in your faith and your Christian love.

2. Be Bold, Joyful, and Triumphant

Do not be afraid to share your belief in Christ. Jesus tells us:

> Therefore, everyone who will acknowledge Me before men, I will also acknowledge him before My Father in heaven. But whoever denies Me before men, I will also deny him before My Father in heaven.[4]

These are the words of our Lord and Savior: they should be taken seriously. We disgrace our God when we are ashamed, embarrassed, or silence about our faith. We should boldly proclaim our faith to all who ask. After all, if they are asking you, they want to know what you truly believe. That probably means they respect you as a person and are interested in your opinion. This is not the time or place to be "sophisticated" or play the part of the cynical pseudo-intellectual. It is your moment to stand for Christ. Be not afraid.

Christians should be as bold in our belief as atheists are in their unbelief. The primary reason we are becoming a post-Christian nation is because those who oppose the teachings of Christianity are more passionate, bolder, and more assertive than those of us who are Christians. When your local school prohibits a brief prayer at graduation ceremonies, for example, fight back. Let the administrators and the school board know that you care about this issue and that you believe it is perfectly legal for a student to give a brief prayer or moment of silence. When schools refuse to permit your child to silently pray or bring a Bible to class, politely inform the school that your child has a legal right to do such things. Most decisions made by schools are not made based on constitutional law—they are made based on whatever leads to the easiest way to silence the loudest complainers! Schools might cite the "separation of church and state" to you, but in reality, very few of them are familiar with the legal rulings. What they are really doing is just trying to make the problem go away. Christians usually lose these battles because the loudest voices come from the few radical atheists. It is time we let our voices be heard, also.

---

[4] Matthew 10:32-33.

Be neither angry nor defensive. After all, as Christians we know we have already won the battle. If one truly believes, we need not behave belligerently or out of fear. Our faith is not so weak that we will crumble under the doubts or questions of others. We may not know the answers to their questions, but we know the truth of Christ resides in our hearts and souls. This should be expressed joyfully and triumphantly. Not the kind of mean-spirited triumph that might exist at a football victory, but the kind of confident and assured triumph that brings peace and patience. Our God is real. We do not need to prove that to anyone. It is nice if we can, but we know the truth remains the truth, whether we are able to convince others of it or not.

Along these lines, do not be afraid to admit when you don't know the answer to a question. The Apostles were all simple men, not well-educated. They were common men, not rabbis or scribes. They were not learned in the law. Yet they transformed the world! They did so not by clever arguments, but by the profound strength of a simple conviction of the truth.

Finally, Christians should be the most joyful of all people. We know we are saved! We know we have eternal life! Rejoice and show joy. It is not convincing to anyone that one has the love of Christ and the assured knowledge of salvation when that person's heart is filled with condemnation and hatred. If one truly believes they have everlasting life, that person should be recognizable by his or her abundance of love, compassion, and patience. Jesus tells us: "By this all people will know that you are My disciples, if you have love for one another."[5]

3. **Join Hands With Fellow Believers…Even If They Are Not Christians**

Christians have every right to be unabashedly pro-Christian, but in this battle for the cultural life of our nation it may be best to also be pro-theist. The battle is primarily between believers and non-believers, not between Christians and Muslims or Christians and Jews. Yes, Christians can and should proselytize the truth of their faith to those of other faiths. But in our efforts to restore a discussion of God in our

---

[5] John 13:35.

public life, and especially in our public schools, we need to focus on just that: demanding that our schools engage in a robust discussion of the history and philosophy of God and religion, which includes the discussion of all concepts of God and of all major religions. We will be better served to ask our schools to offer classes on theology, faith, and religion than simply on Christian education. After all, we are at a point in our culture where "separation of church and state" has come to mean, in the minds of many, an absolute prohibition on *any* discussion of anything even remotely resembling a discussion about faith or religion, even going so far as removing from the central role faith has played in the history of the world.

What we need to strive for is not Christian indoctrination, but a common-sense return to the discussion of the importance of religion and faith in such topics as world history, philosophy, and government. This discussion should be fair and balanced, and should include a discussion of the philosophies of all faiths. To simply teach Christianity in public schools is a violation of the First Amendment. But to teach Christianity along with other faiths, as a part of a world religions class, or as philosophy or history, is most certainly not a violation of the Constitution.

Towards that end, we should join hands with fellow believers from different faith groups. The enemy is not those who have a different conception of God, it is those who want to stamp out every trace of even the mention of God in our schools. It is not fellow theists who are demanding our schools prohibit discussion of God—it is atheists. And the atheists are winning. All believers in God—all theists—should join forces to battle the atheists. Atheists know that by prohibiting any discussion of God they are promoting atheism. The false narrative may be that prohibiting the discussion of any faith is a neutral and unbiased policy. It is not. Prohibiting the discussion of all faiths is tantamount to promoting atheism. This is what has happened in our public schools and we have all seen the disastrous consequences. It is time to join hands with other believers, who, in good conscience, are interested in promoting a fair and balanced discussion of all faiths and philosophies. The Constitution does not prohibit such a discussion, and good education demands it.

The Roles of Our Courts, Our Schools, and Our Churches

Aside from our personal involvement, there are three institutions that are essential to the fight: our courts, our schools, and our churches. And while we may not be a judge or a school board member or a pastor, it is incumbent upon us to influence those who are because these three institutions will have an enormous impact in freeing us from the grips of totalitarian secularism.

Our Courts

The courts need to return to the jurisprudence that was practiced in this nation for almost 200 years prior to the *Everson* decision, and specifically the Supreme Court needs to overturn the failed "separation" test they established in 1971 in *Lemon v. Kurtzman*. As we discussed, the *Lemon* tests determines whether something violates the imaginary "separation of church and state" doctrine using the following 3-pronged test:

1. The statute must have a secular legislative purpose.
2. Its principal or primary effect must be one that neither advances nor inhibits religion.
3. The statute must not foster an excessive government entanglement with religion.

I join former Chief Justice William Rehnquist in calling on the Court to overturn this decision. It is a decision based on the most erroneous constitutional interpretation and its results have been disastrous.

First, the entire "separation of church and state" fiction should be abandoned. The Constitution does not call for a separation of church and state. Rather, it says the Congress shall not establish a religion. Establishing a religion is a very different standard than attempting to make sure there is an "impenetrable wall of separation" between church and state. As we have seen, there was not really a wall of separation between church and state, much less an impenetrable one for most of the history of the United States.

Second, there is nothing in the Constitution (nor in the first nearly 200 years of our nation's history or jurisprudence) to suggest that a statute must have a "secular legislative purpose." Nothing. We were not founded as a "secular" nation. We were founded as a nation that was to not favor any one particular religion. That is entirely different than embracing secularism. Indeed, by embracing secularism we are favoring one particular religious belief: atheism.

Third, there is not one word in the Constitution that suggests "the principal or primary effect of legislation must be one that neither advances nor inhibits religion." Legislatures are constitutionally permitted to enact legislation that advances religion so long as they do not favor one religion over another. Again, the Congress and the state legislatures had done this over and over since the Founding until relatively recently in our nation's history. Not to mention, that any prohibition on prayer, Bible reading, or the discussion of one's faith in the classroom most certainly "inhibits" religion. So, any such prohibition fails even *Lemon's* own ludicrous standards.

Finally, it is almost impossible to know what is "an excessive government entanglement with religion," but it is certainly something the Framers would have scoffed at. And again, prohibiting a teacher from silently reading a Bible on his or her break is hardly something that creates "an excessive government entanglement with religion."

Overturning *Lemon* is something that not only believers should desire, but that any unbiased constitutional scholar should desire. The decision was clearly the result of a certain perverse animus that the Supreme Court held against religion. It is time for the Court to correct this constitutional folly. To overturn *Lemon* would not be judicial activism, but just the opposite: correcting a terrible decision made by a misguided Court bent on removing all vestiges of religion from our public lives. The current Court has shown very positive signs that they are ready to abandon the unworkable and unconstitutional *Lemon* test. Let us hope and pray that they find the courage to do so and to return to the standard that was followed from the inception of the First Amendment until the 1960's. That constitutionally required standard is not to ask whether a statute or behavior violates an imaginary separation of church and state, but rather to ask: Does this legislation "establish a religion?" This would be a much easier question to answer, not to mention it would be consistent with the Constitution.

Our Schools

Even with horrific decisions such as *Lemon*, our schools remain quite free to engage in many forms of religious study. They simply cannot proselytize. But while public schools are not (and should not be) allowed to force school prayer or have teachers proclaim the Good News of the Gospel, they most certainly can discuss matters of meaning, purpose, and morality. And when discussing such things, they would be derelict in their duties if they did not examine the views of the Old Testament, the Bible, the Koran and other seminal religious texts in such discussions. It is also perfectly legal for schools to teach the Bible as literature, poetry, or history. The fact that most schools do not engage in these kinds of studies is almost unbelievable. I say that not as a Christian, but as an educator.

The obstacle for schools is not so much the law as it is fear of the law. School principals and school boards are notoriously risk-averse and often the default position is to simply prohibit anything that even remotely looks like religious conversation in the classroom. This is not what the law requires, but it is often the easiest path for schools to take. We can change this by informing our educators what the law is and by becoming active in our schools and presenting possible courses of study to the school board that have withstood judicial scrutiny. Good information on such courses is provided by The Family Research Council at their website: frc.org/ReligiousLibertyInSchools.

Our Churches

Our churches must take the lead in these battles. For Christians that means, first and foremost, to become a member of a church. A Christian without a church is like a soldier without an army. We need to become more active in our churches and our churches need to become more active in our communities. The church can no longer behave passively as a place where the faithful gather to worship and have donuts. The church needs to recapture its historical role as the most important institution in the community. We need bold, courageous, and committed leadership in our churches to make them once again the most vibrant and important voices in the culture.

Yes, the church is more than an activist organization. But it should not be less. The church was given a uniquely important role by God to educate, inform, and transform our communities. No church should settle for merely being a place where people gather one hour a week to sing a few songs and listen to a sermon that is more about pop-psychology than it is about the Gospel. A great church should be vibrant and meaningful and should be one of the first places that any public official would go in search of guidance on public policy. Pastors should be, as they were in times past, considered among the most important leaders in the community.

Finally, the church needs to begin educating its parishioners on Christian theology. Yes, churches should be places of worship, but God tells us to worship Him with all of our heart and soul and strength and *mind*. It is true that our children are not going to be taught anything about Christianity in most of our public schools. But that does not stop the church from engaging in robust programs of Christian education. Not only should churches offer meaningful Bible study courses for people of all ages, but the pastor should regularly educate his congregation from the pulpit. Such sermons need not be boring lessons on theology. Indeed, some of the most inspiring and exciting sermons I have heard preached have been on the incredible and amazing philosophy of Christianity. We must remember, it was not modern technology or feel-good sermons that changed the history of the world—it was the direct and unapologetic preaching of the Good News. And that Good News included the exciting and transcendent *theological* message of Jesus. There is nothing more inspiring—or relevant—than that original message. A message that requires not only the transforming of our hearts and souls—but of our minds.

The Battle Will Be In Our Homes, On Our Streets, and In Our Schools

Christianity has never been easy. It is a demanding faith. It is demanding to us internally and externally. Internally, Christ asks us to die to ourselves. This is no small request! Externally we are asked to go to all the world and preach the Gospel, even though we know the world will not be receptive. Jesus does not hide the difficulties His followers will have. Sadly, we have often ignored these passages in the Scriptures. A brief recitation of some of those may be helpful in introducing us to what an authentic Christian life might entail:

> You will be hated by everyone because of my name.
> Matthew 10:20

> If the world hates you, understand that it hated Me before it hated you.
> John 15:18

> I came to bring fire on the earth, and how I wish it were already set ablaze! But I have a baptism to be baptized with, and how it consumes Me until it is finished! Do you think I came here to give peace to the earth? No, I tell you, but rather division!
> Luke 14:49-51

> If anyone wants to come with Me, he must deny himself, take up his cross, and follow Me. For whoever wants to save his life will lose it, but whoever loses his life because of Me will find it.
> Matthew 16:24-25

This is the Christian message, although it is seldom preached. Is Christianity about peace, love, and eternal life? Yes. But Christianity is essentially a paradox. It is about peace, love, and eternal life through division, denial, and death. This struggle is not only internal, but also external. We must battle daily within our own souls to submit to Christ, and we must battle externally with a world that does not know, and does not want to know, the truth.

Where will this battle take place? Everywhere. It rages within us and outside of us. We dare not embrace the secular worldview that our lives are divided into the religious and the secular. That Christianity only requires that we adhere to our Christian worldview on matters of faith and religion, but we cede to the secular world all else. This understanding of "separation of church and state" is as unchristian as any policy I can imagine. It is what leads to the cultural attitude that so long as I am a "good" person and attend church on occasion, I have fulfilled my Christian obligations. This is most assuredly not what Jesus called for. The Gospels are clear: Jesus does not want us to give Him the "religious" part of our lives—he wants *all* of us. The great Christian apologist C.S. Lewis writes:

> The Christian way is different: harder and easier. Christ says, 'Give me All. I don't want so much of your time and so much of your money and so much of your work: I want you. I have not come to torment your natural self, but to kill it. No half-measures are any good. I don't want to cut off a branch here and a branch there, I want to have the whole tree down. I don't want to drill the tooth, or crown it, or stop it, but to have it out. Hand over the whole natural self, all the desires which you think innocent as well as the ones you think wicked—the whole outfit. I will give you a new self instead. In fact, I will give you myself: my own will shall become yours.[6]

It is essential for Christians to understand that our trust in Jesus shapes *everything* in our lives. We will continue to lose Christians if we succumb to the secular view that there is a place for our belief and a place for everything else. Christians in Europe and the United States have accepted this unchristian philosophy and we have seen the result: Christianity has been almost completely removed from every aspect of

---

[6] C. S. Lewis, *Mere Christianity*, 196-97.

our lives except the church—and even there it is under attack. Christians must not continue to allow their faith to be compartmentalized to the periphery of their lives. True Christian faith is at the center of our lives; indeed, it is how we should define ourselves. We are not lawyers and teachers and waitresses who also happen to be Christians; we are Christians who happen to be lawyers and teachers and waitresses.

This is why the battle for the soul of the nation does not exist only in church on Sunday morning. Church is not where we go to fulfill our Christian obligations and duties. Church is the place we go to find fellowship, education, and support to help us live as Christians in an unchristian culture the rest of the week. But our Christian behavior should not begin when we enter the church door and leave when we exit.

Perhaps the church has been too willing to conform to the culture. Often, when ministers, pastors, and priests speak of behaving as Christians, they refer only to the Christian virtues of love, forgiveness, patience, and kindness. Certainly, Christians should be loving, forgiving, patient, and kind. But those are not the only virtues Christ called us to. He also asked us to speak the truth of the Gospel, to defend our faith, and to introduce others to Him. Christianity did not grow from twelve lonely disciples to over three billion people because Christians attended church once a week! Christianity became the world's largest and most influential worldview because it was taken to the streets—and taken to the streets as the *truth*—not merely as a religion.

How do we engage in such a movement? We begin acting like we *actually believe* what we say we believe. That means talking to our friends, our relatives, our neighbors, and our co-workers about Jesus. It means boldly proclaiming that, yes, you actually believe the truth of the Gospels when their truth is questioned. It means teaching your children about your faith and correcting what they have been taught in school when the teacher or professor unfairly assails Christianity. It means voting for candidates and causes that are consistent with our faith. To the extent one is able, it means financially supporting our churches and parachurch groups and organizations that promote and defend Christianity. It means defending Christianity when a local teacher, principal, or school board infringes upon the rights of our children. Such rights include:

- The right to pray, read their Bible and other religious material, and discuss their faith in school.
- The right to organize prayer groups or religious clubs.
- The right to express their faith in class work and homework.
- The right to go off campus to engage in religious studies during school hours.
- The right to express their faith at school events.
- The right to express their faith at their graduation ceremony.[7]

We can do all of these things, as Peter requested, with gentleness and respect. We do not need to be annoying, arrogant, or angry. We can defend our faith with the calm that comes from being secure in our beliefs. We can promote and protect Christianity and be loving and kind at the same time. Jesus, our Lord and Savior, as He was dying on the cross, said, "Father, forgive them, for they know not what they do." Christ died for us, but showed love even to those who wrongly executed Him. This is our model.

As we go forward with all courage and conviction, let us remember that God has not given us a spirit of fear and timidity, but of power, love, and self-discipline.[8] Be strong and of good courage, do not fear nor be afraid of them; for the LORD your God, He is the One who goes with you. He will not leave you nor forsake you.[9]

Go forward with courage and conviction, knowing that while the days may be difficult and the nights may look dark, that we have already won the battle through Jesus. At John 16:33 our Savior tells us: "I have told you these things so that in Me you may have peace. You will have suffering in this world. Be courageous! I have conquered the world."

Onward Christian Soldiers!

---

[7] This information comes from the Department of Education's document, "Guidance on Constitutionally Protected Prayer in Public Elementary and Secondary Schools." More information may be found at frc.org/ReligiousLibertyInSchools, a project of the Family Research Council.

[8] 2 Timothy 1:7.

[9] Deuteronomy 31:6.

Discussion Guide

Chapter 1: Man As God: The Triumph of Secularism in American Culture

1. Do you feel that something has gone amiss in our nation? In your own spiritual life? In you devotion to Christianity? If so, why do you think that is?

2. Where you surprised to learn of the dramatic decline in the number of people who now consider themselves Christian? Before you read the chapter, what did you attribute that decline to? After reading the chapter, do you agree with the author's reason for the decline, or do you think there are other reasons? What are they?

Chapter 2: Secular Totalitarianism: Relegating Religious Thought to Irrelevancy

1. Did you know the United States was so thoroughly religious until very recently?

2. Were you surprised to learn that most of the Founding Fathers were devout Christians? That almost all colleges and universities were founded by Christian churches?

Chapter 3: A Shift in Worldviews: From Theistic to Atheistic

1. Have you ever thought about your "worldview" before? How would you describe your worldview?

2. A worldview that denies the supernatural is inherently atheistic. Did you ever think about how atheistic our culture is, regardless of church attendance or proclamations of being a Christian nation?

3. What areas of your own worldview would you consider to be "atheistic"?

Chapter 4: Separation of Church and State: The Myth of a Secular America

1. Did you know that the phrase "separation of church and state" is *not* in the Constitution?

2. Were you surprised at how "co-mingled" the church and the state were for the first 150 years of our nation's existence?

3. Did you know that some states had "religious tests" to determine who could run for office?

Chapter 5: The First Amendment: A Maligned Masterpiece

1. Were you aware that the Bill of Rights (including the First Amendment) did not initially apply to the *state* governments?

2. How is the phrase, "Congress shall make no law establishing a religion" different than the phrase "separation of church and state"?

3. What do you believe would be a sensible interpretation of the meaning of "establishing a religion" that would keep an appropriate balance between the government forcing religion on a person and a person's right to practice their religion?

Chapter 6: The Academic Assault on Education: Removing Theistic Thought from The Classroom

1. Do you think schools have too much influence on the lives of our children?

2. If so, what can be done to correct that?

3. In what ways can we work to ensure that discussions of religion and faith are permitted in our classrooms?

Chapter 7: The Fall of Christian Thought: The Indoctrination of a Nation

1. Were you surprised to learn the depth of atheistic thought at most colleges and universities?

2. If you attended college, did you notice any secular bias? If not, do you notice it in hindsight?

3. If your children have attended or are attending college, have you noticed any bias in what they were or are being taught?

Chapter 8: The Academic Worldview: I Am An Atheist; Therefore, I Am An Intellectual

1. Do you think the theistic worldview should be offered as an alternate worldview when an atheist worldview in being taught?

2. Why do you think so many college professors are atheists?

3. Why do you think professors are opposed to presenting a theistic worldview alongside an atheistic worldview?

Chapter 9: A Scientific Assessment of Scientific Materialism

1. Were you surprised that so many scientists believe in God?

2. Do you think science will ever be able to prove the existence of God? Why or why not?

3. What other ways do we know things without using the scientific method? Do you know certain truths that you cannot prove using the scientific method?

Chapter 10: A Rational Discussion of The Supernatural

1. How would you explain the supernatural? Do you think supernatural things exist?

2. Is belief in the supernatural irrational? Why or why not?

Chapter 11: Has Science Proven the Existence of the Supernatural?

1. Prior to the Big Bang, *nothing* existed. Not time, not space, not matter. Do you believe this? Can you comprehend this? If this is true, how did anything come into existence where there was no time, space, or matter?

2. Do you find the "fine-tuning" of the universe to be a compelling argument for the existence of an intelligent Creator? Why or why not?

3. What are the strengths and weaknesses of the "multiverse" theory?

Chapter 12: Moral Relativism: A Brief Discussion of Secular and Christian Views

1. Do you think morality is relative?

2. Do you believe that certain things are true? What things?

3. People certainly creates laws and social norms and customs. Are laws, social norms and customs the same thing as "morality"? Discuss.

Chapter 13: Moral Truth v. Moral Relativism: Judging God and Finding Him Wanting

1. If there are not absolute moral truths, who decides what is moral?

2. If a person or group of people decide what is moral, does that make it moral? If not, why should one be obedient to a morality invented by some other person?

3. Is it possible for God to do something immoral? Based on whose standards?

Chapter 14: The Truth About Truth

1. Why do Christians insist that there is such a thing as truth?

2. Does any worldview really adhere to the belief that there are no truths?

3. The author posits that there are 3 kinds of statements: 1) statements of opinion; 2) statements of judgements; and 3) statements of fact. Discuss.

4. Jesus said that He was the way, the truth, and the life. What did He mean?

Chapter 15: The Intolerance of Tolerance

1. In what ways can tolerance be intolerant?

2. Is Christianity a tolerant religion? How so and how not?

3. Is Secular Materialism tolerant of opposing views?

Chapter 16: Gorging on the Tree of the Knowledge of Good and Evil

1. There are many views on the Fall of Adam and Eve. What do you think the story means? Is your version consistent with the Bible?

2. Do you think that Adam and Eve were real people? Does it make a difference?

3. How does our culture decide what is good and evil? Is this consistent with the Bible's view?

Chapter 17: What Now Should We Do?

1. Do you believe that Christians and Christianity are under attack in our current culture?

2. The author gives several ideas to combat the secular worldview. What other ways can you think of that would help support Christianity?

Appendix A

Suggested Books on Christian Apologetics

Blue Like Jazz. Donald Miller engages in his inimical light and humorous style to introduce his readers to a non-threatening and joyful Christian lifestyle. Perfect for those who find Christians to be smug and self-righteous. Thomas Nelson Publishers (2003).

The Case For Christ. Lee Strobel, an investigative journalist, undertakes a critical examination of the evidence for Jesus. An excellent book for those who doubt the veracity of the story of Jesus Christ. Zondervan (1998).

Death on a Friday Afternoon. Richard John Neuhaus uses the last words of Christ from the Cross to engage his readers in a brilliant social commentary on what Christianity means and the hope it offers to a broken world. Basic Books (2000).

The Defense of the Faith. Philosopher Cornelius Van Til makes the case for a *presuppositional faith* in Jesus. An intellectually engaging argument for *a priori* faith. Presbyterian and Reformed Publishing (1955).

The Devil's Delusion. David Berlinski does an excellent (and often humorous) job in demolishing the scientific pretensions of atheism. Crown Forum (2008).

The Great Divorce. The incomparable C.S. Lewis in one of his lesser-known works takes his readers on a fanciful examination of heaven... what it is like and why so many will reject it! A short, witty, and entertaining book that examines our stubborn refusal to believe the truth. Touchstone (1946).

I Don't Have Enough Faith to Be an Atheist. Norman Geisler and Frank Turek make a compelling (over 400 pages) case against atheism. This book refutes atheism and supports the Christian worldview using secular arguments based on reason and logic. Crossway (2004).

The Intolerance of Tolerance. D.A. Carson deconstructs the modern fallacies of tolerance and diversity and reveals them as little more than attacks on Christianity. Eerdmans (2012).

The Language of God. Francis S. Collins, one of our foremost living scientists, makes the case that science itself, particularly biology, proves the existence of God. Free Press (2006).

Mere Christianity. C.S. Lewis' classic work on why Christianity makes sense. An excellent book for those seeking to understand Christianity, written with the usual flair and eloquence of the great Christian apologist. Zondervan (1952).

The Naked Public Square. Richard John Neuhaus engages his readers in an intellectual examination of the totalitarian outcome of removing religion from public discourse. Written in 1984, Neuhaus' thesis has proven to be prophetic. Eerdmans (1984).

No Doubt About It. Dr. Winifried Corduan makes an excellent case for the reliability and veracity of the New Testament. Broadman & Holman (1987).

The Pursuit of God. This small book contains pearls of inspiration wrapped in intellectual commentary by the famous Chicago pastor, A.W. Tozer. Christian Publications (1982).

The Return of the Prodigal Son. Henri J.M. Nouwen takes his readers on a profound journey of inspirational thoughts as he contemplates the story of the Prodigal Son. A short but eloquent work that penetrates the heart of its readers. Doubleday (1994).

The Screwtape Letters. C.S. Lewis provides a highly entertaining imaginary conversation between the Devil and his young apprentice. The insights are both enlightening and comic. Zondervan (1996).

Truth Decay. Professor Douglas Groothuis reveals the logical failure of postmodernist thought. A brilliant demolition of the postmodern views that truth and morality are relative. InterVarsity (2000).

Why I Am A Christian. An outstanding collection of writings from some of the world's best thinkers on why they believe. It includes excellent essays by scientists on creation; philosophers on truth; and theologians on faith. Edited by Norman Geisler and Paul Hoffman. BakerBooks (2006).

Appendix B

Legal Resources for Christians

These organizations defend the rights of Christians. If you feel your First Amendment rights have been violated, please contact one of the following organizations.

Alliance Defending Freedom
15100 N. 90th Street, Scottsdale, Arizona 85260
1-800-835-5233

American Center for Law and Justice
P.O. Box 90555, Washington, DC 20090-05
1-800-342-2255

Christian Legal Society
8001 Braddock Road, Springfield, Virginia 22151
703-642-1070

First Liberty Institute
2001 West Plano Parkway, Suite 1600, Plano, Texas 75075
972-941-4444

Bibliography

Amar, Ahkil Reed. *Bill of Rights*. New Haven, CT: Yale University Press, 1998.

Barna, George.

Barton, David. *Original Intent: The Courts, the Constitution, & Religion*. Wallbuilders. Aledo, TX: WallBuilders, 2000.

Berlinski, David. *The Devil's Delusion: Atheism and Its Scientific Pretensions*. New York: Crown Forum, 2008.

Bloom, Allen. *The Closing of the American Mind*. New York: Simon & Schuster, 1987.

Bradley, Walter. "The 'Just-so' Universe: The Fine-Tuning of Constants and Conditions in the Cosmos," in William Dembski and James Kushiner, eds., *Signs of Intelligence*. Grand Rapids, MI: Baker, 2001.

Bork, Robert H. *Slouching Towards Gomorrah*. HarperCollins, New York: 1996.

Brody, David. *The Teavangelicals: The Inside Story of How Evangelicals and the Tea Party Are Taking Back America*. Zondervan, Grand Rapids, MI: 2012.

Carson, D.A. *The Intolerance of Tolerance*. Grand Rapids, MI: Eerdmans, 2012.

Collins, Francis S. *The Language of God: A Scientist Presents Evidence for Belief.* New York: Simon & Schuster: 2006.

Comte, Auguste. *A General View of Positivism.* London: George Routledge & Sons, 1848.

Craig, William Lane. *Reasonable Faith.* Wheaton, IL: Crossway, 2008.

Davies, Paul. *The Mind of God.* New York: Touchstone, 1992.

Dawkins, Richard. *The Blind Watchmaker.* New York: Norton, 1987.

Dyson, Freeman. *Disturbing the Universe.* New York: Basic Books, 2001.

Eastland, Terry, ed. *Religious Liberty in the Supreme Court: The Cases That Define the Debate Over Church and State.* Washington, DC: Ethics and Public Policy Center, 1993.

Egan, Kieran. *The Educated Mind.* Chicago: University of Chicago Press, 1998.

Eidsmoe, John. *Christianity and The Constitution.* Grand Rapids, MI: Baker, 1987.

Gaustad, Edwin S. *Sworn on the Altar of God: A Religious Biography of Thomas Jefferson.* Grand Rapids, MI: Eerdmans, 1996.

Geisler, Norman L. and Turek, Frank. *I Don't Have Faith Enough to Be an Atheist.* Wheaton, IL: Crossway, 2004.

Giberson, Karl W. *The Wonder of the Universe: Hints of God in Our Fine-Tuned World.* Downers Grove, IL: IVP Press, 2012.

Gingrich, Newt. *Rediscovering God in America.* Grand Rapids, MI: Thomas Nelson, 2009.

Gross, Neil. "How Religious are America's College and University Professors?" http://religion.ssrc.org/reforum/Gross_Simmons.pdf. The Social Science Research Council, February 06, 2007.

Haiman, Franklyn S. *Religious Expression and the American Constitution.* East Lansing, MI: Michigan State University Press, 2002.

Hawking, Stephen. *A Brief History of Time.* New York: Bantam, 1998.

House, H. Wayne and Price, J. Randall. *Zondervan Handbook of Biblical Archaeology: A Book by Book Guide to Archaeological Discoveries Related to the Bible.* Grand Rapids, MI: Zondervan, 2017.

Jastrow, Robert. *God and the Astronomers*, New York: Norton, 1978.

Johnson, Byron R. *More God, Less Crime: Why Faith Matters and How It Could Matter More.* West Conshohoken, PA: Templeton Press, 2011.

Lasch, Christopher. *The Revolt of the Elites and the Betrayal of Democracy.* New York: W.W. Norton, 1995.

Lewis, C.S. *A Grief Observed* San Francisco: HarperCollins, 1961.

Lewis, C.S. *Mere Christianity.* San Francisco: HarperCollins, 2001.

Lichter, Robert S., Lichter, Linda, and Rothman, Stanley. *The Media Elite: America's New Power Brokers* New York: Hastings House, 1990.

Little, Bruce A. Little. *God, Why This Evil.* Lanham, MD: Hamilton Books, 2010.

MacDonald, George. *Your Life in Christ: The Nature of God and His Work in Human Hearts.* Grand Rapids, MI: Bethany House, 2005.

MacIntyre, Alisdair. *After Virtue*. South Bend, IN: Notre Dame, 1981.

Mansfield, Stephen. *Ten Tortured Words*. Nashville: Thomas Nelson, 2007.

Meyer, Stephen. *Signature in the Cell: DNA and the Evidence for Intelligent Design*, New York: HarperCollins, 2009.

Middleton, Richard. *Colonial America*. Oxford: Blackwell Publishing, 2003.

Moreland, J.P. "How Should A Christian Relate to a Scientific Naturalist?" The Apologetics Study Bible, Nashville: Holman, 2007.

Munoz, Vincent Phillip. *Religious Liberty and The Supreme Court*. Lanham, MD: Rowman & Littlefield, 2013.

Neuhaus, Richard John. *The Naked Public Square: Religion and Democracy in America*. Grand Rapids, MI: Eerdmans, 1984.

Olasky, Marvin and Smith, Warren Cole, ed. *Prodigal Press: Confronting the Anti-Christian Bias of the American News Media*. Phillipsburg, NJ: P&R Publishing, 2013.

Pinkney, T.C. *Southern Baptist Convention Data,* "Remarks to the Southern Baptist Convention Executive Committee," Nashville, Tennessee, 2001.

Plantinga, Alvin. *God, Freedom, and Evil*. Grand Rapids, MI: Eerdmans, 1977).

Plantinga, Alvin. *Knowledge and Christian Belief*. Grand Rapids, MI: Eerdmans, 2015.

Plantinga, Alvin. *Where the Conflict Really Lies. Science, Religion, & Naturalism*. New York: Oxford University Press, 2011.

Price, Randall. *The Stones Cry Out: What Archeology Reveals About the Truth of the Bible*. Eugene, OR: Harvest House, 1997.

Ross, Hugh. "Why I Believe in the Miracle of Divine Creation," in *Why I Am A Christian,* eds. Normal L. Geisler and Paul K. Hoffman. Grand Rapids, MI: Baker, 2006.

Scalia, Antonin. *Scalia Speaks: Reflections on Law, Faith, and Life Well Lived.* New York: Crown Publishing, 2017.

Schaeffer, Francis. *How Then Should We Then Live: The Rise and Fall of Western Thought and Culture.* Wheaton, IL: Crossway, 1976.

Shalev, Baruch A. *100 Years of Nobel Prizes.* London: Atlantic Publishers & Distributors, 2003.

Stark, Rodney. *God's Battalions: The Case For The Crusades.* New York: HarperCollins, 2009.

Stelter, Mark A. *The Gospel According to Christ: The Message of Jesus and How We Missed It.* Eugene, OR: Wipf & Stock, 2011.

Surin, Kenneth. *Theology and the Problem of Evil.* Eugene, OR: Wipf & Stock, 1986.

Tribe, Laurence. *American Constitutional Law,* 3d ed. Mineola, NY: Foundation Press, 1988.

Van Til, Cornelius. *The Defense of the Faith.* Phillipsburg, NJ: Presbyterian & Reformed, 1967.

Wells, David F. *God in the Wasteland: The Reality of Truth in a World of Fading Dreams.* Grand Rapids, MI: Eerdmans, 1994.

Wright, N.T. *Evil and the Justice of God.* Downers Grove, IL: InterVarsity, 2006.

Zacharias, Ravi. *Jesus Among Other Gods.* Nashville: Thomas Nelson, 2002.

INDEX

A

Adams, John 25, 41
Anthropic Principle, The 180, 184
Atheism 4, 7, 11, 12, 13, 15, 28, 36, 37, 38, 39, 40, 41, 42, 43, 54, 73, 93, 94, 103, 104, 105, 106, 107, 108, 109, 110, 111, 118, 120, 130, 132, 134, 138, 139, 140, 142, 171, 184, 225, 246, 247, 248, 269, 278, 280, 293, 294, 299
Augustine 16, 25, 34, 103, 117, 128, 159, 222, 236, 237, 263

B

Barnes, Fred 18
Barr, William 91
Barton, David 299
Big Bang, The 154, 175, 176, 177, 178, 179, 180, 182, 187, 290
Black, Hugo 61
Board of Education of Westside Community Schools v. Mergens 89
Bork, Robert 18, 299

C

Cannon, Carl 19
Carson, D.A. 294, 299
Chesterton, G.K. 204
Chopra, Deepak 157, 158
Christ xi, xii, 22, 23, 27, 31, 32, 34, 35, 49, 78, 80, 112, 157, 158, 159, 168, 169, 189, 190, 198, 199, 207, 220, 221, 225, 227, 234, 235, 236, 237, 238, 239, 242, 243, 244, 245, 248, 249, 251, 252, 254, 255, 264, 269, 271, 274, 276, 277, 283, 284, 285, 286, 293, 301, 303
Collins, Francis 25, 107, 300
Comte, Auguste 111, 132, 300
Constitution, U.S. 73
Crick, Francis 184
Crossan, John Dominic 157, 158

D

Dalai Lama 246
Danbury Baptist Church 57, 59, 60
Dawkins, Richard 41, 42, 108, 158, 183, 186, 242, 300
Dylan, Bob 218
Dyson, Freeman 183, 300

E

Edwards v. Aguillard 89
Egan, Kieran 113, 300
Epperson v. Arkansas 86

Establishment Clause 57, 64, 66, 67, 68, 69, 74, 75, 88, 90
Everson v. Board of Education 61, 67, 69

F

Fine-Tuning of the Universe 180, 182, 184, 186
First Amendment 18, 21, 48, 50, 51, 52, 53, 54, 55, 57, 58, 59, 60, 61, 62, 63, 64, 65, 66, 67, 68, 70, 71, 72, 73, 74, 75, 78, 86, 87, 88, 89, 90, 92, 99, 266, 278, 280, 288, 297
Founders xiii, 50, 51, 82, 182, 184
Founding Fathers 21, 50, 51, 54, 57, 61, 73, 218, 287
Framers, The 18, 47, 48, 49, 50, 51, 52, 53, 54, 55, 56, 58, 61, 65, 69, 71, 75, 78, 90, 93, 99, 218, 266, 280
Free Exercise Clause 64, 66
Freud, Sigmund 78, 107, 111, 112, 115, 117, 132

G

Gardner, Martin 185
Giberson, Karl 181, 300
Good News Club v. Milford Central School 89
Gorgias 194, 195

H

Haiman, Franklyn 301
Hawking, Stephen 107, 183, 301
Haynes, Charles C. 88
Heaven 3, 6, 32, 35, 141, 153, 162, 164, 166, 167, 168, 169, 175, 222, 239, 244, 250, 255, 260, 263, 267, 271, 276, 294

Heisenberg, Werner 25, 114
Hell 6, 35, 153, 161, 167, 168, 205, 263, 271, 274
Hoyle, Fred 176, 183
Hutson, James 60

J

Jastrow, Robert 182, 188, 301
Jefferson, Thomas 22, 48, 59, 60, 78, 88, 115, 300
Jesus xi, xii, xiii, 3, 6, 13, 15, 16, 23, 24, 27, 31, 32, 34, 35, 43, 61, 78, 85, 110, 112, 130, 157, 158, 159, 161, 162, 163, 164, 165, 166, 167, 168, 169, 189, 190, 198, 199, 208, 220, 221, 225, 226, 227, 228, 229, 230, 234, 235, 237, 238, 239, 240, 241, 242, 243, 244, 245, 248, 251, 252, 254, 255, 263, 268, 271, 273, 274, 275, 276, 277, 282, 283, 284, 285, 286, 291, 293, 303
Jesus Christ xi, 23, 32, 34, 35, 78, 169, 190, 198, 199, 220, 221, 225, 227, 234, 235, 237, 239, 242, 243, 245, 248, 251, 252, 254, 271, 293
John, The Apostle 170

K

King, Martin Luther 25, 115, 117
Kiryas Joel School District v. Grumet 89

L

Lamaitre, George 176
Lasch, Christopher 18, 301
Lee v. Weisman 89
Legal Realism 213

Lewis, C.S. 269, 284, 294, 295, 301
Lichter, S. Robert 19
Luther, Martin 25, 33, 115, 117

M

MacIntyre, Alisdair 229, 302
Madison, James 25, 41, 48, 60, 62, 79, 88
Mansfield, Stephen 61, 302
Marx, Karl 41, 107, 111, 112, 114, 117, 132
Maslow, Abraham 107, 109
McConnell, Michael 73
Mitchell v. Helms 89
Morality 3, 5, 6, 7, 8, 23, 37, 38, 40, 43, 44, 48, 79, 85, 87, 95, 96, 105, 106, 123, 126, 127, 131, 154, 191, 192, 193, 194, 195, 196, 197, 198, 199, 200, 201, 202, 204, 205, 206, 207, 208, 209, 210, 211, 212, 213, 214, 215, 216, 217, 218, 219, 220, 221, 222, 223, 224, 225, 229, 230, 235, 236, 248, 252, 256, 259, 262, 264, 266, 267, 268, 281, 290, 291, 295
Moral Relativism 4, 5, 6, 37, 132, 135, 191, 192, 193, 194, 196, 200, 201, 202, 209, 210, 211, 212, 213, 214, 215, 216, 217, 218, 219, 220, 221, 222, 223, 224, 225, 230, 236, 266, 290
Multiverse, The 184, 185, 186

N

Neuhaus, Richard John 229, 269, 293, 294, 302
Nihilism 12, 37, 40, 76, 194, 195, 196, 213, 214, 220, 223
Nobel Prize 26, 107, 114, 176, 303

O

Open Syllabus Project, The 114
Original Sin 109, 204, 206, 257, 259, 263, 264, 272

P

Pascal, Blaise 25, 172
Penzias, Arno 176, 182
Peter, The Apostle 270
Plantinga, Alvin 144, 302
Pluralism 79, 250
Postmodernism 10, 130, 210

R

Rehnquist, William 62, 74, 279
Religious Irrelevance 4, 5, 36, 265
Rothman, Stanley 19, 301

S

Sagan, Carl 107, 141
Santa Fe Independent School District v. Doe 89
Satan 3, 35, 156, 161, 163, 263
Schaeffer, Francis 303
School District of Abington Township v. Schempp 86
Scientific Materialism 4, 6, 37, 105, 132, 135, 136, 139, 140, 141, 142, 143, 144, 145, 149, 150, 151, 155, 156, 159, 167, 170, 171, 191, 216, 225, 266, 289
Secular Materialism 4, 5, 6, 7, 9, 10, 12, 13, 14, 15, 16, 29, 31, 35, 36, 37, 38, 39, 40, 41, 42, 43, 44, 45, 46, 52, 73, 77, 78, 84, 91, 94, 103, 104, 105, 110, 130, 132, 133, 134, 135, 139, 144, 149, 152, 158, 159, 167, 190, 191, 225, 230, 246, 248, 256, 257, 265, 267, 268, 269, 291

Separation of Church and State 6, 10, 36, 46, 47, 48, 49, 53, 54, 57, 58, 59, 60, 61, 64, 67, 69, 70, 71, 72, 74, 75, 76, 77, 79, 82, 85, 91, 98, 100, 129, 171, 276, 278, 279, 280, 284, 288
Sin 3, 6, 14, 31, 32, 35, 109, 124, 127, 128, 129, 130, 159, 166, 169, 190, 198, 203, 204, 205, 206, 240, 257, 259, 260, 261, 263, 264, 271, 272
Spong, John Shelby 156, 158
Stelter, Mark A. 303
Stone v. Graham 88
Supernatural 3, 5, 6, 7, 8, 27, 32, 35, 37, 38, 43, 44, 101, 105, 106, 131, 132, 139, 144, 148, 149, 151, 152, 153, 154, 155, 156, 157, 159, 160, 161, 162, 164, 165, 166, 167, 169, 170, 171, 172, 173, 174, 176, 177, 178, 179, 183, 184, 186, 187, 188, 189, 190, 191, 220, 252, 256, 263, 264, 266, 267, 268, 288, 290
Supreme Court, U.S. 18, 73

T

Tipler, Frank 180
Tribe, Laurence 78, 303

V

Van Til, Cornelius 293, 303

W

Wallace v. Jaffree 88
Washington, George 22, 41, 58
Wells, David 21, 303
Wilson, Robert 176

Z

Zacharias, Ravi 248, 303
Zelman v. Simmons-Harris 89
Zobrest v. Catalina Foothills School District 89

Made in the USA
Monee, IL
01 April 2024

56148655R00192